IN WILDEST AFRICA

The Record of a hunting and exploration trip through Uganda, Victoria Nyanza, the Kilimanjaro Region and British East Africa, with an account of an ascent of the snowfields of Mount Kibo, in East Central Africa, and a description of the various native tribes.

By

PETER MacQUEEN, F. R. G. S.

Illustrated by sixty-four plates from original photographs, taken chiefly by the Author's travelling comrade

PETER DUTKEWICH

fond of wild life and of hunting, and Central Africa was a new field which would naturally be interesting. Furthermore, I had just completed a long lecture tour and was looking about for a new subject for my lectures; so I at once decided to go.

We were each familiar with the details of preparing for a long trip, and in six weeks had our cameras, kinetoscope, tents, rifles and maps well under way. We started for London on October 26th, 1907, and, after an extended visit in England, sailed for Zanzibar. Reaching Zanzibar early in 1908, we made a study of the island from a scenic and romantic point of view, and then followed the trip up the Uganda Railway, the expedition to Kilimanjaro, and the travels in the Mount Kenia and Victoria Nyanza regions, all made in the latter half of 1908, and in January and February of 1909.

Mr. Dutkewich made nearly all the pictures in the book. He was the acme of trained precision.

I have written as well as I could, in the midst of busy labours, regarding our travels and experiences in that wild Africa, which is the newest theatre for the achievements of the white race; but, from an eight months' stay in a continent so vast, varied and interesting as Africa, one could not write a very comprehensive book; and therefore I have to acknowledge my indebtedness to former

Preface

writers on Africa, especially to the works of Lugard, Sir Harry Johnston, Professor Gregory, Dr. Henry Drummond and others. I also wish to thank the librarians of the Boston Library, Sam Walter Foss of the Somerville Library and Miss Alice Meyers of the Lowell Library for their courteous assistance.

Equatorial Africa is one of the most fascinating and mysterious countries in the world. It allures and repels; it is beautiful as an opium dream, baneful as nightshade. One day a man is well and strong; the next he is dead and buried. The faultless climate of Nairobi and Nakuru is side by side with the deadly shores of Victoria Nyanza and the fatal sudd of Bahr-el-Gazal.

But just as the Americans improved the conditions in Cuba and Panama, so will the English, French and Germans probe into the sombre mysteries of Africa, dispel the clouds with which it has been draped for five millenniums, and make it, in a few decades, a land of light, learning and liberty.

Few seem to realize that Africa is no longer the Dark Continent *per se*. In the North, France has the great, successful commonwealths of Algeria and Tunisia. Italy rules Tripoli and part of Somaliland. England has her colonies almost unbroken from Cairo to the Cape, and her splendid Cape to

Cairo Railway is within sight of completion. Of the six thousand miles of rail and steamship connections necessary, five thousand are already finished. The trains run from Cape Town to Broken Hill in Northern Rhodesia, two thousand miles; while the rail and steamboat connections are practically unbroken from Alexandria to Jinja, so that the Nile is now as much an English river as the Thames. Germany is doing grand colonial work at Kilimanjaro and on Lake Tanganyika, as well as on the East Coast and the western shores.

It is to this superb country of the present and the future that the pictures and text of this book are devoted.

Contents

CHAPTER		PAGE
	PREFACE	v
I.	SOME GEOGRAPHICAL OUTLINES OF AFRICA	1
II.	THE ROMANCE OF AFRICAN EXPLORATION	14
III.	THE ROMANCE OF AFRICAN EXPLORATION (*continued*)	38
IV.	ZANZIBAR, THE GATE OF EAST AFRICA	59
V.	MOMBASA	79
VI.	THE UGANDA RAILWAY	99
VII.	IN THE COUNTRY OF THE BIG GAME	121
VIII.	SOME TRIBES AND CUSTOMS	139
IX.	ACROSS THE SERENGETI PLAIN	158
X.	IN THE TAVETA FOREST	168
XI.	THE PROVINCE OF MOSCHI	183
XII.	AN AMERICAN ASCENT OF KILIMANJARO	194
XIII.	PHASES OF JUNGLE LIFE	217
XIV.	NAIROBI — CAPITAL OF EAST AFRICAN PROTECTORATE	234
XV.	PORT FLORENCE	254
XVI.	THE MOUNT KENIA DISTRICT	263
XVII.	THE KAVIRONDO PEOPLE	276
XVIII.	THE VICTORIA NYANZA	288
XIX.	THE UGANDA PROTECTORATE	298
XX.	ENTEBBE THE ENGLISH CAPITAL	320

Contents

CHAPTER		PAGE
XXI.	KAMPALA THE HISTORIC CAPITAL	330
XXII.	THE DEVELOPMENT OF UGANDA	345
XXIII.	SLEEPING SICKNESS IN UGANDA	361
XXIV.	AT THE FOUNTAINS OF THE NILE	374
	BIBLIOGRAPHY	391
	INDEX	395

List of Illustrations

	PAGE
WACHAGA HUT (*see page* 190) . . .	*Frontispiece*
MAP	iv
MASAI WOMEN BUILDING A HOUSE	6
KAVIRONDO WARRIORS IN FULL PANOPLY . .	12
THE WATERFRONT OF MOMBASA	26
WHERE THE NILE LEAVES VICTORIA NYANZA .	44
THE ETERNAL SNOW AT AN ELEVATION OF 19,000 FEET ON MOUNT KILIMANJARO	55
ON A CLOVE PLANTATION OF BUBUBU . . .	65
THE AUTHOR IN THE AMERICAN CONSULATE AT ZANZIBAR	69
SULTAN ALI BIN HAMOUD AND THE ENGLISHMEN WHO FORM HIS GOVERNMENT	70
LIVINGSTONE'S FORMER RESIDENCE, ZANZIBAR .	73
NATIVE WOMEN WORKING ON A NEW HIGHWAY .	76
GHARY SYSTEM OF STREET CARS IN MOMBASA .	82
A SAFARI BRINGING IVORY TO MOMBASA . .	87
SERANI POINT AND THE FORT OF MIR ALI BEY .	91
TRAIN, DRAWN BY A BALDWIN LOCOMOTIVE, AT CHANGAMWE STATION	105
NAKURU STATION	110
MOUNT KENIA; PHOTOGRAPHED FROM NAIROBI, 60 MILES AWAY	116
KIKUYU WOMEN BRINGING WOOD FOR THE ENGINES	118

List of Illustrations

	PAGE
The Approach to Fort Ternan	120
Elephant Hunting Near Njoro	122
A Successful Hunt in the Bukedi Country, Mount Elgon District	127
A Leopard Trap in Ugan a	129
German Hunters at Moschi after a Buffalo Hunt	134
Game in the Naivasha Country	139
Medicine Men of the Masai in Consultation	144
A Group of Wise-men Among the Nandi	153
Dance of Young Men of the Kikuyu Tribe in Honour of Their Coming of Age	154
Game Shot by the Author and Mr. Dutkewich on the Serengeti Plain	160
Mr. Dutkewich and His Carriers in the Taru Desert	164
Wataveta Warriors Ready for a Lion Hunt	166
A Mission Among the Waparri	173
Four Belles of the Taveta Forest	178
Playing the Game of "Bao"	181
Dance of Wachaga Women	186
Sultan Sulima and His Wives	194
On Mount Kilimanjaro at 8,000 Feet Elevation	198
The Expedition at 15,000 Feet Elevation	202
Mr. MacQueen at 19,200 Feet Elevation	206
Zebras Tamed and Trained to Harness	224
A Masai Encampment near Nairobi	236
Governor Sadler Receiving the Honourable Winston Churchill at Nairobi	244
A Waterfall near Nairobi	250
The Railroad Station at Port Florence. — Steamer at Port Florence	255
King Wamboogu and His Wives	258

List of Illustrations

	PAGE
MASAI WARRIORS ON THE TRAIL OF GAME	266
ON THE ROAD FROM NAIROBI TO MOUNT KENIA	270
KAVIRONDO VILLAGE	276
KAVIRONDO WOMEN CULTIVATING THE GROUND	278
THE PECULIAR HEAD-DRESSES OF THE KAVIRONDO WARRIORS	280
KAVIRONDO WOMEN DRAGGING A FISH NET	284
A FIRST GLIMPSE OF VICTORIA NYANZA	288
A NATIVE BOAT ON VICTORIA NYANZA	293
IN THE NANDI COUNTRY, NEAR MOUNT ELGON	300
BUSOGA HUNTERS BELOW THE RIPON FALLS	309
GOVERNOR BELL OF UGANDA AND TROPHIES OF THE CHASE	315
ENTEBBE	320
THE RESIDENCE OF GOVERNOR BELL	326
CATHOLIC SCHOOL OF THE MILL HILL MISSION. — FATHER PRENTISS AT THE ALGERIAN MISSION	334
DAUDA CHWA, KING OF UGANDA, REVIEWING HIS TROOPS	338
ARCHDEACON BUCKLEY TEACHING THE SONS OF THIRTY-SEVEN CHIEFS TO READ	350
A FOREST OF UGANDA	357
FAMINE SUFFERERS IN UGANDA, RELIEVED BY BISHOP HANLON AND ARCHDEACON BUCKLEY	360
TAKING BLOOD FROM THE NECK OF A SUSPECTED MAN. — DR. MARSHALL INJECTING ATOXYL	372
THE RIPON FALLS	380

In Wildest Africa

CHAPTER I

SOME GEOGRAPHICAL OUTLINES OF AFRICA

AFRICA is a vast irregular triangle with no indentations, and few islands or bays. But three great inlets, three mighty rivers, piercing to its very heart, have been supplied it by a benign nature, one to each of its solid sides. In the north is the river of the past, the Nile, flowing through Egypt, as Leigh Hunt says, "like some mighty thought threading a dream;" on the west, the river of the future, the not less mysterious Congo; and on the east, the river of the present, — the mighty Zambesi.

The physical features of this great continent are easily grasped. From the coast a low, scorched plain, infested with malaria, extends in unbroken monotony inland for nearly a hundred miles. This is succeeded by a plateau some three thousand feet high; and this again, hundreds of miles farther inland, shapes itself into a second plateau as high again. This last plateau, some six thousand feet above sea level, may be said to comprise the whole of Central Africa. It is only in a general way, however, that these can be called plateaus at all. When traversing these uplands nothing appears to the beholder but hills, valleys, plains and forests — waving in a green sea of grass, interspersed with trees of which the umbrella-shaped acacia tree forms the chief variety.

In looking over the map of Africa, another point to be noticed is the number and size of its great lakes. The most casual study of the map shows that the lakes are grouped in the Eastern Tropical region, and that they are here developed in two forms. There are those, such as Victoria Nyanza and Lake Mweru, which are of circular form and have level shores; and those long and narrow with precipitous shores, such as Tanganyika, Nyassa and Lake Rudolph. Further study shows, moreover, that these lakes are not distributed haphazard, but are on a certain definite plan. The long ones are arranged in two lines which pass on either side of Nyanza and meet at the north end of Lake Rudolph. Thence a line of lake-dotted lowland, in places below the level of the sea, runs up to the Red Sea.

Geographical Outlines

Africa is about three times as large as Europe in extent, but infinitely more varied than either Europe or America as to surface and climate. It is nearly four times as large as the United States, and has healthful areas of land, where the white man can live and thrive, equal to twice the extent of our own country. The surface variety of Africa is remarkable. One finds the desert of Nevada in the Sahara; the steppes of Eastern Russia in Masai land; the Castilian Uplands in Unyamwezi. The best parts of France are represented by Egypt; Switzerland by Toro; the Alps by Kilimanjaro, Kenia and Ruwenzori. Brazil is duplicated in the Congo Basin; the Amazon in the Congo River, and the immense forests of South America are rivalled by those of Central Africa.

There is a deep rift, extending through the heart of the continent on the west side of the lake district. It begins with Lake Nyassa and stretches for over two thousand miles down into the valley of the Nile. In it are included Lake Tanganyika, the Semliki Valley and the Albert Nyanza. The East African Protectorate contains a part of this Rift Valley. British East Africa is practically a high plateau falling away toward German East Africa on the south and toward this great chasm on the west. On the north it descends towards Lake Rudolph and the Nile Valley. The elevation averages from five thousand to six thousand feet. This great altitude makes the country between the coast and Victoria Nyanza the most fertile in Africa.

Thirty-five per cent. of Africa is drained toward the Atlantic, fifteen per cent. to the Mediterranean, eighteen per cent. to the Indian Ocean and thirty-two per cent. has no outlet. The highest lands are of igneous origin, like the mass of Ruwenzori (18,000 feet) or the active volcano of Kirunga near Lake Kivu, on the Western Rift Valley; or recent volcanic peaks as Elgon (14,000 feet), Kenia (19,000 feet), and Kilimanjaro (19,800 feet), near the Eastern Rift Valley. (These heights are not yet definitely determined.)

South of the Sahara live the antelopes, zebras, giraffes, buffaloes, elephants, rhinoceri, and other herbivorous animals. Ostriches run on the savannas; hippopotami and crocodiles inhabit the rivers; and lions, panthers, hyenas, leopards and other beasts of prey prowl in the swamps and jungles. The natives possess herds of cattle and fat-tailed sheep. In the extreme south the merino sheep, ostrich, goats, cattle, donkeys, and horses live and thrive. In the dense forests monkeys of many species, man-like gorillas and chimpanzees abound. The mosquito, the chief means of spreading fevers; and the tsetse fly, whose bite is often fatal to horses and spreads the dreadful sleeping sickness; the spirillum tick which infests the native huts and is the cause of a virulent fever; the mbwa fly, whose bite produces a painful swelling — are among the dangerous pests.

The white inhabitants outnumber the blacks north of the Sahara, while the blacks predominate south of it. There are fewer men of European descent in Africa than on any other continent; and these are chiefly located on the Mediterranean seaboard and in the extreme south. The other white men are the Berbers and the Arabs, — the latter descendants of Asiatic invaders. These races, however, are not pure, but mixed, — often with negro blood.

Of the black men the inhabitants of the Sudan are classed as true negroes, while those of the Congo Basin and of East and South Africa are known as Bantus. The dialects of the latter are all closely related, but the different tribes do not possess the same physical characteristics. There is some admixture of white blood in many of the Sudanese negroes, who differ in appearance and language among themselves. The Swahili language is the Lingua Franca of East and Central Africa and the Hausa of the Sudan and West Africa. The Swahili tribe on the East Coast is an admixture of Arab and negro blood. These have a language which contains twenty thousand words, and is a mixture of Arab and Bantu.

A tribe of dwarfs inhabit the tropical forests.

The East African Protectorate lies between the Juba and Umba rivers, and ascends by a series of terraces from the coast to the Kikuyu Escarpment. The coast is hot, moist, malarial and productive; but farther inland the climate is cooler and drier and in the higher regions grass lands prevail on which the semi-nomadic, pastoral and military Masai and other tribes wander with their herds. Three thousand white colonists have taken up holdings in East Africa. They are the vanguard of a great Caucasian migration to the equator.

The Uganda Protectorate extends from the Rift Valley to the Albert and Albert Edward Nyanza, and from the middle of Lake Victoria Nyanza to 5° north. The average elevation is over four thousand feet, but the lower valleys are marshy and malarial. In the west the oil palms and bananas are cultivated, especially in the kingdom of Uganda proper, northwest of Victoria Nyanza. The chief British centre is Entebbe, but the native capital is Mengo. The merchant and missionary centre is Kampala. The eastern region of the Nandi Plateau is lofty and healthful.

German East Africa contains three hundred and

MASAI WOMEN BUILDING A HOUSE.

Geographical Outlines

eighty-five thousand square miles, and eight million inhabitants, of whom about two thousand five hundred are German colonists. It comprises the coastal plain between the Umba and Rovuma rivers and the terraces which rise between the coast and Lake Tanganyika. The Germans have started plantations near the coast and are already invading the interior lands formerly cultivated exclusively by the natives. Dar-es-Salaam is the chief port, but neither it nor Bagamoyo, opposite Zanzibar, nor Tanga, opposite Pemba, are so accessible for large vessels as Mombasa. A railway is built from Tanga to Karagwe, and is being extended to Mombo on the way to the new colony of Kilimanjaro. The importance of these colonies is indicated by a recent appropriation of ten million dollars by the German government to complete its system of railways in East Africa. The termini of the important branches will be at Mwanza on Victoria Nyanza and Ujiji on Lake Tanganyika.

The Nile, where it issues from Victoria Nyanza, is a deep broad stream from five hundred to eight hundred yards wide, with a strong current towards the Ripon Falls. The scenery is very beautiful, for the banks of the river are high and densely wooded, and back in the lake many small islands dot the bay which is called Napoleon Gulf. Schools of hippopotami snort and grunt in the water and the strange cry of the kwazi fish eagle is heard, while the vast expanse of water to the far horizon reminds one of the ocean.

The Nile rushes from Victoria Nyanza at a height of about three thousand eight hundred feet above sea level; flows on, forming rapids and waterfalls, to the Albert Lake; then runs more smoothly to the Fola Rapids, whence the river is navigable for a distance of nearly fourteen hundred miles to Khartum, receiving on its way thither the waters of two other large rivers, the Bahr-el-Ghazal and the Sobat.

The more special features of the East African plateau are Kilimanjaro, Mount Kenia, Mount Elgon and the plains that lie around the bases of those great mountains.

Kilimanjaro may be described as a great, irregular pear-shaped mass, with its major axis in a line running northwest and southeast, the tapering point running into the heart of the Masai country. Its minor axis, running at right angles, extends only thirty miles. The mountain separates into the high central peak of Kibo and the lower conical peak of Kimawenzi. Towards the northwest it slopes away into a long ridge, which gradually tapers horizontally and vertically till it becomes merged into the Masai plain.

The southern side of this stupendous mountain

forms the country of Chagga, which may be described as a great platform, base, or terrace from which the dome and peak abruptly rise. This platform rises from four thousand to six thousand feet, covers over ten miles of rounded ridges; and is characterized by deep glens at its broadest part. The foothills of Kilimanjaro, although in themselves rich and pleasing, and presenting a smiling aspect with luxuriant verdure, yet somewhat detract from the imposing grandeur of the mountain, since the vision must stretch more than fifteen miles before Kibo is discerned twelve thousand feet higher.

It is from the north side, however, that the grandest view of the whole system can be obtained. Standing a short distance off, on the Njiri Plain, we see the entire mountain horizontally and vertically, without moving the head. Rising from an almost level sandy plain, the altitude of which is about three thousand feet, it springs at an even angle to a height of fifteen thousand feet, unbroken by a single irregularity or projecting buttress. No cones or hills diversify its surface. Neither gorge nor valley cuts deep into its sides. You see on your left the great cone of Mawenzi, with only one or two slight indentations, sweeping around in a saddle-like depression, to spring up into a dome of the most perfect proportions. The snow face shows here to great advantage, forming a close-fitting glittering helmet artistically laid on the massive head of Kibo.

The only inhabited part of this region is the Chagga platform, which offers favourable conditions for agriculture in the projecting terraces, rich soil and the numerous streams which lend themselves profitably to irrigation one of the features of the land.

Mount Kenia rises as a great volcanic cone, nearly thirty miles in diameter at its base, from a thorn-clad plain five thousand seven hundred feet in altitude. Up to a height of fifteen thousand feet the angle is very low, and the slope is unbroken, comparatively, by ridge or glen. From that level the mountain suddenly springs into a sugar-loaf peak, the resemblance being made all the more striking by the glittering facets of snow which characterize the uppermost three thousand feet. The sides of the peak are so steep that the snow cannot lie on many places, the unclad parts showing through the white as black spots. Hence its Masai name of Donyo Egare, — the speckled or gray mountain.

The Masai country is very markedly divided into two quite distinct regions — the southern or lower desert area and the northern or plateau region. The southerly part is comparatively low in altitude, that is to say from three thousand to four thousand feet. It is sterile and unproductive in the extreme. This is owing not to a barren soil, but to the scantiness of the rainfall which for about three months in the year barely gives sufficient sustenance to scattered tufts of grass. The acacia and mimosa have almost sole possession of these dreary plains, except near the base of some isolated mountain or other elevation, where small rivulets trickle down to be speedily devoured by the arid sand. No river traverses this region, and many parts are covered with incrustations of natron, left by the evaporation of salt-charged springs. It is not, however, to be regarded as a monotonous level. Far from it. The colossal Kilimanjaro and the conical Mount Meru belong to it.

The northerly or higher plateau region of Masai land rises from an elevation of nearly five thousand feet on either side and culminates in the centre at an elevation little short of nine thousand feet. On the eastern half of this divided plateau rises the snow clad peak of Kenia and the picturesque range of the Aberdare Mountains, which run almost parallel with the central line of depression. A more charming region is probably not to be found in all Africa. Though lying at a general elevation of six thousand feet, it is not mountainous but extends out in billowy, swelling reaches, and is characterized by everything that makes a pleasing landscape. There are dense patches of flowering shrubs and noble forests; now you traverse a park-like country enlivened by groups of game; further on great herds of cattle or flocks of sheep and goats are seen wandering knee-deep in the splendid pasture.

The largest lake of Africa, the Victoria Nyanza, covers an area of nearly thirty thousand square miles, being second in size only to Lake Superior. Its banks are formed of grassy hills, sloping towards the shore, or of rugged stretches of rock soon giving place to higher mountain ranges or plateaus. The shore at the north, west and south, along the lake from Uganda to Mwanza, displays the character of a hilly country with occasional weather-worn cliffs; while in the southwest, east and northeast there are actual ranges of mountains and extensive plains.

A part of Uzukuma's country and great stretches of land farther on by the River Ruvana, in Ugaya and Kavirondo, consist of vast plains and grassy slopes. Elevations of a considerable height are found in the ranges to the east. The northern, western and southwestern regions are, as a rule, more fertile than the others. The shores themselves abound in bays, large and small, and at the south the Speke, Smith and Emin Pasha gulfs cut

Photograph by Peter Dutkewich, copyright, 1909, by Underwood & Underwood, N. Y.

KAVIRONDO WARRIORS IN FULL PANOPLY.

Geographical Outlines 13

deep into the land. The shallow water in the bays has generally a dull, dirty colour, and is traversed by broad stretches of dense papyrus, the haunts of numerous hippopotami and crocodiles. Where a brook or stream enters the lake there is found around its mouth a singular mud swamp, which in some places shows no considerable difference of level between land and water; and it is by no means one of the pleasures of life to have to pass through a fetid swamp of this kind near the lake among papyrus stems twenty feet high. To one who stands on the shores of the lake, and allows his eyes to range over the broad expanse of blue water, the Nyanza gives an impression similar to that of the ocean.

There are sixteen hundred miles of navigable waterways in the centre of Africa, and the whole region is being penetrated and permeated by the steamship and the railway. In fifty years, ten millions of white men will have their homes in Equatorial Africa.

CHAPTER II

THE ROMANCE OF AFRICAN EXPLORATION

UNTIL the latter half of the nineteenth century, Central Africa was almost a sealed book to the historian and mapmaker. This fact, while not remarkable in the case of some parts of South America, Australasia, and other savage or inaccessible territory, is astonishing in the case of Africa when we consider that civilization had one of its cradles in Ancient Egypt, and Africa has for ages paid enormous tribute in slaves, ivory, gold, precious stones, and other treasure to the rest of the world.

Ancient Egypt entered into the arena of life, love and war, of human knowledge and concentred power, full statured and armed, wise and terrible as Pallas Athene springing into being from the temples of Zeus. Her history was cut on pages of stone, and the books that tell of her are the pyramids and obelisks, constructions colossal and enigmatic, the granite epitaphs of buried dynasties.

Without record of previous barbarism or dependency, we find her first known monarch a man of letters and his first work a medical treatise.

While we may not certainly fix the chronology of the more ancient Egyptian dynasties, and authorities differ widely as to the date of the reign of King Menes — from 5702 B. C. (Boeck) to 2000 B. C. (Sharp) — there is no doubt that, fifty centuries ago, "Egypt, mother of nations," ruled the larger part of the Nile Valley, and, by forced tribute or peaceful barter, controlled the commodities of the Upper Nile far to the southward of Khartum, which, within the memory of living men, was considered the furthest outpost of civilization on the White Nile.

We know also that the Pharaohs maintained a corps of Pahars or scouts, who in peace and war explored the outlands and recorded and reported all that the ruler of Khem needed to know of lands, rulers, and conditions which might offer rich booty or remunerative trade. These officers had chariots, horses, boats, camels, galleys, and assistants of all kinds, and were trained to endurance and speed beyond the wont of modern adventurers. Simple in their habits, well educated for their respective fields of labour and adventure, they explored Asia and Africa beyond the furthest outposts of Egyptian power and influence.

We are apt to greatly underrate the immense

distances to which primeval and rude methods of barter will lead men, who willingly risk life and goods to obtain greater wealth; to consider as impossible the ordinary journeys of Asiatic and African caravans over terrible deserts, across lofty and intensely cold mountain ranges, and through tropical jungles. We know little of the practical geographical knowledge of the rude fishermen, trappers, miners, traders, and slavers, who in all ages and all lands have boldly adventured and penetrated far beyond the limits mapped out by discoverers whose names and fame are household words. In more recent times the whalers, fur-sealers, fur-traders and pearl fishers' logs have often chronicled in scrawly, simple phrases, discoveries which years later made the reputation of some naval commander or professional explorer. Indeed they were often utterly silent as to the existence of islands and shores which they carefully but covertly indicated on charts that should thereafter guide the owner back to riches of which he alone had knowledge.

Even when there was no especial desire to conceal discoveries, the rude adventurer often cared not to speak of strange lands, of people, and curious fauna and flora, well knowing that some closet cartographer, naturalist or wiseacre, would be almost certain to give the lie to any tale not in accordance with his own knowledge or pet theories; — such men for instance as those who greeted with innuendo and depreciation Stanley's simple, straightforward account of "How I Found Livingston," who denied that Speke had found the sources of the Nile, and flouted Rebmann's discovery of snow on Kilimanjaro.

The discoveries and trading-voyages of the Norsemen along the North Atlantic coast, five or ten centuries before the coming of Columbus; the wonderful caravans which, for ages past, have traversed every part of Asia and much of Europe, Africa and South America, impress upon us the fact that men of courage and endurance, seeking wealth or fame, defy the hardships and dangers which we consider a bar to transportation of goods, or successful exploration. For ages, of whose extent we have no reliable estimate, traders and warriors of Coptic, Hamitic, and Semitic descent have spread southward throughout Africa, drawing thence gold, ivory, spices, incense, slaves, and many other precious commodities.

The impress of ancient Egypt is still seen in the human face, in dress, and musical instruments, even in the deep jungles of Central Africa. The priests of Meroë, when they told Herodotus how the "Fountain sources of the Nile" welled up under the ranges of the "Mountains of the Moon," doubtless only related facts that had been gathered from some perfectly reliable explorer, and perhaps from the secret archives which held the formal reports of the Pahars of Pharaoh. Perhaps some adventurer, whom success had made rich and bold, came back, from a last and fatal quest, to die, happy in knowing that his rich gifts and his great secrets should buy the embalmers' best skill and a happy entrance for the fleeting soul into the kingdom of Amenti.

It is also certain that many interesting accounts of travel, adventure, and geographical and historical fact, that once existed in records known only to the few, have been destroyed or lost, or, like Solon's story of Atlantis, set forth in a splendid prologue, whose untimely ending reminds one of a priceless jewel of which only the exquisite clasp remains.

But we learn authentically that Pharaoh Necho, about 600 B. C., completed a canal from the Nile to the Red Sea, and sent a number of Phœnician galleys down the East African Coast with orders if possible to circumnavigate Africa, and come back to the Nile delta through the Mediterranean Sea. This task they completed in three years, stopping from time to time, as did Stanley, to raise grain and pulse from seed for their further provision.

About 500 B. C., Sataspes, a Persian noble, sailed

from Carthage to explore and settle the West Coast, and apparently went as far south as the Congo, or Zaire River.

From various sources, Ptolemy of Alexandria, about 150 A. D., described and mapped out the "Sources of the Nile" and the "Mountains of the Moon," which for many centuries after him were accepted by scholars who followed Edrisi, Ibn Batuta and other Arabian sages and cartographers, who doubtless had good occasion to believe that the records of the great Alexandrian Library, destroyed by the fanatical Mahmoud, contained accounts of the Egyptian, Carthaginian, Grecian, Persian and Roman discoveries, some fragments of which remain in spite of the barbarous holocaust of that magnificent treasure-house of the world's literature.

It is written that Nero sent two Roman centurions southward up the Nile from Cyrene, who kept on until they found themselves baffled by that vast mass of floating vegetation called the Sudd, which has more than once in our day closed the White Nile to navigation, since its rediscovery by an Egyptian exploring party in 1839-1840.

The redemption of the Arabians from idolatry by Mahomet, and the fierce Jehad, or Holy War, which gave them control of immense territories in Asia, Europe and Northern Africa, inspired an energy and spirit of adventure in the children of Ishmael which sent out in every direction legions of brave fanatics, bent on proselytizing the nations. Hand in hand with religious fervour and lust of battle, went a keen eye for commercial advantages and a system of combined trade and pillage which for many centuries has laid half Africa under contribution. Their light-armed dhows and ships crossed the Persian Gulf and the Red Sea, coasted as far south as the Zambesi, and eventually settled the islands and many harbours along the Pacific Coast line, and for many centuries held Madagascar, Mozambique, Zanzibar, Pemba, Mombasa, and in fact every civilized and half-civilized city in East and Northern Africa.

By A. D. 1134, Arabian and Moorish wealth, wisdom and luxury had a world-wide reputation, and modern science still perforce must acknowledge its great debt to the alchemists, physicians, architects, armourers, and skilled artisans of that race and era. Among them was that Edrisi, already spoken of, who in his map of Africa set down with considerable accuracy not only the "Fountains of the Nile" and the "Mountains of the Moon" but the great inland seas of the lake region, with the general courses of the Nile and Congo.

Two hundred years later Ibn Batuta of Tangier

travelled as far south as Zanzibar, and from Fezzan penetrated southwest to the headwaters of the Niger, which so far as he traced it he believed to be a branch of the Nile. On his return to Tangier he visited Timbuctoo, the great market town of north Central Africa.

In the sixteenth century an astronomer, later known as Leo Africanus, a Moor of Grenada, removed, after the conquest of his people, to Fezzan, where he devoted himself to Arabian science, and especially all matters relating to Africa. He himself accompanied caravans into the interior, and finally went to Rome, where, under the patronage of Pope Leo X, he published a record of his travels. Since the visit of Ibn Batuta, two hundred years before, the traffic of the Niger country had enormously increased, drawing from the Foulahs and Bambarras immense amounts of gold, ivory, and slaves.

Timbuctoo, the residence of King Izchia, had become the metropolis of many powerful and wealthy traders, who lived luxuriously and even paid immense sums for choice manuscripts. There was a disciplined army of six thousand foot and horse, largely archers. The king had great treasure in gold, including one nugget weighing thirteen hundred ounces, worth about twenty-one thousand dollars. The palaces, mosques and mansions were of stone, but most of the common people lived in huts of wattle.

Until the sixteenth century European nations had little traffic with Africa at any point. Spain had expelled the Moors and the check of Turkish conquest by Russia and Poland set up barriers to Mohammedan rule within which the fires of race hatred and religious fanaticism burned with deadly intensity.

The whole northern coast of Africa was a stronghold of piracy which spared no people, sex, or condition, except those sailing under some flag which paid tribute to Algiers and Tunis, or were strong enough to meet their forces in naval battle. That within a hundred years the United States paid such tribute and ransomed its citizens from slavery with gold instead of steel, proves that Mohammedan Africa was until then almost a sealed book to European investigation. Turkey closed both the Hellespont and the Nile to infidel travel and only the more savage lands of South Africa were open to naval exploration.

In 1415, Prince Henry, called the Navigator, son of John I of Portugal, became a brilliant patron of African exploration. His ships carried Portuguese discovery slowly but surely beyond the Moorish settlements until finally the Cape of Good

Hope was attained. The islands of Porto Santo and Madeira were discovered, 1418-1420; Dom Gilsanez doubled Cape Bojador in 1433; Elmina was settled on the gold coast in 1471; and many minor discoveries gave renown to Prince Henry, who died without visiting the last and most valuable of these acquisitions. One great object of his search was the mythical kingdom of Prester John, whose wisdom, dominion and almost supernatural attributes were believed throughout Christendom to be little less than divine. Expeditions were sent inland from the coast, some as far as Timbuctoo, where caravans arriving from all parts of Africa furnished the Portuguese cavaliers with stories of many kingdoms and strange men and beasts but no tidings of Prester John.

In 1484 Diego Cane sailed south from Elmina and, on the cape at the southern bank of the Congo, erected a pillar bearing the royal arms of Portugal; hence the Congo was long called the River of the Pillar. Guided by native chiefs, he ascended the Congo, but soon returned home, carrying away his native guides, but leaving an equal number of his men as hostages for their return. The Africans were received with great honour, were loaded with gifts, and the next year returned to their people, who in the meantime had kindly entertained the Portuguese.

On a second trip Dom Diego ascended the river to the capital of the king, who welcomed him and finally agreed to adopt the Catholic faith, and send some of his chiefs to Lisbon to be educated there. These at the end of two years were received into the church with great pomp, the king himself and his chief nobles acting as their sponsors in baptism. They were restored to their people in 1490 by Ruy da Souza.

In 1486 Bartholomew Diaz rounded the Cape of Good Hope, reached the Great Fish River and, on his return, explored the Cape of Storms, which Holland afterwards christened the Cape of Good Hope. Meanwhile John II of Portugal sent Pedro da Covilham and Alonzo da Piava to find a safe route to India via the Isthmus of Suez and the Red Sea. At Sinai Da Piava left and crossed into Ethiopia to search for Prester John, from which quest he never returned.

Da Covilham visited Malabar, studied the trade of Calicut and Goa, and visited Mozambique, Sofala and other Arabian ports on the coast of Africa and the Red Sea. Returning to Cairo, he gave his notes and maps to Rabbi Ben Beza, a learned Jew, the messenger of John II, and set out for Abyssinia. The king of that country gave him a royal welcome but would never allow him to return home. Thirty-five years afterwards a Portuguese ambassador met him, honoured, wealthy, married to a noble lady, and surrounded by luxury, but utterly inconsolable because he might never see Portugal again.

Da Covilham's report and map determined King John to send Vasco da Gama to circumnavigate Africa and visit the rich ports of the Indian coast. Da Gama sailed from Rastella on Saturday, July 8th, 1497, in the Sam-Gabriel, 120 tons, with his brother Paulo da Gama, in the Sam-Raphael, 100 tons, and Nicolo Coelho in the Berrio, 50 tons, as well as a large transport, commanded by Pedro Nunez, laden with supplies and merchandise. Every precaution was taken to make the outfit complete, but the force, although carefully selected, numbered only one hundred and sixty men.

Da Gama doubled the Cape of Storms, November 19th, 1497, and, on the 25th, anchored and destroyed the transport, after her lading and crew were distributed among the other vessels. They reached Natal on January 10th, 1498, where they first met the Kaffirs, tall, strong men, armed with long-bows and iron-headed assegais, but so friendly and hospitable that Da Gama called their country Terra Da Bon Gente, — the Land of Good People.

Further north they met two Mussulman traders and a young man who said that he came " From a far country where there were ships as large as those of the king," probably meaning India.

On March 10, 1498, they reached Mozambique, where the Vizier Colytam came on board several times and was magnificently entertained. Later, however, he learned that his new friends with whom he had discussed the trade and resources of the country were not true believers but infidels, at which he was terribly incensed and planned to seize and slay Da Gama and his people. The Portuguese discovered the plot, trained their guns on the city, forced the Vizier to supply them with fresh water, and later captured two richly laden ships, whose cargo was distributed among the sailors.

On April 4th they reached Mombasa, but the fleet wisely dropped anchor in the roadstead and did not enter the harbour. In the night a lighter with a hundred men attempted to board Da Gama's flag ship, but were refused permission.

The King of Mombasa, having received news from Mozambique, treacherously invited Da Gama to establish a factory at Mombasa and offered him a full cargo of spices and incense. Da Gama sent two men to announce his entry and the next morning weighed anchor, but the wind was unfavourable and the anchor was dropped. At once all the Moors on board, except two, quitted the ship, the Mozam-

THE WATER FRONT OF MOMBASA.

bique pilot sprang into the sea and the few men who were left confessed a plot to capture the fleet as soon as it entered the harbour. Da Gama prevented several attempts to board his ships or cut their cables, procured supplies by threats and left the inhospitable port.

A few hours later Da Gama captured a Mombasa bark laden with provisions and treasure and next day arrived at Melindi. The king at first resented the capture of the Mombasa vessel, but, on learning the circumstances, confessed the justice of the retaliation. A treaty of peace was ratified by oaths on the Bible and the Koran, and everything done to make the stay pleasant. Artillery was then unknown on the East African Coast and the Portuguese target practice excited great astonishment. After nine days' stay at Melindi, Da Gama sailed for India and the story of his African discoveries ended.

After the voyage of Da Gama many Portuguese expeditions made settlements at Angola, Sofala, Mozambique and Mombasa in East Africa. Many a caravan started for the interior, seeking gold, ivory and, later, slaves. Treaties were made with native chiefs, especially with King Monomapata, whose empire, it is written, extended from Abyssinia to the Cape of Storms. These treaties are recorded in the Portuguese archives, but the empire and most of the Portuguese territory in Africa have wasted away with the centuries.

In 1772-1776, MM. Sparrman and Thunberg journeyed among the Boers, who had replaced the Portuguese at the Cape of Good' Hope, and described the Hottentots, Bushmen and the fauna and flora of the Cape Colony.

An English naturalist, Lieut. William Patterson, explored Caffraria north of the Orange and Great Fish Rivers. Vaillant, a French naturalist, set out from the Cape in 1781 and thoroughly explored the Cape Colony, as far north as the Schewenberg ranges. He visited the Karoo desert and the Buffalo River, and returned to Cape Town in April, 1783, having collected over one thousand specimens. In June, 1783, he started on another exploration, traversing nearly the whole of South Africa to the northern boundary of the Transvaal. He brought back some plants, a load of specimens, a mass of ethnological and geographical information and the first giraffe ever imported into Europe.

Francisco Jose da Lacerda left Mozambique in 1797 to explore the interior. Starting from Sana, on the lower Zambesi, he visited the Cazembe of the country about Lake Bangweolo, two hundred and seventy leagues inland, but died of the fatigue and diseases incident to African travel. His notes were returned to Europe and, although Portuguese traders and Dr. Livingstone have since reached this section, little has been added to what he then recorded.

James Bruce, a Scottish lawyer, lived some years in Spain, giving much time to the study of Arabian and Moorish antiquities. Returning to England, he decided to look for the sources of the Nile. In June, 1768, he left England for Egypt and reached Massowah, on the borders of Abyssinia, September 17th, 1769. Entering Abyssinia, he discovered the Province of Tigre. He also discovered many ancient pillars and sphinxes of Egyptian origin and some remains of Grecian architecture. He visited Sare and arrived at Gondar, whence he made a number of excursions, in one of which he discovered the sources of the Blue Nile. It was a moment of triumph to the lonely traveller, who believed he was "Standing opposite the sources which had baffled the genius and courage of the most celebrated men for three thousand years." He was in error, he was not at the sources of the true Nile, but at the head of the Blue Nile, its greatest affluent. He had, nevertheless, added greatly to the geographical knowledge of his era, and later discoverers have indorsed the truth and vigour of his report.

English discovery begins with the Rev. Thomas

Shaw's great work on Numidia, the result of twelve years' residence in Algiers. In 1798 Frederick Conrad Horneman, disguised as a Mohammedan, having agreed with the African Society of London to explore North Africa, left Cairo for the Oasis of Siwah, once the site of the Temple of Jupiter Ammon. He later went to Fezzan, and, after a journey to Tripoli and back, started for Bournou, where he died in April, 1800.

Major Houghton, in 1790, attempted to explore the Niger, visiting Timbuctoo and Houssa, returning across the Sahara. He followed the Gambia River from its mouth for a thousand miles and crossed Senegambia, but lost his outfit, and was never heard of, after sending a note from the little town of Tisimbing, stating that he was trying to reach Timbuctoo.

In 1795 Dr. Mungo Park, a young Scotchman aided by the African Society, sailed for the mouth of the Gambia, and set out with two negro interpreters for the town of Medina; thence he went to Bondou in Senegal. At Kassan the king desired to detain him until the wars then raging were ended. Mungo Park proceeded and finally reached Segou, the Bambarra capital on the Niger. The town would not receive him, but the king sent him a guide to Sandig. Park returned to the Gambia, having determined that the Niger ran eastward.

He then sailed for England, where his discoveries were impatiently awaited.

On January 30th, 1805, Mungo Park sailed on a second expedition with Dr. Anderson, George Scott, a draughtsman, and thirty-five artillerymen. He was joined by a Mandingo merchant and four carpenters, but when Park arrived at the Niger only six soldiers and one carpenter remained alive. At Sansandig he opened a large store and built a boat to ascend the Niger. The death of Anderson left him alone to start on his voyage down the Niger, November 16th, 1805. Eight or nine days afterwards, having already beaten off several attacks directed by the chief Yaouri, he perished.

In 1816, Majors Peddie and Campbell were engaged by the British government to explore Central Africa by way of Senegal. Major Peddie died early in the journey, and Major Campbell also succumbed, together with most of the officers. A few survivors only returned to Sierra Leone.

In 1819 Messrs. Ritchie and Lyon left Tripoli for Fezzan, reaching Murzuk, where Mr. Ritchie died November 2d, 1819. Capt. Lyon recovered from the fever and brought back much valuable information about the desert, towns, oases, caravans, and the Tuaric Arabs of the Great Sahara.

Another British expedition, consisting of Major Denham, Lieut. Clapperton, Dr. Oudney and Mr.

William Hillman, the last a carpenter, left Tripoli in November, 1821. With a Moorish escort and a passport from the Moorish authorities, they reached Murzuk, the capital of Fezzan, in April, 1822, being hospitably received all along the route. Here, however, an attempt was made to prevent their further progress south, but Denham returned to Tripoli and told the Bey that he should go back to England and report his bad faith to the English authorities. Having procured a proper permission, the expedition set out from Murzuk to Tegerry, escorted by two hundred Arabs. At Tegerry, a walled city, they entered the great desert by the ancient caravan route. Their road was marked by the skeletons of men and beasts. At several small oases, water and rough forage were supplied. Kishi, the largest of these, paid tribute money to the Tibboos, a race of splendid horsemen, so dexterous with their javelins that Denham records a range of 145 yards.

On February 4th, 1823, they reached the city of Rilari, at the northern end of Lake Tchad, an inland sea of fresh water.

Passing west of the lake, they reached Kouka, the capital of Bournou, to be received by four thousand disciplined cavalry, including the Sultan's body-guard, wearing chain armour. Kouka was a city of one thousand people, whose markets abounded in all kinds of provisions, slaves, ivory, brass, copper, amber, coral, and linen. Sheikh El Kahnemy, the real ruler of Bournou, tried to dissuade Denham from proceeding farther, but finally allowed him to accompany Bou Khaloum on a raid against the infidel Fellatahs, also known as Foulahs and Fans in later accounts. They attacked and destroyed the first town reached, but at Muspeia the assailants were utterly routed. Denham, wounded and taken prisoner, was stripped of his clothing and barely escaped with his life to Kouka. There he was joined in December, 1823, by Ensign Toole, and visited the country south of Lake Tchad. Here the Ensign died of fever, and Denham returned to Kouka, where Lieut. Tyrwhitt arrived May 20th, 1824, as resident British Consul, with costly presents for the Sultan.

In the meantime Messrs. Clapperton and Oudney had visited Kano, a city of the Fellatahs, and were well received. Dr. Oudney's health failed rapidly and he died January 12th, 1824. From Kano, the capital of Houssa, a city of forty thousand inhabitants, Clapperton went northwest to Sockatoo, a walled city with twelve gates guarded and closed at nightfall. Sultan Bello was greatly delighted with the gifts brought him by Clapperton, and returned to him the books, journals, and clothing lost by Major Denham in his raid on the frontiers.

Clapperton and Denham returned to England, having discovered Lake Tchad and visited the great empire of the Confederacy of the Fellatahs.

In 1825, Clapperton, Drs. Dickson and Morrison, and Capt. Pearce, sailed for the Bight of Benin. Dr. Dickson tried to visit Sockatoo with a Portuguese merchant, named Sousa, and Denham's servant, Columbus. They left Whydah, visited Dahomey and were traced to various villages, but Dickson quarrelled with the native chiefs and was killed with all his followers. Clapperton, being warned of the enmity of the natives to all Englishmen, gave up the ascent of the Quorra River and, with Houtson, an English trader, went through a part of Dahomey to Jenneh, sixty miles from the coast, where Capt. Pearce and Dr. Morrison died of African fever.

Clapperton proceeded alone and was met by an escort of King Yariba at Katunga, a town three miles in length and palisadoed with growing trees, at the base of a granite mountain. In 1826, he encountered a Housa caravan, consisting of thousands of men, women, horses, asses and oxen, all marching in single file, a motley assemblage of naked slaves, porters, merchants, armed escorts, veiled ladies and the like. At Boussa, on an island of the Quorra River, the Sultan evidently did not wish to answer his questions about the death of

Mungo Park in 1805. Finally he learned that Park was murdered and that his books, etc., were in the possession of a Mohammedan devotee who had left the country. In 1826, Clapperton reached Kano to find that Bournou had cut off communication with Fezzan and Tripoli. Shortly after, Sultan Bello, after receiving the presents sent him by the English government, took by force the gifts and despatches sent to the Sultan of Bournou. Capt. Clapperton with difficulty retained his own arms and ammunition, and his servant, Richard Lander, came only in time to care for him in his last illness. Lander tried to return to Benin by way of the Niger but finally had to take another route, adding much to the results of Clapperton's last exploration.

In 1816 Capt. James Tuckey sailed in the frigate "Congo" with the "Dorothea" transport via the Congo, and ascended the river, first in his ship and then in boats, two hundred and eighty miles, when disease in the rainy season compelled him to return to his ship, on board of which he died, October 4, 1816.

In 1817, the Messrs. Bowditch were sent on an embassy to Coomassie, the capital of the Ashantees, who since 1807 had ravaged the country and broken up the English trade. On their entrance into Coomassie they found thirty thousand men under arms, and a hundred bands pouring forth martial and not unpleasing music. The king's messengers, with golden breastplates and long canes, led the ambassadors past the Caboceers, clad in Ashantee cloth, made by unravelling highly coloured silks and weaving them into rich and heavy robes worn like the Roman toga.

The description of the court of Ashantee, given by the travellers, reads like an account of the Court of King Solomon, when barbaric Israel was at the height of its pride and power.

The record of early discovery adds to its tragedies the expedition of Gaspard Mollian, a nephew of Napoleon, Minister of Finance, who started from Djeddeh and penetrated to the sources of the Senegal. He was followed in 1824 by René Caillie, who lived for sometime among the Moors, and in 1827 left Freetown, Sierra Leone, ascended the Rio Nunuz, crossed to the Niger and near its source found it nine hundred feet wide with a current of nearly three miles an hour. In April, 1828, Caillie reached Timbuctoo, eight miles from the Niger, in a desert whose only product is salt. He was not the first to reach Timbuctoo, which Major Alexander Gordon Lang reached from Tripoli in 1826. Caillie was later beaten almost to death and robbed by the savage Tuaricks. He attempted to go home via Senegal, but he was strangled and left unburied in the desert simply and solely because he was not of the faith.

In 1830 Richard Lander and his brother John explored the Senegal from its source to its mouth, and returned in safety to England. But Richard Lander, having attempted to ascend the Niger in a river steamboat, was attacked and killed in 1834.

CHAPTER III

THE ROMANCE OF AFRICAN EXPLORATION (CONTINUED)

MODERN African exploration may be said to have begun with the expeditions of David Livingstone, born March 19, 1813, at Blantyre, Scotland. Of all the names that have come to us in the romance of African exploration no one is better known or more beloved than that of this simple Scottish weaver. From a humble walk in life he rose to be the most famous man of his day, and earned at last from his grateful country a tomb in Westminster Abbey. There, written upon his gravestone by the thrilled hand of the affection of a mighty nation, are his own words as he lay dying amid the swamps of Tanganyika:

"May the blessing of God descend upon the man, be he an Englishman, an American or a Turk, who will heal the open sore of Africa." The open sore of Africa was the slave trade, and to the nation that produced Livingstone we must award the credit of having almost unaided annihilated slavery in Africa.

Educated as a minister, physician and surgeon for missionary labours, he met at London Robert Moffatt, the pioneer of South African frontier missionary enterprise. Landing at Algoa Bay in 1840, he settled at Kuruman, a mission station, whence for two years he explored the country, securing the good-will of the great chiefs Sekome and Sechele. He finally settled at Mabotsa, among the Bechuanas, among whom he laboured until 1846, when he took up his residence at the chief village of Sechele, chief of the Bakwains. In 1849 with Mr. Oswell he crossed the Kalahari desert to Lake Ngami, which was reached in August, 1849.

In April, 1851, in company with Mr. Oswell, he reached the Chobe, the southern branch of the Zambesi, where he met Sebituane, the great chief of the Makololo, among whom he was given the greatest liberty of action. Finding no suitable place for a permanent missionary station, Livingstone sent his family to Scotland and pursued his labours alone. In the attempt to find some locality not infested by the tsetse fly he determined to take a party of natives and make a way to the Atlantic coast.

Ascending the Leeba to Lake Kilolo, they struck due west, crossing the Congo in April and reaching

Loanda on the west coast May 31st, 1854. Here they were well treated by the Portuguese and, returning home, reached Linyanti in September, 1855. In November, with Sekeletu, the chief of the Makololo, he descended the Zambesi, and on November 22, 1854, discovered the Great Victoria Falls. At this point he parted from Sekeletu and, with one hundred and fourteen men, sailed down the great river and reached the Portuguese settlement of Tette on March 2, 1856, whence he returned with his native following to Kilimane. He soon after sailed for England, where he arrived in 1856.

In 1858, he was appointed British Consul at large and given command of an expedition for exploring Central and Eastern Africa, sailing from Liverpool and reaching the Zambesi, May 14th, 1858. He now explored the Zambesi and the great rapids in 1858, the Shire and Nyassa in 1859 and made a journey to Victoria Falls in 1860.

In July, 1861, Livingstone went with an escort to show Bishop Mackenzie the country, and liberated several slave gangs. The Ajawa, a tribe of slavers, attacked the party and Livingstone was obliged to put them to flight by a volley. Bishop Mackenzie and his party of missionaries settled in the hills south of Lake Shirwa, while Livingstone explored the shores of Lake Nyassa, but found nearly the whole coast lined with burned villages, wasted crops, and multitudes of corpses, until he was turned back by the presence of large bodies of slavers who were carrying on the infernal work.

In January, 1862, Mrs. Livingstone and the ladies of the new missionaries arrived at the Zambesi, but before the ladies reached the mission station they learned of the death of Bishop Mackenzie and of the Rev. Mr. Burrup. This great blow to Livingstone's hope of establishing a mission was followed by the death of Mrs. Livingstone April 27, 1862. In the "Lady Nyassa" he explored the Rovuma River and further delimited Lake Nyassa. But the horrors of the Arab and Portuguese slave trade made it impossible to establish peaceful missions and he returned, via Zanzibar and Bombay, to England in 1864.

During this time Burton had discovered Lake Tanganyika; Speke, the Victoria Nyanza; and Baker, Lake Albert Nyanza, with Nilotic feeders, and it seemed that Livingstone's dream of finding the sources of the Nile must be abandoned. In 1866, he left Zanzibar on another expedition and, following the shore of Lake Nyassa, set out to reach the southern end of Tanganyika, over a totally unexplored and very swampy country. He had only four or five mission boys, his medicine chest was stolen and he was fearfully ill and emaciated. However, he reached Tanganyika in

March, 1867, and obtained some supplies from Arab slave traders. In November he reached the northern end of Lake Mweru, and thence the Cazembes' town on Lake Mofwa, where he learned much about the travels of Lacerda, Pereira, Monteiro, and other Portuguese explorers. Returning, he visited the Lualaba, an affluent of Lake Bangweolo, which ultimately becomes the Congo River, but which Livingstone, unfortunately for him, believed to be the upper waters of the Nile. Indeed his belief that the Fountains of Herodotus lay far west of Lake Bangweolo became so fixed in his mind that his efforts to find them undoubtedly led to his last fatal expedition.

Later, he circumnavigated Lake Bangweolo for a part of its length, finding it almost surrounded by those spongy marshes which he believed to be a part of the real sources of the Nile. Here he was again detained by Arab slave hunters; but finally he marched eastward to Lake Tanganyika and sailed up its western shore, reaching Ujiji, March 14, 1869. Here he found that most of the stores forwarded from Zanzibar had been stolen and that the men sent to aid him were perfectly unreliable. However, he again crossed Tanganyika into Manyuema, trying for nearly a year to reach and cross the Lualaba. In July he settled down to rest at

Bambarra, where the natives were very kind to him in spite of the brutalities of the Arab marauders.

In 1871, he reached Nyangwe on the Lualaba and tried for four months to cross the river. Suddenly on a market day a party of Arabian slavers attacked the people, shooting down men and women by hundreds, while Livingstone with great difficulty, and realizing his own utter helplessness, refrained from using his own revolver on the miscreants. Almost utterly helpless, he retreated, barely escaping an attack from the Manyema, reaching Ujiji, October 13, 1871. Here on the 18th of October he was surprised by the arrival of the New York Herald expedition, sent out by Mr. Gordon Bennett under the command of Mr. Henry M. Stanley, who brought him full supplies for all his needs and another year of exploration.

Together they explored the north end of Tanganyika and proved that it had no outlet. Thence Livingstone accompanied Stanley to Unyanyembe to secure some supplies awaiting him there, but found them largely stolen and spoiled. At Unyanyembe they separated, March 15, 1872, after Stanley, having in vain besought Livingstone to return to Europe, had given him all his extra supplies and agreed to send him men and needed articles from Zanzibar. In August, 1872, fifty-seven men and boys arrived at Unyanyembe with the supplies forwarded by Stanley.

On August 15th, Livingstone set out and followed the eastern shore of Tanganyika for Lake Bangweolo, which he hoped to pass at its southern extremity, and thence to march westward to find the sources of the Nile. January, 1873, found his party wading day after day through treacherous bogs and swampy jungles, east of Lake Bangweolo. Livingstone's old chronic dysentery again seized him, but he would not give up his quest for the elusive Fountains of the Nile which he was never to behold. By the middle of April he had to be carried in a litter, but kept up his journal and observations until April 27th, although very weak. On April 29th, 1873, he reached Chitambo's village in Ilala on the southern shore of the lake, but the next day he was very feeble and with difficulty wound up his watch.

On the morning of May 1st, 1873, his faithful boys found him kneeling by the side of his bed but he had been dead for some hours. Susi, his body servant and his faithful companion, preserved the body as well as he could; and, swathing it in many wrappings, bore it with all his papers, instruments and property down to the coast. From Zanzibar the body was removed to England and on April 18th, 1874, was laid to rest with every tribute of

WHERE THE NILE LEAVES VICTORIA NYANZA.

national and international sorrow and respect in that Pantheon of England's departed worthies, Westminster Abbey.

Livingstone's explorations on the Zambesi inspired Messrs. Galton and Anderssen, who, in 1850-1851, penetrated from Walfisch Bay into Namaqualand, as far as Lake Ngami. Carl Mauch explored the Matabele country north of the Limpopo River, and discovered in the Transvaal the great gold reef and placers which have since proved the richest in the world. Here also he found the ruins of Zimbabye, where walls thirty feet high and seven to ten feet thick, and towers thirty feet in height still contain rude furnaces, motors, pedestals, gold bearing ore and slag, with evidences of heathen worship long since obsolete.

Another German explorer, Edward Mohr, with Mr. Thomas Baines, set out from Natal in 1870, crossed the Limpopo and reached the Victoria Falls. The same country, in 1872-1879, was also partially explored by Dr. Emil Holub. In 1884, Mr. Walter M. Kerr came from Cape Town to the Zambesi. Part of the way he was accompanied by Mr. F. C. Selous, a famous African hunter, who secured permission from King Lo-Bengula to cross his territory into Mashonaland. Going on to Lake Nyassa, Kerr found the mission at Livingstonia utterly deserted, seven of the people having died and the rest having removed to another station. But at last he was taken on board the steam launch Itala, was carried to the mouth of the Zambesi and so home.

In 1877, Major Serpo Pinto of the Portuguese army went from St. Paul da Loanda to the headwaters of the Zambesi, thence down the river to Victoria Falls, and southward through Mashonaland, Matabeleland, and the Transvaal to Natal, arriving at Durban in the spring of 1879.

In 1855, Major Gafarini started from Cape Town to cross the Kalahari desert, wherein he barely escaped dying of thirst. Arriving at the Orange River, he explored and photographed the Hundred Falls and the cascades, the deep glens and towering cliffs of those wonderful gorges through which the headwaters of the Orange River flow downward to the sea.

In 1862, Sir Richard Burton ascended the Gaboon River to visit the N'bongwe or Fan cannibals and the habitats of the gorilla, previously described by M. Paul Du Chaillu. In 1863, he ascended the Congo as far as the lower cataracts.

In November, 1874, Stanley, with two brothers, named Popock, and Mr. Fred Baker, left Bagamoyo for Ujiji. The expedition, financed by the London Daily Telegraph and the New York Herald, had a small army of carriers and guides, and everything that experience could suggest, including many donkeys and a large sectional boat, the "Lady Alice." The expedition reached the Victoria Nyanza in the Kagehyi country in February, 1875. Selecting a picked crew and leaving his expedition under the command of Frank Popock and Fred Baker, Stanley sailed in the "Alice," March 8, 1875, heading eastward and intending to circumnavigate the great inland sea. On the 10th, Stanley reached the river Shikkeyu, supposed to be three hundred miles long, whose headwaters are forty-two hundred miles from the delta of the Nile, through which its waters eventually reach the Mediterranean Sea. Sailing west and north, the boat passed a large number of islands and at several points, especially at the Bavuma on the northern coast of Lake Victoria Nyanza, the little crew narrowly escaped death from the treacherous natives. But on the 30th of March, the expedition reached the outlying territories of M'tesa, the King of Uganda.

On April 3d, six canoes, under a chief named Magassa, met the "Alice" and invited Stanley to become the guest of the Kabaka. The "Alice" was received at Usavara, the favourite sea side resort of M'tesa, and, amid the shouts of thousands of people and the discharge of volleys of muskets, Stanley landed and was received by the Katakiro, or chief subordinate of the king. In the afternoon, after having received a vast amount of provisions from the king, the party was presented in due form to the most powerful and intelligent ruler of the most civilized natives of East Central Africa.

On the 10th of April, M'tesa returned to his capital. Stanley followed him and was assigned a comfortable house with quarters for his men and a liberal allowance of provisions. Here on the 11th, at a reception of M'tesa, he met M. Linant Bellefonds, who had just come up the Nile with an escort of Nubian soldiers. The two travellers were greatly pleased with each other and spent much time together when not in attendance upon the Emperor. And, while Stanley returned to Usavara on his way to bring up his men and baggage from the other end of the lake, M. Linant Bellefonds agreed to remain with M'tesa at Uganda, during his absence.

The canoes sent to attend and aid Stanley in bringing up his expedition were diverted from this purpose by the jealousy or insubordination of the chief in charge, and finally the "Alice" was left alone. While landing on Bumbireh Island to purchase food they were attacked by the natives, their boat seized by main force and run up on the shore, and the whole party narrowly escaped massacre by running the boat forcibly into the lake and paddling away with pieces of the lining of the boat, while Stanley with his elephant rifle destroyed canoes and killed a number of the natives. On May 6, after having passed through a terrible tempest, Stanley reached his camp, to his great joy, which was saddened by the death of Fred Baker, who had been buried twelve days before.

On returning to Uganda, many canoes were secured, but the chief of Bumbireh attempted to prevent them from passing. Stanley, having exhausted negotiations, attacked the natives at Bumbireh, and punished them so severely that they sued for peace. Arriving at Uganda, he made a long stay at the capital and took part in a great war on the hostile Bavuma Islanders, who though greatly outnumbered kept the Uganda people at bay.

Finally, Stanley constructed a floating fort on three canoes lying side by side, which, containing a body of picked troops and flying several gay banners, mysteriously moved on the face of the waters across the strait. From within a herald summoned the islanders to surrender and to pay tribute, announcing that otherwise the island would be blown out of existence. Overcome by the mystery and impregnability of this marine monster, the Bavuma people gave hostages and tributes and the war was over.

After a long stay in Uganda, Stanley went westward and discovered Lake Albert Edward, and then along the shores of Tanganyika to Ujiji. In July, Stanley in the "Alice," with a great canoe hired from the Arabs, started to circumnavigate Lake Tanganyika, exploring the bays and rivers and satisfying himself that the great lake is deepening so rapidly that in a few years at most it will force its way through the Lukuga into the Livingstone and sweep out an ample passage through the Congo into the Atlantic.

On July 31st, 1876, Stanley returned to Ujiji, having sailed eight hundred and ten miles, the extreme circuit of the Tanganyika being nine hundred and thirty miles. Then Stanley headed northeast to the town of Nyangwe on the lower Lualaba River, where Cameron and Livingstone had in vain attempted to cross or follow its waters and ascertain its course. Here, late in October, a few miles north of the junction of the Lulindi, Stanley joined a large encampment of Arabs just returned from a forage amongst the Manyema. Here he met the famous Tippu Tib, who had escorted Cameron until, unable to obtain canoes of the native chief, the gallant officer was forced to return.

Stanley induced Tippu Tib to escort his party sixty marches of four hours each in any direction for the sum of five thousand dollars. Starting on November 5, 1876, Stanley marched with one hundred and fifty-four men, women and children, and sixty-four rifles and guns. Tippu Tib had seven hundred persons, but, after marching about two hundred miles, on December 22, 1876, he announced that he could go no further, but consented to aid the expedition to start on the river and encouraged the men to follow and obey Stanley. Having paid the Arab twenty-six hundred dollars for his services and having given him and his chiefs costly gifts for their assistance, Stanley began with twenty-three canoes and one hundred and forty-nine men, women, and children the most daring adventure of modern times.

Almost immediately they came upon the continuous villages of the Lualaba tribesmen, most of whom were cannibals and greeted the coming of the expedition as soldiers would an enemy's convoy of fat cattle. On December 29th they had their first skirmish. On the 30th a canoe was lost with two men and four guns, and on January 1st, 1877, another big fight cleared the river of the cannibal fleet. On January 2d the expedition fought four hours, but next day found a friendly reception and a good supply of food, only to be attacked later by a fleet of forty canoes, some from sixty to eighty-five feet long. Being just above the first cataract, Stanley was obliged to anchor and fight the fierce cannibals and finally to land and build a fortified camp. In the fighting next day the natives were repulsed with difficulty, Stanley losing two men killed and ten wounded. On January 8th, having hauled their canoes around the first cataract, they found, a few miles lower down, the second cataract, where they had to drive out the hostiles from an island. From January 10th to the 13th, by alternate fighting and labour, a three mile portage was effected around the second cataract. On the 15th another portage was overcome, only to find another fleet of canoes ready for battle. Stanley retaliated by landing, capturing two villages with all their contents; and the natives, finding that their women, children and property were unharmed, made peace and supplied the expedition with food. On the 25th the seventh cataract was reached and near it the villages of the Wenya, who attacked with great impetuosity but could not penetrate the stockade. On the 26th, Stanley decided to attack their villages but found them abandoned, although they must have held six thousand people. On the 27th the expedition was again attacked, but on the 28th the river lay open before them at the foot of the last cataract of the Stanley Falls.

From this point the river trended more and more toward the west but at last flowed nearly southwest towards the Atlantic. There was much fighting and privation, but Stanley, now certain that he was on the Congo, kept up the spirits of his men and of his only surviving white companion, Frank Popock, who had become crippled and unfit for active work.

On June 3d, in the absence of Stanley, Frank Popock, as if urged on by fate, ordered a picked crew to carry him down the left side of the Livingstone Falls. Stanley's men declared it was sure death to attempt it, but he taunted them with cowardice and at last they consented. They could not reach the left side of the river and were compelled to take a terrible plunge in midstream. Only eight escaped alive and, although Uledi attempted to save Popock, he was unable to grasp his body and with difficulty saved himself. After this they rapidly drifted and sailed towards the Atlantic until on July 16, at the great Ngombi Falls, the natives themselves drew the "Alice" and canoes on the sand beaches for the last time.

During the last days the natives, although not hostile, were very selfish and indisposed to sell food, and the expedition was on the verge of starvation. Some stole food and were ransomed at great cost, and later, some, thus seized, were left behind as slaves. When within five days' journey of Boma, the nearest European trading post, the "Alice" was for the last time drawn ashore and left to decay, having travelled on the lakes and the Congo nearly seven thousand miles. On August 4th the men had suffered so much from want of food that Stanley finally decided to send messages to Boma, whence Europeans would surely send food and aid. A prompt answer was received on the 7th accompanied by ample supplies of food and clothing for the people and luxuries for Stanley himself. The account given by Stanley of this timely relief is one of the most simply touching in all the literature of travel and adventure. One of the most striking features is an extemporaneous song by one of the men describing the adventurous journey and its happy ending. Each verse being followed by the chorus:

> "Then sing, oh, friend, sing, the journey is ended.
> Sing loudly, oh, friend, sing to this great chief."

On August 9th, 1877, they reached Boma, and on the 11th, took passage on the steamer "Kabinda" on their way to the Atlantic, whose waters they were the first of all men to reach from the East Coast by way of the Congo.

Mr. Joseph Thompson, previous to 1882, after the death of Mr. Keith Johnston, pushed on with his expedition around the north end of the Nyanza to Lake Tanganyika and thence into unknown countries to the west. In 1883, he was sent by the Royal Geographical Society to explore the country lying between Lake Victoria and the East Coast.

His accounts of the Masai, then a much more turbulent and dangerous people than now, of Kili-

Photograph by Peter Dutkewich, copyright, 1909, by Underwood & Underwood, N.Y.

THE ETERNAL SNOW, AT AN ELEVATION OF 19,000 FEET, ON MOUNT KILIMANJARO.

manjaro, Mount Kenia and the great plateaus between the Nyanza and the sea are still looked upon as unsurpassed in interest and reliability. In over twenty thousand miles of African travel, among some of the most turbulent and warlike tribes of Africa, it was never necessary for him to sacrifice a single human life.

Krapf and Rebman, German missionaries, in 1849 discovered Mts. Kenia and Kilimanjaro. In 1889 Dr. Hans Meyer ascended Kilimanjaro to the summit, 19,800 feet.

I could not close this sketch without mention of two very recent and romantic names — Chinese Gordon and Lord Kitchener.

Charles George Gordon was born in 1833 and served his country with great distinction in China. In 1882 he commanded the Royal Engineers in Mauritius, where he attained the rank of major-general. From March to October, 1882, he was connected with the Cape Government in an attempt to terminate the Basuto trouble, but resigned in indignation at the intrigues of Mr. Sauer, Secretary for Native Affairs. The year 1883 he spent in the Holy Land. He had undertaken a mission to the Congo for the King of the Belgians when the catastrophe to. Hicks Pasha's army, which was overwhelmed by the forces of the Mahdi, made the Gladstone Government insist on the Khedive's abandonment of the Sudan. Gordon was commissioned to effect the withdrawal of the scattered garrisons and the evacuation of the country. He arrived at Khartum in 1884 and received a warm welcome; but his first battle with the hostile Sudanese was unsuccessful, owing to the treachery of two pashas. The capture of Berber by the rebels cut Gordon's communication with Cairo and he was beleaguered in Khartum. He successfully repelled the besieging hordes for over ten months, but on January 26, 1885, Khartum fell through the treachery of Ferig Pasha, and Gordon was slain.

Horatio Herbert Kitchener, first Viscount Kitchener of Khartum, was born near Ballylongford, Ireland, Sept. 22, 1850. Educated at The Royal Military Academy, Woolwich, he entered the Royal Engineers as a lieutenant in 1871, having already seen some active service on the French side in the Franco-Prussian war. In 1874-8 he was engaged on the survey of Palestine under the auspices of the Palestine Exploration Fund Committee, and in 1878-82, except for a short period as vice-consul in Anatolia, carried out a survey of Cyprus. In 1882 he was appointed to a cavalry command in Egypt, served in the Nile expedition of 1884-5, and for his services was made a brevet lieutenant-colonel and received the Khedive's star and the second class

Medjidie. He was governor of Suakin, 1886-8, and distinguished himself in the latter year by the bravery and skill with which he led the Egyptian troops against Osman Digna at Handoub. In 1889 he was in command of mounted troops on the Sudan frontier, and, for his bravery, was created Companion of the Bath. From 1888 till 1892 he was adjutant-general and second in command of the Egyptian army, and in 1892 became Sirdar. He commanded the Anglo-Egyptian force which recovered Dongola for Egypt in 1896, and his services were rewarded by promotion to the rank of major-general. He was also made a Knight Commander of the Bath and awarded the first-class Osmanieh order. He utterly destroyed the power of the Khalifa by the battle of Omdurman on Sept. 2, 1898, and for this was raised to the peerage (1898) as Baron Kitchener of Khartum and of Aspall, in the county of Suffolk, receiving also the formal thanks of Parliament and a grant of £30,000. He was appointed governor-general and commander-in-chief of the Egyptian Sudan in 1899, but resigned this post and that of Sirdar of the Egyptian army in the latter part of the same year in order to accompany Lord Roberts to South Africa as chief of his staff in the war with the Boers. When Lord Roberts left South Africa to become commander-in-chief at home, Kitchener succeeded him as commander-in-chief of the forces in South Africa, and carried on the war to its conclusion. He was then created viscount and appointed commander-in-chief in India in the same year, 1902.

CHAPTER IV

ZANZIBAR, THE GATE OF EAST AFRICA

A UNIQUE centre of trade and diplomacy is Zanzibar, and the most pleasant and convenient gate through which the explorer, merchant or traveller can enter upon the study of the great plateaus and interesting kingdoms of East and Central Africa. The student of travel cannot understand darkest Africa without first visiting the scene of the preparatory labours of Livingstone, Burton, Speke, Grant, Cameron, Emin and Stanley and other less-known, yet not less devoted and courageous, men who have "taken up the white man's burden," sought out humanity's waste places and made straighter and easier the path by which their successors might, with peaceful trade and Christian education, supplant the murderous wars of ten thousand years. To Zanzibar, moreover, have returned the explorers and missionaries of Africa to receive the applause of a grateful world; or, less fortunate, have come back from the great and terrible wilderness mere wrecks of the splendid manhood which had set out with indomitable zeal, a few months before. Sometimes, like the heroic Livingstone, they have been borne hither on the shoulders of a few faithful black men from the scenes of their last brave battle with relentless fate. And then in Westminster Abbey, or in the peaceful village where, as boys, they played, they have received the homage which appreciative Europe seldom fails to accord manliness and achievement.

In my boyhood I read in my child's geography: "Mozambique and Zanzibar, West of Madagascar." These resonant names of far-away and then little known lands brought before my glowing, childish fancy visions of sultans bearded and turbaned, on golden thrones; birds of paradise, veritable flying jewels traversing fairy arcades through the umbrageous foliage of tropic forests; the gorgeous, sensuous, mysterious East showering on war-like kings and on queens of unutterable beauty, musk, sandal, attar, and barbaric pearl and gold. But in my wildest imaginings I never hoped to visit such an earthly paradise, such lands of eternal summer, such Islands of the Blest lapped in the silvery seas.

After having seen all these lands of unfamiliar names and of my early dreams, there still remains to me something of the splendour and mystery, the glamour of my childish fancy. They are colonies now, of England, France, Germany and Portugal, but at their names rise up an airy mirage of past and present associations — tales of the great freebooters and petty pirates of the Indian Ocean, of Tippu Tib and the slave-hunters who raided Africa with armies for ivory "white and black;" the perils and sufferings of the Arab and half-breed adventurers; their destruction of hundreds of villages and myriads of human beings; the utter misery and horror of the long journeys on the slave trail to the coast; the dying captives cloven by scimitar and axe from the chain; and the living pulled down by the dying. And in that shadowy empire of fancy one sees again the terrors of the spear-flight and arrow storm of hostile and powerful clans, the pangs of insatiate thirst and destroying hunger, the nameless crimes of men left to their lusts and avarice; the sorrows of the slave-mart and the crowded dhow; the swift pursuit of infidel cruisers and the merciless drowning of the whole human freight when escape seemed impossible; the screams for mercy and the rush of ravening sharks. All this commingled in my brain as, from the deck of the English steamship "Swaledale," I first saw, close at hand, the gray sands and white walls of the ancient Arab city of Zanzibar, for centuries the greatest slave-mart of the East, now a centre of peaceful commerce, a city of freedom for ever.

Set in a sea of sapphire blue, her graceful contours outlined in tenderest green, her rounded hills crowned with dainty palms which lazily nod to the sea-birds and the white surf, the Island of Zanzibar slumbers beneath the brilliant glory of a tropic sun. It is the ideal land of the Lotus-eater. I know no fairer spot on earth than this.

The city rises abruptly back from a beach of yellow sand in a succession of high white walls. A row-boat, managed by noisy Swahili boys, puts you ashore on a shelving beach, and you face an impenetrable and mysterious mass of snow-white houses. You get your baggage passed through the customs house, where you meet a courteous, white-turbaned officer; you breathe the aromatic odour of cloves and the sweet, sickening scent of copra; a native guide drags you through a twisting canyon in the wall, past great doorways of carved teakwood, between whitewashed walls, and suddenly you emerge into the light and glow and colour of Zanzibar.

The lanes and narrow streets are aglow with all the hues of the rainbow; all the primal colours of the passionate, luxurious Orient — gorgeous, unshaded, violent. Cobalt-blue, greens, reds and yellows glow on frame-work and door-way like colour-photography. Orange and black, blue, yellow, purple, white, scarlet, golden; such are the costumes of the men and women — fifty thousand of the most picturesque people ever brought together; Indians,

Arabs, Swahilis, Somalis, Goanese, Parsees, Europeans. It is the brightest, richest in colour, as well as the most energetically commercial of all the East African ports.

All is noise, activity, glitter. Here the Indian merchant beseeches you from his bazar; there children swathed in silk, and decorated with costly jewels and bangles, stumble under your feet. Black women, draped below their shoulders in the colours of the butterfly, their necks and bosoms gay with chains and beads, their plump arms clasped by bracelets, with fingers and brows dyed purple, balance on their heads water-jars made out of American oil-tins.

These dusky maidens, chattering around the pumps, filling their five-gallon tins with beautifully clear water from the Sultan's Spring, form a scene one could watch for hours. They are so clean, so eager and merry. The spring is two miles away, but the water comes by an iron main and is distributed to the many pumps throughout the city. One of the former sultans, old "Barghash, the Builder," brought the water to the people, and made a law that no water-tax should be imposed for ever. When the British government took the island, it agreed to keep the Sultan's will, and so there is no water-tax in Zanzibar.

All drink from the fountains of Barghash.

Water costs one cent for a five-gallon tinful brought to your house by the water-women.

Zanzibar is an Arabian Nights city — a comic opera capital. There is no street nor house which does not suggest the scenic artist and the limelight. We expect the water-girls to appear as slaves in the next act, and that the Sultan's band down in the palace square will presently strike up an operatic tune.

Outside the city there are wide and beautiful roads between rows of mango and palm trees of richest green. The gardens and deserted palaces of departed sultans give glimpses of kiosk and encircling wall through the greenery. We enter the one belonging to Sultan Seyyid Said, he who conquered the Mombasa Arabs and moved the capital from Muscat in Arabia to Zanzibar. The great roadway that leads to the palace is worthy of Fontainebleau or Windsor. The walls are tastefully laid out and carefully kept. A high tower overlooks the sea and from it can be had a vista of gem-like islands. Here, under cool palms, amid tinkling waters and the songs of tropic birds, the brave old corsair sought rest after his many wars. We can see he loved his home and made it the cozy refuge of a lover of nature and beauty. He was a fierce fighter, and in war his scimitar knew no brother. He could

ON A CLOVE PLANTATION OF BUBUBU.

hate well and he could love. Peace to his soul in Paradise.

In our drives about Zanzibar we also come upon Hindu Temples, the little white-washed cottages of the Swahilis, each with its tiny garden of fruits and vegetables, the curtained verandahs of "the white exiles" — the twenty-odd Englishmen who with the Sultan form the Zanzibar government, half a dozen Americans representing the ivory and clove trade, the electric lighting company and the seven mile railway to Bububu, the Germans who do the largest share of the trade, and the European consuls. There are about two hundred in all, and the English have their club with the inevitable tennis, golf and cricket grounds. The Germans, who do not associate with the English at all, have their own club.

It is ridiculous, however, to talk of these people as "exiles," for it is a Mohammedan paradise to which they are exiled, and one young American who has been living there for five years told me he had lost all wish to return home. He said he was afraid of being run over in New York! Such is the fascination of this half-barbaric capital. And I think the charm of Zanzibar lies in the fact that, while the white men have made it clean and healthy, have given it safe highways, good laws and a firm government under a benign Sultan, they have done all this without destroying one flash of its local colour or one throb of its showy, sumptuous, sensuous Oriental life.

The good things of civilization are here, but they are unobtrusive, and the evils of civilization have not yet begun to appear. The great ships from Madagascar and the Cape touch here, and the passengers come ashore for a holiday; but, while they are assailed by vociferous boys, their judgment and good taste are not insulted. The native does not wear a bowler hat and a kimona, as he does in Japan; nor offer you souvenirs of the city made in Birmingham or Rhode Island, as they do in Cairo.

It may be interesting to Americans to know that Zanzibar and East Africa were first opened to the enterprise of the West by American traders. About 1830 the famous ivory house of Arnold, Cheney & Co. of New York opened their stores in Zanzibar. In 1833 a treaty was made by the United States with the Sultan Seyyid Said, protecting the lives and property of Americans sojourning in the Sultan's dominions; and in 1836 the American government established the first consulate ever located there. Being the first in the field, the Americans have dispersed their hardware and their cottons throughout East Africa, so that, even in remotest Congo, cotton cloth is called by the natives " Mericani." In 1839 Great Britain established a con-

Zanzibar

sulate here. At that time fifteen to twenty thousand slaves were sold yearly in the market-place.

England originally came to East Africa for the prevention of the slave trade. Her first treaty with the Sultan was made in 1822; and to England unaided we must accord the credit of practically abolishing the slave trade of the Zang coast.

The early Sultans of Zanzibar grew rich and powerful through the exportation of slaves and ivory from the mainland. The one trade was developed by the other. The Arab slave-trader would pay the Sultan a certain tribute for the privilege of dealing in ivory. He would then take an expedition into the interior and bargain with the local chiefs for so much ivory and so many men to carry it to the ships upon the coast. Without transport the bargain was useless. Accordingly, the chief would select a village that had not paid its taxes, and tell the trader to help himself. Then would follow a horrible midnight massacre of the women and children and the selection of all the able-bodied males. These poor fellows, chained together and each bearing a heavy load of ivory, would be driven down to the coast. It was not till the ivory had reached the sea-board that the idea presented itself of selling the carriers as well as the ivory. In later days the bearers became of greater value than the ivory, and the raiding of native villages and the taking of women as well as men to be sold into slavery became a great industry. The slaves were called "black ivory."

The "dhows" that carried slaves are still used a great deal in the coast trade, and they go as far as Persia and India. They are swift boats, and often in the slave days were able to sail faster than a man-of-war. Some have even made two hundred and forty miles in a day. A pear sharpened at the larger end and cut in two longitudinally will afford two models in all essential respects resembling a slave-dhow. The prow of a dhow sinks deeply into the water, while the stern floats lightly upon it, the sail is a right-angled triangle, and the dhow does not "tack" but "wears" when beating to windward. While the dhow reverses all the conditions sought in an American or English craft, one can hardly say that it is not seaworthy and effective. All its fittings are of the rudest sort; nothing seems to be finished.

These dhows are very leaky, and when they carried slaves even the water tanks were so badly made that the fresh water leaked out and the salt water leaked in, so that the slaves suffered terribly from thirst — but often hardly more than the captain of the ship. In many respects the captains were humane enough.

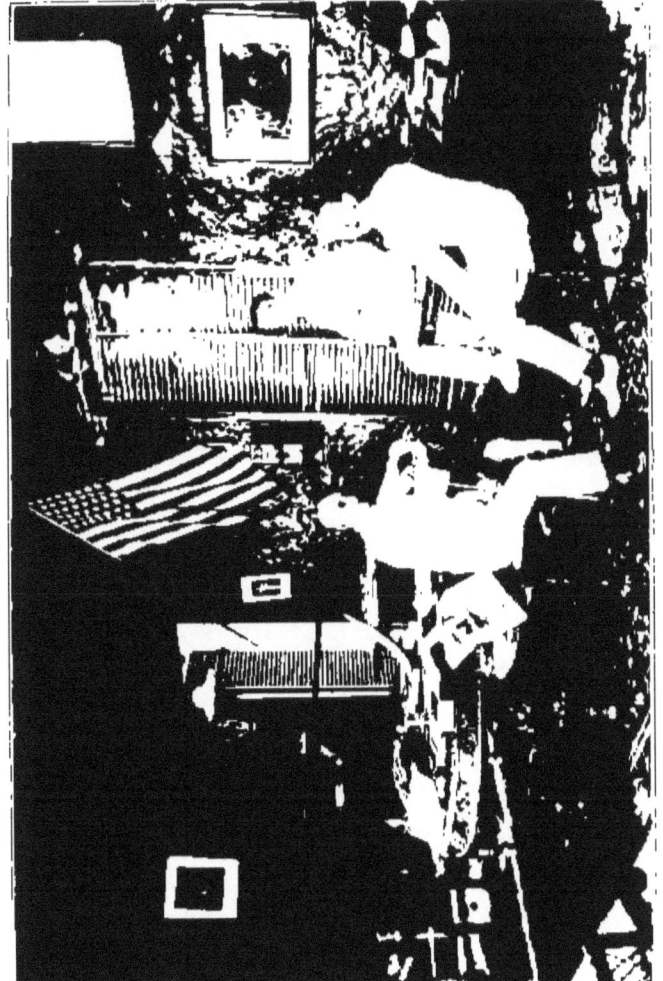

THE AUTHOR IN THE AMERICAN CONSULATE AT ZANZIBAR.

Zanzibar 69

Up to 1908, a mild form of domestic slavery was recognized in the clove plantations or "shambas" in the islands of Pemba and Zanzibar. But even that is no longer permitted by the British government. The big Arab farmers threaten to let the plantations go to waste rather than pay wages to their former slaves, and the end is not yet.

The export value of cloves from Zanzibar in 1907 was over eighteen million dollars, two million dollars' worth of which came to America. Nine-tenths of all the cloves in the world are raised in Pemba and Zanzibar. Copra yields six million and ivory two million a year. From the mainland about twenty-five million dollars' worth of ivory is exported per year, most of which is now shipped from Mombasa and Dar-es-Salaam upon the mainland. The island derives its main revenue from an export duty of thirty per cent. on ivory and copra. American kerosene lights the huts and homes; American electrical plants illuminate the Sultan's palace and the main streets; Americans have built and run the seven-mile railway to Bububu and the clove "shambas." It was really Americans who brought this part of East Africa in contact with the brilliant civilization of the West.

Although there are only a handful of Americans here, yet the American consul takes precedence to all other consuls except the British. It was therefore with some pride that we accompanied our vice-consul, Mr. W. B. Arnold, to the palace for an interview with his Highness Ali bin Hamoud, the Sultan of Zanzibar, Pemba and the Lamu Archipelago.

The palace is massive and modern on the exterior, but within it is fairyland, with silk draperies, tapestries and handpainted curtains. There is a great square in the centre, and around this are the various suites belonging to the Sultan. The harem is in a square, plain building connected with the palace by a bridge. The reception hall is hung with portraits of former rulers and an especially fine picture of the Emperor of Austria and his beautiful Empress, Elizabeth. The floors are covered with splendid rugs from Persia and India, and there are priceless treasures of ebony, ivory, lacquer-work, gold and silver, among them two chairs made of silver dragons with glittering scales and studded with jewels, a gift from Queen Victoria.

With his retinue, a few dignified Arabs, and Mr. Ellis, his English aide-de-camp, the Sultan received us. Ali bin Hamoud, a young man twenty-two years old last June, was educated at Eton, and shows his English education. Not a large man, but refined and dignified, he looks older than his years and has a kindly, off-hand way that recalled the student friends of my old college days. The Sul-

SULTAN ALI BIN HAMOUD AND THE ENGLISHMEN WHO FORM HIS GOVERNMENT.

tan's features are decidedly Arab, and he has the strong intelligence that marks his race, but his accent is that of an Englishman of the upper class. He talks of travel, books, scenery, the things a polished traveller and elegant gentleman is interested in.

His Highness was dressed in an English suit of white duck and wore a red fez. He rose and shook hands with us, asked us to be seated and ordered coffee and cigarettes to be set before us. Almost his first words were: "I am greatly interested in your big country, and planned to visit the United States last year. I was not able to go at that time, but I am going to America as soon as I can make my arrangements."

I told him he would see wonderful things and receive a very hospitable welcome in the Republic. He turned the conversation upon China and Japan, and took great interest in Mr. Dutkewich's travels in the far East. It was raining, and as we could not photograph the palace on that day, the Sultan gave us a kindly invitation to return two days later. This we did, and made pictures of his Highness and of the princpal rooms. We returned a third time and made moving pictures of the Sultan and his body-guard of Uganda Rifles. On one occasion we brought him a set of Underwood's stereographs of New York City, and he was as delighted as a boy, and sent them to the Sultana. In fact we found the Sultan of Zanzibar one of the most refined and intelligent of rulers.

There have been Sultans who were not so wise as Ali bin Hamoud. One of these, Said Khaled, in 1897 defied the British empire as represented by several gun boats, and dared them to fire on his fleet. The gun boats were anchored about four hundred yards from his palace, and, at the time declared in an ultimatum, fired on the fleet of Khaled and destroyed his ships, including the old "Glasgow," a converted tramp steamer whose masts still protrude above the water in front of the new palace. Most of the old palace was destroyed in the forty-five minute bombardment, and one of the rooms burned which contained invaluable curios, including the finest set of clocks in the world. To complete the ruin, most of the Sultan's collection of rare articles of vertu were looted. The Sultan was compelled to take refuge in the German consulate. The "bombardment" is still spoken of with awe by the people of Zanzibar.

For two months, in the rainy season of 1908, I roamed about this ancient Arab town. The heavy rains fall in April and May, and when it rains it seems as if a lake were tipped over on your head. The Africa Hotel and the Tippu Tib Hotel are fairly comfortable places; and, while I was at the

Photograph by Peter Dutkewich, copyright, 1909, by Underwood & Underwood, N. Y.

LIVINGSTONE'S FORMER RESIDENCE, ZANZIBAR.

former, the Duchess of Aosta stayed for a week at the hotel after her famous trip up the Nile from Alexandria to Lake Victoria. She had travelled to Mombasa on the Uganda Railway and had come over from the mainland to complete her African trip and take the boat to Naples.

I never tired of Zanzibar. When the rain stopped and the clouds lifted there were fascinating walks out past the English Club house, beyond the tennis courts and the wireless telegraph station to the sea shore. The great " Meseeka," the southwest monsoon, lashes the brine into one's face, the fisher boats come in each morning full of shining treasure. The boats are dug-out canoes with outriggers and a lateen sail. The sailors drive this frail skiff straight upon the rocks with wonderful skill. I made a picture of the Swahili fishermen dragging their nets. Some of the fish were red-snappers and other varieties often seen in our own markets. They are sold in the market place, which is as clean and sanitary as any in our own cities.

A walk to the north of the city brought us past Livingstone's former residence, a big white Arab house, looking toward the coast of Africa. My Arab boys took off their hats and said as they pointed to its old weather-worn walls: " Bwana Ingreza Mzuri Sana Pasha," " The English Master was a very good man,"

The clove plantations are beautiful, sunk in a sea of verdure around the hamlet of Bububu, seven miles from the town of Zanzibar. The old palaces of former Sultans line the shore toward Bububu. In olden times, whenever the Sultan died his palace was abandoned and a new one was built for his successor. These picturesque ruins are covered now with the thick tangles of a jungle vegetation. The walls are broken, the gates are gone, and beside the ruined bastions that surrounded the homes of these pirate-kings the peaceful shepherd watches his flock of sheep and goats along the shore.

> "They say the lion and the lizard keep
> The courts where Jamshyd gloried and drank deep;
> And Bahram that great hunter, the wild ass
> Treads o'er his grave, but cannot break his sleep."

The copra trade is in the hands of French merchants. Copra is the kernel of the cocoanut; and the natives carry the copra in bags to little factories where it is made into cocoanut oil. The mill for making the oil is a very interesting contrivance. It is a little machine like a cider-mill to which a camel is attached by a whiffle-tree. The camel is blindfolded and walks around in a circle, turning the machinery as he goes. A boy feeds the copra into the machine, where it is ground up. The oil runs into a tin can set for the purpose. It is then put in barrels and sent to France;—and in France it is manufactured into that lovely French olive-oil of which we are so fond on salads!

The Swahili men and women do a good deal of work, and are paid from five to fifteen cents a day. These Swahili are interesting people. Their mothers are negresses and their fathers Arabs; and they are one of the very few instances in history where a strong race has been produced by the mixture of a superior with an inferior people. Stanley and Livingstone, Grant and Cameron, and nearly all the great explorers in the last half of the nineteenth century took Swahili men with them on their expeditions because the Swahili are strong, versatile and good natured; and, though they have many roguish ways, yet on the whole they understand the white man and do his work better than any other of the tribes of Africa.

The religion of the Swahili is Mohammedan, but they greatly respect the work of the Christian missionaries, especially of David Livingstone and his successors. Though Livingstone was a Presbyterian yet the mission that he founded in Zanzibar is now successfully carried on by the Church of England Missionary Society. The missionaries of this station are self-devoted men and women, teaching the natives the handicrafts, industry, cleanliness and morality. There is a beautiful church, a hos-

76 In Wildest Africa

pital, a school, and several missionary buildings. The mission is embowered among beautiful trees and shrubbery and the high altar of the church is unique in that it is the slave-block that formerly stood in the centre of the slave market of Zanzibar.

None of the native races are prone to energetic labour; but one sees a busy throng in Zanzibar every day among the bazars, in the market-place and along the many roads and avenues that lead in from the country. One morning I went outside the city and on the famous Mnazi Moji road I came upon a gang of women at work upon a new highway. The manager of the work told me that the women labour from 6 A. M. to 3 P. M. and receive thirteen cents per day. They live on bananas, maize, sugar-cane and white-ant pie, the latter a delicacy made by mixing up white ants in banana-flour and forming a kind of nougat. The young ladies kindly consented to sit in front of the camera and I saw while making the picture that one was looking at her dainty, dusky face in a handglass with as much interest as that shown by women of more favoured nations. These dark, equatorial beauties have a huge comb like a pitchfork to coiffure the hair with; and they have as many and as romantic ways of arranging the hair as a white girl, notwithstanding that they do not use the curling tongs, rods, rats, or marcel waves,

Zanzibar

Although Zanzibar is an English colony, yet the German merchants do the most of the business. They bring their merchandise from Tanga on the coast, and from Dar-es-Salaam. They have large ivory houses and German ships come twice a month from Naples and Hamburg. There is also a direct line of French steamers from Marseilles every two weeks. The American merchants do a big trade in ivory although they are transferring the ivory houses to Mombasa in English territory and Dar-es-Salaam in the German colony.

The largest exporters of ivory in the world are Arnold, Cheney & Co. of New York, in whose warerooms at Zanzibar or Mombasa can oftentimes be seen twenty-five thousand dollars' worth of tusks in one small corner. They have entertained nearly all the great explorers of Africa, and the tales that have been told at their table of pirate dhows, native wars and terrible jungle marches would make valuable and romantic reading. The other great ivory traders of Zanzibar and Mombasa are Childs & Co., also of New York City.

I saw in Zanzibar, in 1900, a long line of Swahili boys, each balancing on his shoulder a great tusk worth from five hundred to a thousand dollars. This is not so common a sight to-day, since the great ivory firms have had their export warehouses at Mombasa and Dar-es-Salaam on the mainland.

But Zanzibar will always have a distinct commerce of its own. As the old Arab centre of East Africa, it will send its dhows to Muscat and Bombay. The clove and copra trade will always flourish here. The ardent African sun, the glowing starry night, the tawny sunsets and the dreamy seas, the quaint, bizarre, old-world folk will be seen by the traveller a hundred years from now as they were seen by Marco Polo five centuries ago — as I saw them in fancy when, in a gray-walled Scotch village, I conned my early lesson in geography.

CHAPTER V

MOMBASA

AFTER we had passed two months in the lucent latitudes of the southern zone, we sailed northward one bright spring morning, into the harbour of Mombasa. A line of white waters breaking on brown reefs backed by a bank of verdure presented to us the coast of Central Africa. Three rounded peaks, a few miles inland, showed the land rising toward the great plateaus. The rains were just finishing and the green was glowing in rare freshets of vegetation. Away on the horizon the white houses of this old Arab capital shone in the fervid light. And as the vessel neared the harbour, we were conscious of the sweet odours wafted to us from the fertile land. Soon we came alongside of the coral reef on which the city is built.

There are two harbours here, the old harbour of Mombasa on one side of the coral island, facing English Point and Frere Town mission; and Kilindini, the new port beyond Serani Point, — the deeper harbour opened by the English government for their new commercial metropolis, at the terminus of the Uganda Railway.

From the ship we saw the white Portuguese-Arab fort, begun in 1498 by Vasco da Gama, the famous Portuguese navigator, who in that year rounded the Cape of Good Hope, and established here the colonial empire of Portugal in East Africa. The Portuguese held the city for two hundred years. It was the scene of constant conflict with the Arabs until in 1698 the Arabs finally wrested it from the palsied hands of that corrupt and weakened empire which had once held half the new lands of the world. The old fort stands in good condition, and we see, clustered around it, modern English bungalows and Portuguese and Arab houses, in white and blue and red, standing out in bold relief against the tropic vegetation of feathery palms, banana trees and fairy greenery along the shore.

On a closer view, the riotous colours of equatorial flowers appear; and, just beyond, huge gouty calabash trees covered with blossoms like the azaleas one sees in florists, at the Eastertime. The Bougainvillea vine throws profusely its purple flowers, like clematis, around the warm, gray walls. The whole landscape is covered with a sky of troubled blue. All the growths are rich and luxurious. We are at the centre of the earth, where nature works her

Mombasa

mighty machinery through long summers that know no winter-time's decay. There are wind blown heights that face the sea, and gentle cliffs arising from the surge that has rolled across the Indian Ocean and here makes a scene of incomparable beauty. For the crested waves, breaking on the coral-reefs, are like blossomed wild-flowers; and the air is soft like that of Al Couchetta in the month of June, as old Da Gama said.

We sailed into a narrow channel and dropped anchor in the harbour of Kilindini. In front of us were the Rabai Hills. On our left, a shore thickly crowded with palm trees down to the dappled shelving beach. On our right, the Bay of Kilindini, the lighthouse on Serani Point, and the red-roofed bungalows of the white men's dwellings embowered among trees and flowers. We were rowed ashore by sturdy, half-naked natives in boats that had six oars each, with awnings to protect us from the torrid sun. These boatmen are the Swahili of the coast, strong, shouting fellows, who carry our luggage to the customs house. Ten per cent. is charged upon our guns, but our cameras and plates are let in free. The customs inspector is a polite and obliging young Englishman.

The heat at first seemed to be very great; but this was only on account of the moist atmosphere, for I learned afterwards that the temperature ranges from 62° to 93°, 62° being the lowest ever registered. From May until September are the coolest months. The hottest months are January, February and March. The rainfall, however, is very great, reaching as high as 74 inches a year. April to June are the wettest months, and August to October the dryest. The rainiest day recorded was May 5, 1906, when 3.91 inches fell.

After a short walk along the shore, we climb a pathway festooned with lovely, creeping flowers, and through an avenue of fire-trees, whose red blossoms were flashing out like flames. We found a little railroad running three miles from Kilindini to Mombasa, across the coral island on which both towns are built. The tracks of this toy-railway are about two feet wide, and upon it runs a trolley called a " ghary." The car consists of a small platform, about five feet square, on which seats are erected, with an awning over the top, and motive power is supplied by two natives who run at the back of the car and push it along. Four people can ride on one car, two on each seat, back to back. Wherever there is a down grade, the human motors hop on the rear of the car and coast with it; and the speed with which you get over the ground by this means is remarkable. The tracks are run to all the principal houses in the suburbs, and everybody of importance has his own private " ghary " and

GHARY SYSTEM OF STREET CARS IN MOMBASA.
(Hon. Joseph Chamberlain in front car.)

maintains "ghary-boys," who are decorated with his family colours in fancy turbans, with sashes, over long, white gowns.

There is also a broad highway running from Kilindini into the main town of Mombasa; and here we begin to see the real African men and women. The women are all dressed in the highly coloured checked or striped sheeting, called "Americani." This cotton cloth they drape gracefully around their bodies from the armpits to the heels; a second piece, highly decorated, is thrown artistically around their shoulders and sometimes covers their heads.

Many of the girls are covered with jewelry of various kinds, mostly brass, iron and copper wire. Some also carry ordinary umbrellas. The men are the sturdy fellows whose ancestors accompanied Livingstone and Stanley on their expeditions; and it is surprising to see the enormous loads they can carry and the amount of work that they can do. When at work they wear nothing but a small bit of cloth tied around the loins, and their perspiring bodies shine like ebony as they move the huge boxes and bear the great packages on their heads.

On our way into the city of Mombasa, we saw on each side of us new houses building under the white man's régime. The English rule here has lasted only about fifteen years, and in that time all these old coast cities have been made wholesome, and given a fair and just government.

One beautiful structure on the Kilindini road is the station of the White Fathers of Algeria, a Catholic mission, where a new convent is being built and a beautiful monastery has already been completed. The Portuguese and Goanese of Mombasa are Catholics, and the audiences at the Catholic mission are very large. I saw about eight hundred worshippers in the church one Sunday evening.

Still further on we come to the magnificent Church of England Cathedral, attached to which is a fine academy, — the Buxton School for boys and girls. Last year there were between three and four hundred students in the institution. The English Cathedral was built to the memory of Bishop Hannington, the heroic young missionary who was cruelly put to death by the orders of Mwanga, the King of Uganda. It is a successful effort to combine Eastern and Western architecture. The interior, with its massive stone columns and Saracenic arch-work, is very restful. The woodwork was all done by the natives. The interior is not yet quite finished, but there is a beautiful pulpit and font of Carrara marble carved in imitation of an old church in Italy. Thus far thirty thousand dollars has been spent upon this church, and as the labour

Mombasa 85

is much cheaper here than in western countries, the value of the work done is equal to about one hundred thousand dollars. The Rev. G. W. Wright is chaplain, and services are held on Sunday at 9 A. M. for the natives, and at 4.30 P. M. for the English residents of the city.

We presently began to see the beautiful calabash or baobab trees growing in the fields nearby, and covered with beautiful clusters of flowers like the blossoms of pink rhododendrons in our northern clime.

As we approached the densely populated part of the town of Mombasa, we noticed among some vacant lots a charming little temple dedicated to the worship of Lingam, an Oriental cult. There are various sects of Mohammedans throughout the city and there is a beautiful Mosque of the Bohras, near the Customs House. The Arabs have a Mosque in Vasco da Gama Street, which street, recalling the Portuguese navigator, is the principal thoroughfare of the business part of Mombasa.

As the "ghary-boy" stopped our car in front of the Grand Hotel, we saw across the way the beautiful gardens named after Sir Arthur MacKinnon, the first English governor of East Africa. On one side of the gardens is the beautiful building of the National Bank of India, and on the other side the fine new structure called the Treasury Building, where the English government has its offices.

From my verandah at the Grand Hotel, I looked down on the municipal buildings, known officially as His Britannic Majesty's Court of Justice. The hotel is one of four or five fairly good ones, and the price is three to five dollars per day. Our rooms opened out on the verandah, and though we had close mosquito nettings, yet the cool breeze from the Indian Ocean tempered the atmosphere, and usually prevented the mosquitoes from being too troublesome. We learned that all the decaying vegetation throughout the island has been removed; that the town has been thoroughly sanitated, and that malarial fever is now very rare in this equatorial capital. Owing, however, to the inconvenience of the heat caused by the moist air of the sea and the monsoon, the various government offices are being gradually removed to Nairobi, 337 miles in the interior, situated on a plateau more than five thousand feet above the Indian Ocean. I usually stayed in my room through the hottest part of the day, but would go out to walk or ride at four o'clock in the afternoon, when the intense heat subsided. From four until half-past six the charm and the glamour of the tropical days were very alluring.

We made our residence at Mombasa for six

A SAFARI BRINGING IVORY TO MOMBASA.

Mombasa

weeks and became acquainted with the Americans and Englishmen, who are either business men, hunters, or officials of the British government. The Mombasa Club, which was founded in 1896, has an attractive building at the end of Vasco da Gama Street, with gardens sloping to the sea. The buildings comprise a fine reading room, billiard room, and residential accommodations for members and their friends. The entrance fee is about seventeen dollars and the subscription about four dollars per month. The Englishmen connected with the Club have cricket grounds, and tennis and badminton courts. They play football on Saturday afternoons and so there is quite a lively European community. Arnold, Cheney & Co. and Childs & Co. of Zanzibar and New York are the two important ivory houses of Mombasa. The Americans mingle freely with the English, but the Germans keep to themselves. There is a good English weekly paper, the "East African Standard;" and the Arabs and Hindoos have clubs and newspapers of their own.

Mombasa Town may be divided into three distinct parts, namely — the old Arab and native quarter, hidden behind and extending inland towards the "shambas" or plantations; the central portion, which is the town proper and where are situated the government offices and the principal shops, and which also forms the residence of the Hindoos;

and, lastly, a stretch of high ground towards the south and facing the Indian Ocean, which is being gradually built over with residences for the government officials and other Europeans. The sanitation at Mombasa is carried on by a Conservancy Department, and is quite satisfactory so far as the European quarter is concerned. Several large cement-lined drains have been put down to carry off the surface-water which accumulates with extraordinary rapidity in heavy rains.

The water supply for Europeans is derived from tanks attached to their bungalows. The quality is good, but in case of an insufficient rainfall there is a shortage. The natives drink well water, which is brackish, and, owing to the porous nature of the coral rock, liable to contamination. There is no proper supply for ships visiting the harbour, and there is no doubt that some scheme for bringing water to the town will have to be carried through before it can take its natural place as a great port of call, and as one of the most important termini of the vast Cape to Cairo Railway system.

No census of the town has been taken, but the population approximately numbers twenty to thirty thousand.

The East African Coast with the adjoining islands was well known to ancient geographers, centuries before the beginning of the Christian era.

Mombasa

The Greek geographer Ptolemy in 150 A. D. gives a detailed account of East Africa as then known, which he calls "Azania," and mentions the promontory of Zingis. The writer of the "Periplus" also describes how he coasted south down "Azania" and the land of the Zans or Zangs, and from this may be derived the word Zanguebar, later Zanzibar.

Arabian historians record the attack and defeat of Said and Suleiman, the chiefs of Oman, by the Governor of Irak. To the defeated, who fled to the "land of Zang," and some Persians who accompanied them, may be ascribed the foundations of the East African Coast towns. (A. D. 684.)

Makdishu has the reputation of being the earliest settlement, having been built according to tradition in the year 908 A. D. No doubt there were some human habitations here in the dim pre-historic world.

Then followed Kilwa; and about two hundred years later (1100 A. D.) Mombasa, Kilifi, Malindi and the settlements of the Lamu Archipelago.

The shores seem to have been visited by the Japanese and Chinese also, in whose encyclopedias it is recorded that "in the country of the Tsengu, in the South West Ocean, there is a bird called 'pheng' which in its flight eclipses the sun. It can swallow a camel and its quills are used for water-casks."

Chinese coins dated between A. D. 713-1170 have also been found.

Marco Polo, the famous Venetian traveller, visited Makdishu and describes it as an exceedingly large city. He also visited Mombasa, which he writes, " is large, abounding with banana, lemon and the citron . . . the people are religious, chaste and honest and of peaceful habits."

The East Coast of Africa was first made known to Europe by Vasco da Gama, when, in 1498, he doubled the Cape of Good Hope and sailed up the Coast, visiting Mozambique, Mombasa and Malindi.

From this time may be said to commence the long record of quarrels and bloodshed which forms the history of Mombasa till the beginning of the last century. Sir Charles Eliot in his book, " The East African Protectorate," has the following graphic description: — " In virtue of the advantage of its position, its good climate and fine harbours, Mombasa was the most important point, yet it cannot be said to have been a political centre for the surrounding country. It was simply the place which was most fought about and oftenest burnt. The native name Myita means war, and never was name more justified by history. There can hardly be any town in the world which has been besieged, captured, sacked, burnt and razed to the ground so often and in so short a time. Mombasa was not so much the

SERANI POINT AND THE FORT OF MIR ALI BEY.

field where important issues were decided as a seaport tavern into which every passing pirate entered to take part in a drunken brawl and smash the furniture; and it is only in quite recent years that it has begun to assume its proper position as an emporium and door for the interior."

From 1498 until 1698 the Portuguese held Mombasa against the Arabs and the wild tribes of the interior. The constant warfare was interrupted by the inroads of a Turkish corsair, Mir Ali Bey, who ravaged the seas and the archipelagoes around it for ten years, and went back to Turkey with fifty Portuguese prisoners and a million dollars' worth of loot. In 1589, the Turkish pirates returned and established themselves at Ras Serani, the end of Mombasa island, which faces the sea. Here they built a fort, but, being attacked by the combined armies of the Zimbas and the Portuguese, the Turks were annihilated and Mir Ali Bey was slain.

The old fort, with rusty cannons, broken port holes and shattered walls, is covered to-day by clinging vines and clustering flowers. I stood one day at the summit of the fort and looked at the double entrance to Mombasa harbour. It was a view of surpassing beauty. To the left, across the harbour, was English Point; and the waves broke on the reefs like wreaths of driven snow. To the right, were the angry waters, surging over the brown bars of coral rocks that make the gateway to Kilindini harbour. The winds as they rushed in from the sea were bending the palm trees; and the ocean's far horizon was like a famous jewel, coquetting with the light of every gem that is known, for the sunset shot flashes of red and green and yellow, the emerald, the amethyst and the topaz lived in a remote cloud.

The Portuguese empire lasted here till 1698, when the Arabs, after a siege of thirty-three months, captured St. Joseph's fort, which had been begun by Vasco da Gama. Then the red flag of Islam floated for two centuries from its stern castellated walls.

The Arabs ruled at Zanzibar and at Mombasa until the English government began to administer Uganda and East Africa. For the past fifteen years the English government has paid to the Sultan of Zanzibar, who is the hereditary ruler of East Africa and the islands of the neighbouring coast, eighty-five thousand dollars a year as a rental.

But the place is now in actuality an English colony. By the Heligoland Convention of 1890 Germany recognized a British Protectorate over Zanzibar, the island of Pemba and the African mainland between the Umba and Juba Rivers, which now comprises the East African Protectorate. Germany paid a million dollars to the Sultan of Zanzibar and obtained in exchange the definite cession of the East African coast and hinterland held in lease from the Sultan. A line was thus drawn between German East Africa and the British Protectorate. It is an arbitrary direct line across to Victoria Nyanza from the country of the Mountains of the Moon (Ruwenzori) on the fourth degree of latitude south and extending from Kavirondo Bay to the Indian Ocean at Usumbara. The line, however, makes one deviation where it passes through Mount Kilimanjaro, giving the German colony control of that splendid mountain region. It is said that this was done at the instance of King Edward, who made the concession as a birthday present to his distinguished nephew.

I often took a walk just as the eventide was coming on, from my hotel down past the old Portuguese fort (which is now a model English prison), and wandered along the water-front beyond the bungalows of the English officials to Serani Point. I was there in the rainy season and during a part of the dry. In that green country the atmosphere is heavy with the perfume of wild flowers and the fresh saltness of the sea. Bright birds and coloured butterflies were in the little valleys, and the air was drowsy with the humming of intoxicated bees. It filled one with the great joy of out-of-doors; and fed the veins with the rich wine of life.

In contrast to this open air delight was the hot city, thrilling with human life — a mosaic of many races and problems. Here a Swahili woman flaunts gay colours in the sunshine; there a Somali warrior brandishes his glistening spear. Natives of the plains bargaining with the city sharps; the workers in bronze and brass; the stores where hunters buy beads and cotton to exchange in their far jungle journeys; an occasional ivory caravan from Congo and the Nile; Indian merchants sitting crossed legged like idols in their little shops; the big stores of the Portuguese; the business houses of the Germans, French, English, Americans; porters carrying skins and ivory, rubber and cocoa, cloves and copra to the great ships in the bay — all this lies close to the quietude of Ras Serani.

Sometimes, as the darkness fell over this strange city, I would adjourn to the English Club for a quiet meal with one of the American ivory merchants or some young Englishman whom I had met at Nairobi, or out along the railway. At night we nearly always heard the music of the "Ngoma," the big drum which the natives beat at their dances. For the dances are usually held in the moonlight, and the "Ngoma" is the great instrument of festivity or woe, rejoicing or sadness, all over equatorial Africa.

One Sunday afternoon we heard the familiar "Ngoma" and went down several narrow streets between the daub-and-wattle houses of the natives, and in a court we saw some forty men and women dancing to wild Somali measures. It was a weird and fascinating sight. The women were dressed in beautiful beads, the men in gorgeous warrior apparel, and, as the circling mazes of the dance went on, the perspiration poured in streams from the black ivory bodies of the dancers. Occasionally, a man or woman, overheated with the furious exertion, would leave the circle and step aside to a great well nearby, where an attendant stood with a big earthen jar filled with water. He would dash the water in cascades over the perspiring terpsichorean, whereat the latter would grunt some grateful thanks and then resume the dance. We tried to make a moving picture of this dance, but a Somali warrior, with a sword of steel long enough to impale both the photographer and myself at once, rushed at us and we beat an inglorious retreat.

Mombasa is growing from year to year; the great trade in skins and ivory and cattle which is being brought to it, by the Uganda Railway, from the Victoria Nyanza, Uganda and East Africa, is bound to make it in the future one of the great commercial cities of the globe. The German colonies around Kilimanjaro send their coffee, cotton and rubber from Moschi by wagon road a hundred miles to Voi station on the railway, and thence to Mombasa to be shipped into the markets of the world. Moreover, the English have nearly all the shipping trade of Lake Victoria; and so their vessels call at Bukoba, Shirati, Mwanza and the other German ports upon the lake, and bring the produce of the German colony which lies between Victoria and Tanganyika, to Port Florence, thence to be transported by rail to the shipping centre at Mombasa.

It was in the old fort that Makelingu, chief of the Wayanika, with three accomplices, was held prisoner, for the murder of Thomas London on December 21st, 1907. The four were tried by a court of native judges and condemned to death. They appealed to the Supreme Court of Zanzibar.

This court is composed of three Englishmen. They upheld the sentence. The condemned men then appealed to King Edward in Privy Council. The council decided that the sentence was just, and Makelingu and his companions were hanged August 28th, 1908.

As I witnessed the solemn execution of the death penalty upon these men I realized how inevitable and accurate was English justice; and could agree with Swinburne's address to Britannia:

> "Thou, though the world may misdoubt thee,
> Be strong as the seas by thy side."

There is a ferry boat which for two cents will carry one across Mombasa harbour to English

Point, where is located the famous Frere-Town mission. This mission lies on a point of land which is cooled on either side by the soft waters of the sea. Here, amid delicious palm groves and cool gardens, I found myself one afternoon at the Church of England mission, and in the hospitable home of the Rev. Dr. Binns and his daughter. There are about a dozen buildings in this mission, and nowhere on my travels did I visit any place that seemed such a fairyland. The mission consists of a fine church, large enough to hold a thousand people, a building for theological students of the native race, school-houses for the smaller children, and the peaceful homes of the missionaries looking toward the water. In the distance one catches glimpses of the white Arab houses of the city. From the dizzy, hot and dusty flurry of Mombasa to this quiet place, not two miles away, one seems transferred into a different world.

This mission was founded by Sir Bartle Frere in 1872, and was the result of David Livingstone's great work in Africa. As I looked around me upon the happy homes of five hundred freed-men in the Frere-Town mission — of men and women rescued by English gun-boats from the Arab dhows, I realized the debt humanity owes to the brave old Scottish weaver.

The missionary took me in among his books and through the gardens of the contented people, among the school children, who were singing, happy-hearted, like the bright birds around them, and then I dined with the kindly minister and his charming daughter, an educated English girl. I do not know what made the viands taste so good, or why a great peace came over me while thus the guest at this good Christian home. It may have been the succulent tropic fruits laid on the table; or it may have been the quiet dignity and strength of this cultivated gentleman, who had transferred his strong English sympathies and work from the ripe civilization of the Old World to the rude barbarism of the New; or it may have been the gentle grace and courtesy of this fair English girl, transplanted from a European college to work a deathless work of womanly compassion out here in the black heart of Africa.

CHAPTER VI

THE UGANDA RAILWAY

THE Continent of Africa, so long a tantalizing mystery to man, is fast becoming civilized. England, France, Germany, Italy, Portugal, Spain and Belgium have all done their quota of work toward the new advance. But England is leading all the nations in colonizing and opening the wild centre of the Dark Continent. From the time of acquiring the Suez Canal to the finishing of the Assouan Dam in Egypt and the surrender of the Boers, the advance of England in Africa has been superb and stupendous. Already the great railway from Cairo to the Cape has reached four hundred miles north of the Zambesi River to Broken Hill, and southward, with steamboat connections, almost to Victoria Nyanza. A new railway has just been projected from Ripon Falls, fifty miles through the forests at the head of the Nile, to connect with steamers lower down the river for Gondokoro and Khartum.

One of the principal branches of this new system

is the Uganda Railway, which runs five hundred and eighty-four miles from Mombasa, on the Indian Ocean, to Port Florence, on Victoria Nyanza. The opening of this railway, in 1902, was justly termed "One of the greatest philanthropic enterprises of modern times," for, aside from its vast political significance, the railway brings into touch with the life of Europe and the markets of the world an immense area of two hundred and forty thousand square miles of territory known as the East African Protectorate, as well as Uganda and the Upper Nile countries. A large part of this region, lying at two thousand to eight thousand feet above sea level, and well watered by plentiful rains, is evidently well suited for the colonization of white men. Already, for hundreds of miles on the high plateaus, there are thriving settlements.

The Uganda railroad cost the British nation twenty-two million dollars, but already it is paying for itself and is managed entirely by the government.

What a contrast is the Africa of to-day to the Africa of twenty years ago! Then it took four months for Emin Pasha or Stanley to journey from the coast to the lakes. Now we traverse the distance in forty-eight hours. We have a comfortable carriage of the Indian style; we dine in the handsome rooms of the dak-bungalows; we look out of our cozy train and watch through our window a land

The Uganda Railway 101

of tropic forest, dense jungle, open prairie. And on this ride we observe the native, undeveloped human beings, from the suave and almost civilized Swahilis of Mombasa and the coast, through the El Moran or Spartan-like soldiers of the Masai, to the docile Kikuyu, the shepherd Nandi, and the stark-naked, but modest Wakavirondo at Port Florence.

It was into this country and across these Equatorial prairies that Ex-President Roosevelt went to attack the last stronghold of big and dangerous game. Even on the railway and in your comfortable car, you are not in the " sheltered home " of Europe and America. Why, the very train I rode upon in the summer of 1908 was stopped by two inquisitive giraffes, who poked their noses across our engine and broke off one of the lanterns serving for our headlight. When the engineer got off to see what was the matter, he found a huge giraffe, with broken legs, dying on the track. A rhinoceros tried conclusions with one of the earlier trains, and the train demolished him.

But it was " Simba," the lion, that gave the Uganda Railway its most thrilling stories. In fact, one of the stations in the region of wild game, between Tsavo and the Athi Plains, is called Simba Station.

Hunters disagree as to the bravery of the lion,

but all credit him with exceptional sagacity. Since the British government has preserved the game along the railway, but allowed the shooting of lions, these latter beasts have disappeared from the vicinity of the line, but are found in great numbers not far from the game lands. Hunters also state that lions have learned that the white man with a rifle is more formidable than the black man with a bow and arrow; and that they will run from the white man; also that a lion can distinguish the man who has shot at it, and will lie in wait for him to be revenged. A lioness, especially one with cubs, is known as the most terrible of antagonists. Stories of the building of the Uganda Railway seem to confirm these theories.

The most famous lion of the Uganda Railway was one of the man-eaters of Tsavo. Tsavo is one hundred and thirty-three miles from Mombasa, and, during the construction of the line, no less than twenty-nine Indians were eaten there by lions. The work was threatened, and a party of three young men — Hubner, Parenti, and Ryal — took a car and lay in wait at night for a bold man-eater, who had stalked up and picked a man off an open railway truck as the train slowed down into the station. Parenti lay on the floor, Hubner was in an upper berth, and Ryal was on watch with his rifle. Unfortunately he fell asleep. At two o'clock in the

The Uganda Railway

morning the very man-eater they were hunting entered the carriage, picked up Ryal, jumped through the window and fled to the forest, where the unfortunate man's gnawed bones were found the next day. An expedition was formed, and the old man-eater was finally killed.

A ride on the Uganda Railway is unique and one of the most interesting in all the world, for we pass through a country where the animal and human life is much the same as it was in Europe two hundred thousand years ago, and here we see primitive savagery walking hand in hand with modern civilization, retaining nearly all of its picturesqueness, but divorced from most of its lust and cruelty.

The fare is six cents per mile, first class; three cents, second class; and three miles for one cent in the third class. The blacks cannot go by first or second, but they swarm in the third. I took this trip twice during the summer of 1908. Settled comfortably in the train, we drew out from the tropical station of Mombasa, and, crossing from the island to the mainland by the Salisbury Bridge, seventeen hundred feet long, we plunged into the heart of Africa. The flora of East Africa as a whole is but meagre and is far different from what I have been accustomed to see in equatorial and tropical regions of the globe. One can hardly imagine that the impenetrable jungles of the Amazon are under the same tropical sun as the commonplace vegetation of East Central Africa. There is no dense forest or matted jungle of undergrowth made by innumerable creeping vines and lianas, with beautiful orchids of all shades of colours, and of perfumes new at every turn. On the other hand the vegetation is but sparse and, except on the coast, there are few edible fruits. This is due to the peculiar climatic conditions of this region.

Along the banks of the rivers and on the nearby plains there occur deep forest belts, and also on the mountains of the interior, where the rain is perennial.

The coastal swamps are covered with wide stretches of Yungi-Yungi or lotus-water-lily with its blue flower mingled with the small yellow bladderwort. Near the coast are to be seen the screw-pines, with mammoth spiral rosettes of leaves, trailing rubber vines and lianas looking like huge ropes or cables. The baobabs are an extremely striking addition to the landscapes, with their massive trunks arching over toward each other, and their irregularly knobbed branches appearing as a whole like ruined arches — relics of the works of man. There are also the silk-cotton trees and branch-dum palms, all of which vary the monotony of the scene.

Most of the trees and vegetation named are found only in the coast zone. On leaving the coast, and after a journey of but a few miles inland, the palms,

TRAIN, DRAWN BY A BALDWIN LOCOMOTIVE, AT CHANGAMWE STATION.

mangoes and all the fruit trees are replaced by the thick stems of huge candelabra-shaped euphorbias and sharp-spiked aloes, saw-leaved sansevieras and, everywhere, the thorny acacia shrub. There is but little else and it is certainly tiresome and monotonous.

After long weary miles of this sameness, it was a relief to arrive at the higher level in the interior, where there is a heavy rainfall and where it is evenly distributed the year round. There is no more of the thorny scrub which is replaced by luxuriant green shrubs, and the occasional tufts of desert grass thicken into fine rich turf. There are meadow flowers such as we see in this country and in Europe, and grand timber trees furnish shade from the tropical sun. The whole appearance of the country is that of the temperate zones.

Professor Gregory divides the flora of East Africa into zones as follows: (1) The Coastal, (2) The foothills, (3) The Scrub, (4) The Prairies, (5) The Mountain forests, (6) Bamboo Zone, (7) Lower Alpine Zone, (8) Upper Alpine Zone, (9) The Snowfields.

The engines on the Uganda Railway are Baldwin locomotives from Philadelphia, and twenty-three of the bridges and viaducts are of American manufacture. When we stopped at the first station of Changamwe, we noted the natives clothed in light cotton and gingham; also Indians and Goanese selling fruit to the passengers.

Our journey on the railway divided itself into three sections. First, the unhealthy, scrubby coast land and interior low plateau, extending to Kiu station two hundred and sixty-seven miles inland, and 4,860 feet in elevation. Natives and Indians can live in this part, but the white man withers and dies. At Voi, one hundred and three miles, elevation 1,830, there is an excellent dak-bungalow, with a restaurant as fine as any I have seen, even on the New York Central lines. Also at Voi parties of hunters leave the train for a trip to the Kilimanjaro district in German territory, one hundred miles away. Nearly all of this first two hundred and sixty-seven miles is covered with short, scrubby jungles, and is infested with malaria. At the very start one begins to see wild zebra and an occasional antelope, and, by the time Tsavo is reached, one hundred and thirty-three miles from Mombasa, game has become common and is seen on every side.

It is interesting also to note the various tribes along the way. Though there are few houses in sight, there are endless numbers of brown footpaths, leading often to thickly settled villages and "shambas," or plantations. The strongest of the tribes are the Swahili. Impudent and assertive, the Swahili have a language containing twenty thousand words, mostly of Arabic derivation. They are the people mostly employed by hunters. The "boys" are dressed in every style, from nothing up to the cast-off riding suit of an English squire.

The first hundred miles of the railway, extending through the province of Seyidie, runs through the territory peopled by Arabs, Indians, and a host of pagan tribes, who call themselves Wanyika. From Tsavo to Nairobi, two hundred miles, is the country of the Wakamba, a people short, stout, and fearless, yet peaceful and industrious. An enormous amount of ornamentation is displayed, and the lobes of the ears are pierced and disfigured. This, indeed, is the case with all the tribes till we come to the Baganda, beyond Lake Victoria. In this first section are the stations of Kibwezi and Simba, lion haunted and infested with leopards; also the home of huge herds of zebra, hartebeest, wildebeest, Grant gazelle, and Thomson gazelle, which graze within a few yards of the train. This is where Colonel Roosevelt saw more game than he ever before encountered; and these vast herds were feeding quietly like cattle over the whole face of the open lands. It is a scene characteristic of the times before Adam. A recent traveller compared this part of the ride to a menagerie through which a railway carries the visitors.

The second section of the Uganda Railway is the real white man's East Africa. It stretches from

Kiu, two hundred and sixty-seven miles, to Fort Ternan, five hundred and thirty-six miles, thus being a territory two hundred and sixty-nine miles wide. The elevation seldom falls below that of Fort Ternan, four thousand nine hundred and eighty feet above the sea, reaching at Mau summit eight thousand three hundred and fifty feet, and at Nairobi, the capital of British East Africa, five thousand four hundred and fifty feet. Kiu, Machakos Road, Kapiti Plains, and Athi River are in the centre of the game reserve.

No one who travels on this road will be disappointed in the marvellous collection of game seen every few hundred yards. Ostriches waddled across the open prairies, the unwieldy rhinoceros blinked at us from the grass, and the giraffe ogled our engine.

At Nairobi, the tin-roofed town, less than ten years old, are the headquarters of the railway as well as of the government of the colony. There was a sense of bustle and of city life as we entered the station. At this place already are a thousand white residents and fourteen thousand natives, Goanese and Indians; good hotels; and hustling markets. Of the three thousand white men in British East Africa, fifteen hundred are located within fifty miles of Nairobi.

Between Nairobi and Fort Ternan lies the best farming land of East Africa, a territory over two hundred miles wide, and reaching practically from German East Africa to Abyssinia, without fever or the dread tsetse fly. Lord Delamere holds a hundred thousand acres near the Njoro station in the Rift Valley, four hundred and sixty-one miles from the coast. He has done more than any one else to improve the breed of the native cattle. Other men with smaller farms are raising sheep and taming ostriches. At Naivasha Lake the government is experimenting with zebras, trying to train them for work on the farms. It is estimated that there are about a million of those beautiful animals in East Africa. If zebras can be used for agricultural work, the lot of the poorer immigrants will be rendered much more hopeful than it is to-day. As yet it is not possible for the man with small means to develop this colony, but every year improves the country for the average white immigrant.

The most picturesque part of the journey is the Kikuyu escarpment, the Rift Valley and the Mau escarpment. In the midst of the uplands at Kijabe station there is an interesting American mission, under the care of Rev. Mr. Hurlburt, of Pennsylvania. Mr. Roosevelt was entertained by the missionaries here, and spoke enthusiastically of their labours and successes. The Ex-President hunted the colobus monkey in the forests near Kijabe. From the train the traveller sees huge birds —

marabous, eagles, kites, vultures. Elephant spoor (marks) are plentiful, Chandler's reed bucks dance away from the engine, and the flat escarpment ranges lie in a blue haze of amethystine horizon. The oryx and the lesser kudu are also seen in this valley.

In the last two years many Boers have been taking up farms, especially near Nakuru station, four hundred and forty-nine miles from the coast, at about six thousand feet elevation. At Nakuru the train stopped for our evening meal. There was an excellent hotel supper for us near the station. An efficient French landlady and her husband purveyed. The way the good lady ordered her husband about made one feel the joy of civilization.

Fifty miles from Molo station is the beginning of the famous Uasi Ngishu plateau, the best grazing country in the Protectorate. Already a good many farms of five thousand acres have been taken by Boer immigrants. The highest station on the line is Londiani, 7,410 feet above the sea. This is the point of departure for a remarkably fine stretch of agricultural country in which lies the "Eldama Ravine," where in forty miles one passes from tropical ferns to all the products of the north temperate zone. Here the days are delightful and the evenings cool. The soil will grow anything, and rains keep the earth fresh and green. At every station

NAKURU STATION.

The Uganda Railway

we met crowds of aborigines, who never cease admiring the trains. The Ukamba tribe extends to Nairobi; the Kikuyu and Masai occupy the high lands farther inland. The former cultivate maize and bananas; the latter are warriors and shepherds.

The third and last section of the railway is the fifty-mile stretch from Fort Ternan to Port Florence. This is the Nandi country, the home of the mosquito and the tsetse fly. Where white men cannot live, Hindus farm the level plains. There are throughout the Protectorate great areas reserved for the natives. It is a green land of open fields and rising hills.

As we approached Lake Victoria, we passed through the most interesting tribe of all — the Wakavirondo, a nation that goes stark-naked. They are modest, however, and are reputed the most moral people of the whole continent of Africa. The central market of the Wakavirondo is at Kisumu, on the edge of the Lake.

A line of boats, six hundred to eight hundred tons, connects at Port Florence with Entebbe in Uganda and Jinja in Usoga at the head waters of the Nile. Every second week a steamer goes around the Lake touching at German ports. This sail is 1,000 miles. Branch lines of railway are projected across the Africa uplands. In a few years the game will be in small reserves, the colonists' farms will blossom from Somaliland to Kilimanjaro, the interesting Wakavirondo will wear clothes and be interesting no longer.

Roosevelt was very popular in Uganda and had a big ovation. He came none too soon. Before the next presidential election, East Africa will be greatly civilized, and with its advancing civilization there will have "passed a glory from the earth."

Some general features of the East African Protectorate should be mentioned. The Uganda Railway crosses this protectorate but does not touch Uganda at any point. From Nairobi good roads on either flank of the railway lead out to European plantations and cattle pastures, the principal one to Fort Hall, the frontier outpost of civilization on the Mbiri River opposite Mount Kenia. Mount Kenia is more of a range than a peak, and seems to shut out all view of the northern lands beyond it. It is crested with a glacier of moderate expanse in midsummer, from which a single sharp, straight snow-covered peak, almost reminding one of a flagstaff, rises heavenward. A great belt of bamboo forest lies between the glaciers and the cultivated foothills. Telegraphic and telephonic communication with Fort Hall and the intervening settlements is a necessary measure of protection as well as of convenience, and, of course, the English and European "planters" and their ladies look upon visits to Nairobi as the great events of the year. The omnipresent Hindu merchant is prominent in local and general trade. Ice, fresh sea fish, tropic fruits and vegetables take only twenty-four hours of refrigerator-car transportation.

There are no tsetse flies at Nairobi, and horses pass safely through the dreaded tsetse belt near the coast by train. Horse-keeping and horse-breeding are quite general, and the races and polo matches, dear to the Anglo-Saxon heart, are enthusiastically attended.

The provision for education has been largely confined to European children, and the missionaries have borne the burden of this important factor in civilization. Without wishing to criticize any of the many gentlemen who so hospitably received me in the various stations of the Protectorate, I cannot but express the wish that, outside of any question of religious belief, the civil and military officials of the colony would more generously recognize the sterling benefits of missionary teachings and labours in their infant empire.

On our way to Nairobi, we made a good deal of the journey by night, which at the equator is nearly as long as the day, leaving about an hour to the very brief transitions which we under northern skies call "dawn" and "twilight." Here, as the day draws to a close, the sun sinks low in the west, and for a few moments the edge of its disappearing disk throws a brazen, lurid glow over sky and hill. Then, as if by magic, all is darkness.

The narrow belt of country between the coast line and the desert is not largely occupied by the tribesmen. The sterile zone between the desert and the prairies has very few inhabitants. The whole district, however, is criss-crossed by the typical Africa "roads," little brown footpaths leading off through copse and jungle to some palisaded or thorn-encircled enclosure wherein the native huts and their inmates are safe from the prowling man-eater and robber.

Colonel Sir James Kayes Sadler, governor of British East Africa; Lieutenant-Governor Jackson, who has the government reserves in special charge; Sir Alfred Pease, who has a tract of land near Machakos, about two hundred miles from Mombasa; and Mr. William N. McMillan, a St. Louis gentleman, who has large holdings, some thirty-four miles beyond Nairobi, have all been most courteous and hospitable to any who have had the slightest claim upon their consideration. Besides these a host of military and civil officers, gentleman planters, experienced hunters and fair ladies, were looking forward to the approaching visit of Ex-President Roosevelt, with a deep interest and expectation which the American people can scarcely realize. I was most hospitably entertained by all the pioneers I met. A hundred questions were asked me about the coming of our Ex-President.

To the English people, Colonel Roosevelt is the ideal English gentleman — a university graduate, an enthusiastic sportsman, a statesman, fearless and incorruptible. On German territory I was asked: "Vill dot Herr President Rooseveldt mit der Kaiser hier komin?" A French officer one day said to me: "Ah, mon Dieu, why are no lions and elephants in Madagascar? Monsieur le President Roosevelt is one grand French gentleman. Oh, my country, my France, it is a ruin by the not to have of the life strenuous." An English planter remarked: "Tell the President that I have on my farm forty or more wild buffaloes. I am keeping away from them so that we can give him a good hunt; when he comes we will kill them all." A very clever hunter told me to direct the Colonel to his house. "I will show him all the game of Africa if he comes my way," said this Englishman, who has killed two hundred lions in the chase.

Beyond Nairobi, the tri-weekly trains go on to Uganda, and three trips per week are not now considered sufficient to carry on the business and travel of the ordinary season. Nairobi is, however, more like a terminus than a way station — a kind of "solar plexus" of the ganglia of nerves, — industrial, social, financial and political, — that radiate through the tribes and satrapies of the Protectorate.

In a country whose natives consider a walk of fifty to one hundred miles a rather moderate promenade, the railroad is not usually a necessity, but rather a luxury to be indulged in rarely. It is a lavish expenditure, and a train ride is a great event to the men of the native tribelets, who come hundreds of miles on foot to the market towns.

Between Nairobi and Mount Kenia to the north, the native population is scanty in certain sections, owing partially to the ravages of the Masai prior to 1885, and later to famine during the great drought of 1897, when many died and whole villages were obliged to seek food in the mountain ranges and valleys.

So great is the variety of savage and half-savage life here gathered that one is tempted to linger among the irregulars, police and wayfarers at this political and social centre of equatorial Africa.

I delayed my departure from the East Africa capital for four short, busy weeks, weeks full of pleasant and curious experiences. At last we trundled out of Nairobi and made our way up the steep gradients. So slowly does the train proceed that here and there a native, decked for a holiday, his half-naked breast and limbs freshly massaged with 'red ochre and groundnut oil, issues from some for-

MOUNT KENIA, PHOTOGRAPHED FROM NAIROBI, 60 MILES AWAY.

est path, and, running briskly after the train, jumps on board the third-class van, and quietly regales himself with a pinch of snuff. Perhaps, if he is short of cash, he hangs on to the rear end of the train until driven off by an irate brakeman.

In the first twenty-four miles beyond Nairobi the road rises two thousand feet, Limoru Station being seven thousand three hundred and forty feet above sea level. Here many acres are cultivated by European planters. The average temperature at this height is about sixty-six degrees Fahrenheit in cool weather and seventy-three degrees in hot weather; the lowest mean, forty-five degrees, being reached in the early mornings of the cold season. Sometimes there are cold winds at night and chilling fogs at midday which call for heavy clothing and great care after becoming overheated, for either sunstroke or chill are serious matters under the equator.

The hot season is from December to April, and the cooler months from July to September. The heavy rains fall from March to June and the lighter in November and December. The yearly rainfall varies from thirty-six to forty inches, but the heavier rains often do much damage and seem to leave the country with little in the way of a reserve supply. "Underground rivers" are, therefore, not exclusively the idea of Rider Haggard in his African stories, for such subterranean water courses seem to be the only adequate explanation of so complete a drainage as exists in some sections. It is hoped that underground basins in the lower sections may be tapped by artesian wells, and thus be made to equalize the general water supply for agriculture.

From Limoru the road descends rapidly to a ledge whereon the Escarpment station overlooks the Rift Valley, fifteen hundred feet below. By daylight this is an exciting ride; for, after rounding curve after curve among the plantations of the Wa-Kikuyu and the swamps west of Limoru, the road suddenly swings around a more abrupt turn and sweeps down to the border of a vast, unpeopled plain, traversed by a tiny thread of silver, the Kedong River. Beyond the river in a dreamy horizon line Mount Longanot towers with a spur partially closing in the Rift Valley, the great depression already mentioned which runs through the heart of Africa from the Zambesi to the Red Sea. Mile after mile the valley rolls in waves whose crests are tossed with the foam of a million flowers.

The road keeps to the side of the Rift, running almost northward under Kijabe Hill. The station earns its native title (the Wind), being a windy, bleak, dusty locality. Thence the road continues to Lake Naivasha, a body of fresh water where the gov-

The Uganda Railway 119

ernmental experiment farm, previously mentioned, is maintained. Considerable attention, I learned, has been paid to the breeding and taming of zebras, and other wild animals, like the eland. Thus far no marked results have been obtained. The Germans at Tanga are more successful, and have produced a fine animal, which they call the "zebroid" — a mixture of donkey and zebra. When young, the zebra is easily tamed and will follow its owner like a dog, even into his house and bed — rather too much of a good thing with a four-footed pet. Young Harry Edgehill of Nairobi claims to have a successful plan of raising tame zebras.

From Naivasha the road ascends the Rift Valley, turning once, in a huge loop nearly due south, to follow the line of the mountains and avoiding the salt lake Elmenteita, then north again, along the northern shore of Lake Nakuru, a round body of bitter salt water. On it goes with many curves, along the Mau escarpment, crossing in this section, in a space of seventy-three miles, twenty-seven huge viaducts measuring altogether nearly two and one-fourth miles. The longest is eight hundred and eighty-one feet and the highest one hundred and eleven feet above the bottom of the ravine it crosses. These bridges were nearly all constructed by an American firm, and promise to stand for ages.

The Boers who have settled on the plains are

fine shots and great hunters. It is said that they teach their fourteen-year-old boys to lie in front of the older men when a lion is charging and to hold their fire until he is within twenty yards and the word is given. They have discovered that the English government is not so bad after all.

At Fort Ternan, seen in the far distance before the train reaches it, the last section of the road begins. It runs through a spongy but fertile country of large and populous villages. Here the Nandi tribesmen for a while interfered with the working of the road and telegraph, not by acts of war, but by appropriating the telegraph wire for female adornment, and the rail bolts and rivets for the making of spears, war-axes, and arrow heads, It was as ridiculously absurd, in the Nandi estimation, for the English to leave such treasures out in the rain and the darkness as it would seem to us to leave bracelets, diamond pins, pistols, and knives, hanging unguarded on poles or fences.

At Kisumu, whose English name is Port Florence, the train ends its long and circuitous journey, five hundred and eighty-four miles from Mombasa.

THE APPROACH TO FORT TERNAN.

CHAPTER VII

IN THE COUNTRY OF THE BIG GAME

IT is a memorable hour in a traveller's life when, riding on the Uganda Railway, he looks out of the car window and sees the dainty paa, tiniest of deer, no larger than a small collie dog; or the big lumbering kongoni; the sprightly Chandler's reed buck; the herds of Grant's gazelle (white and black streaks on a roan skin); the sweet little Thomson's gazelle, called by the sportsmen the "Tommy;" the shaggy gnu; the rough wart-hogs; or the sly jackal; among the white and black of the zebra herds. I counted in one brief day 959 head of game. They grazed as quietly near our camp as domestic animals at home, and there are as many of them as there are of cattle on the farms of our richest Western States.

One of the best trips in the game country is the one from Voi, on the Uganda Railway, to Moschi, in the Kilimanjaro region. It is an even hundred-mile walk; and fifty miles is across the Taru, a waterless desert, but for the whole way it is lion infested, full of game and leopards. At the end of the route lies Lake Djipe, on the borders of German East Africa, swarming with hippopotami. The Parri Mountains, in German East Africa, have colobus monkeys in addition to other wild animals. All along that Taveta road, which has a regular service of donkeys and camels, the hyenas come around the camp every night, and lions roar within two hundred feet. At every turn in the road one starts coveys of partridges, guinea fowl, and wild pigeons. As for ostriches, gazelles, and kongoni, they are everywhere.

The game license in British East Africa is two hundred and fifty dollars, and if the hunter enters Uganda it is two hundred and fifty dollars more, and in the Sudan two hundred dollars in addition, or seven hundred dollars through these three territories. Now in German East Africa the game license is only three dollars and thirty cents. The Germans, however, charge thirty-three dollars and thirty-three cents for each elephant shot, ten dollars for each rhinoceros, six dollars and fifty cents for each buffalo or gnu, and one dollar for each of the smaller game.

Between Kilimanjaro (19,800 feet) and Mount Meru (12,000 feet) there is a thick forest for ninety miles, abounding in elephants. When I was there nine of these animals were shot in one week. The

ELEPHANT HUNTING NEAR NJORO.

In the Country of Big Game 123

Boer, Van Roy, and the brothers Trichard, also Boers, got three elephants between them in as many days. Monchardi, a young Italian, shot two lions one morning before breakfast at a settlement called Marangu. Fleischer, a famous Hungarian hunter, bagged a couple of elephants in an afternoon near Moschi. Several fine young rhinoceros cubs were caught by Max Klein and sent to Bostock's in Hamburg.

But in British East Africa there are to be found the biggest herds of game in the world. The British government has three game reserves in East Africa, aggregating nearly fifty thousand square miles. The whole East Africa Protectorate is only 240,000 square miles, so that the white settlers complain that there are too many game reserves. Lord Delamere and Mr. Bailey, two of the Governor's council at Nairobi, were expelled in 1908 by Governor Sadler for insisting on the reduction of the game reserves and also of the reserves set aside by the British government for the natives. Nevertheless, outside of the reserves there are sufficient game herds to draw the most famous hunters of the world, and this year the licenses will yield the government more than fifty thousand dollars. On one license the hunter may kill two elephants, two rhinoceri, two hippopotami, two zebras, six rare antelopes and gazelles; also two of the rare colobus monkeys and two smaller ones, two male ostriches, two marabous, two aigrets, common antelopes and gazelles to the number of ten, ten wildcats, ten jackals, ten wild pigs, two wolves, and two cheetahs. As to lions, leopards, and crocodiles, one may, without payment, shoot as many of them as one can get.

A young American woman, Mrs. Ismay (née Schieffelin, of New York), killed one of the biggest man-eating lions ever bagged.

At Simba, on the Uganda Railway, there are lions within two miles of the station. On the Kapiti and Athi plains one sees herds of game as far as the eye can reach across the open country.

In the African fauna the big mammals hold the most conspicuous position. The mind at once recalls the giraffe, elephant, lion, hippopotamus, rhinoceros, zebra, as well as the numerous species of antelope; and few scenes leave a deeper impression on the mind of the traveller than the numerous herds of game, gambolling and feeding on the vast plains of the interior.

The relative importance of the great mammals is increased by the scarcity of the small ones. This reminds us at once of Darwin's famous comparison of the mammalian fauna of Africa and that of South America. He pointed out that the barren steppes of the former are inhabited by vast herds of enormous animals, whereas the luxuriant vegetation of the latter supports only a few small forms. Darwin's statement of the facts is undoubtedly correct, and his conclusions just and instructive, but he gave no explanation of the anomaly. Professor Gregory suggests that Africa may be described as the land of migratory mammals, instead of the habitat of large mammals. The rains fall at two special periods of the year, which differ in different parts of the country, and at other times the steppes are burnt and foodless. In the dry season the soil is baked so intensely hard that small mammals cannot burrow into it. The result is that the only animals that can live are those that have sufficiently rapid power of locomotion to follow the rains, or are sufficiently strong to hold their own in the fight for water around the pools or to survive long periods without drinking.

Unless animals are followed one cannot realize how far they will wander. They walk slowly, feeding as they go, but often journeying twenty or thirty miles from one night's resting place to the next. Only animals of considerable size can travel such distances, and, since these journeys are necessary in Africa, the continent has gained the name of the "home of the large mammals."

The buffalo is very dangerous, being far more formidable than the American bison. He hunts instead of being hunted, and is said to have ten times the vitality of the lion. In fact the lion is not only cowardly, but he dies easily. Mr. McMillan, the American millionaire, who has a farm of twenty thousand acres thirty-four miles from Nairobi, has animals of all kinds upon his farm. Mr. McMillan is one of the most kindly men in the colony.

Thirteen miles from Nairobi is the farm of Mr. Heatley. Heatley had just shot a magnificent specimen of buffalo the day I met him at McMillan's house. He said there was a herd of forty near his place. He has the best model farm in East Africa.

There are one thousand white men in a circle of twenty-two miles from the centre of Nairobi, and farms and farm-houses in the regular English style are springing up all around. Nairobi is in the very heart of the game lands. The game oftentimes comes right into the town. Fifty miles away all sorts of big game can be found, and Mr. McMillan said he would procure for Col. Roosevelt, buffaloes, lions, leopards, and rhinoceri, all in the vicinity of his house. This he seems to have done.

To the northward of Nairobi and the Mount Kenia region lies the Sucota game reserve in Naivasha Province; and near this is the Eldama Ravine. Some of the level land at this point rises to between eight and nine thousand feet. Many herds of wild game fatten on these great meadows. The

A SUCCESSFUL HUNT IN THE BUKEDI COUNTRY, MOUNT ELGON DISTRICT.

plateau, near Mount Elgon, is perhaps
spot of all this upper hinterland.
...ed and well-watered valleys and good native
roads and new highways, constructed by the English
government, lead the hunter to Mount Elgon. All
the way from Nairobi to Mount Elgon, fourteen
thousand feet high, game of every kind abounds
on every hand.

The most picturesque and thrilling journey from
British East Africa into the Uganda Protectorate
is to turn away from the beaten track, walk across
the Uasi Ngishu plateau to the Mount Elgon region,
take in the almost untouched hunting grounds in
the neighbourhood of this great mountain, and by
a six days' journey reach Jinja, at the head waters
of the Nile, near the famous Ripon Falls. From
the railway station at Londiani to the Eldama Ravine is twenty-two miles. Thence to Mumias, forty
miles, the highlands offer charming scenery; and
kudus, tetals, nellats, antelopes, giraffes, harte-
beestes, as well as rhinoceri and elephants are thick.
From Mumias to the Nile a good road passes
through the Elgon district, where we found some
tribes of cave men.

Mbale, on the western slopes of Mount Elgon,
is eighty-six miles from Jinja. The two kingdoms
or principalities of Bukedi and Usoga lie on this
route. Perhaps the two men who understand this

country best are Bishop Hanlon, of the Catholic mission, who has a diocese of eighty-six thousand Christian natives; and Archdeacon Buckley of the Church of England missions. These good men will often ride alone for hundreds of miles through the lion infested forests of the Uganda Protectorate.

A trip around Lake Victoria is a rare treat to the man who loves an outdoor life. This body of water is said by the most recent surveys to be larger than Lake Superior. Hippopotami and rhinoceri are seen among the papyrus reeds; lions and leopards are in the woods; and the red colobus monkey (the rarest in the world) is found in the trees. At Bukoba there is a German commander and several German officers, and at Mwanza, the most southerly port, there is a fine set of German officers. "Good hunting" is always the watchword in this part of Africa. There is a herd of elephants on the island of Ukerewe, — "Ukerewe" was the original name of Victoria Nyanza.

Returning to Entebbe, one can proceed by 'rickshaw to Lake Albert Nyanza, about two hundred miles distant. All the way through this Uganda country one falls in with chimpanzees, colobus monkeys, zebras, buffaloes, and every kind of African antelope. There are wild asses in Uganda, and the three-horned and five-horned giraffes. Sir Harry Johnston claims that there are okapi in the West of

A LEOPARD TRAP IN UGANDA.

the Protectorate. Of course lions, leopards, hyenas and jackals are in every bush and swamp and wood.

The rigid preservation of so large a game reserve in the East African Protectorate has largely increased the number and decreased the timidity of the reed-bucks, zebras, giraffes, ostriches, antelopes and larger animals, who feed almost as fearlessly as tame cattle, close up to the railway tracks. Naturally the lions, leopards, hyenas and jackals, who prey upon them, gather in the same district and grow bold also. Game is frequently killed by the locomotives, and the station masters, section hands, and switchmen take chances of sudden death from accidents unusual in normal railroad employment.

When one turns up the virgin soil of Africa one disturbs more angry and pugnacious insects and reptiles than one ever imagined could exist. Ants that can grip the flesh like tiny forceps, bees and hornets like those that drove out the Anakim before Moses, are stirred into "pernicious activity" at the first turn of the spade. The immediate loss of life from serpent bites is slight, but the presence of such reptiles near the camp is disturbing. The python, the gaboon adder and the cobra are in the dense grass jungles; but they keep away from man.

Much more frequent have been the ravages of lions, leopards, and hyenas. At Voi a few years ago a gentleman named O'Hara killed a lion and brought in his skin as a trophy. The lioness trailed him from the despoiled body of her mate to his tent. When all were asleep, the hunter reposing between his wife and child, the great cat crept up through the darkness, unobserved, to where O'Hara lay, seized him and, without harming Mrs. O'Hara or the baby, carried him out among the provision boxes, where his mangled body was found next morning.

At Simba station we naturally hear much about lions, for Simba means "lion," and the lions of Simba keep up the record for enterprise and daring. A short time ago two Englishmen, Messrs. Dean and McLeod, were hunting near this station and came across a lion and his mate. Disregarding the latter, they followed the lion and slew him, but on their homeward path the lioness lay in wait to avenge, if she could not save. The victorious sportsmen were unaware of her presence until, with one resistless leap, she launched herself upon McLeod and tore him into shreds. During 1908, a Hindu flagman, who went out to set his signals, saw a lion coming towards him, and saved himself by hastily climbing a telegraph pole. Several comrades of the brute appeared in the station yard. The lion, growling his dissatisfaction, crouched at the foot of the pole, while the flagman communicated existing conditions to the station master. He, in turn, wired to a station fifty miles down the line: " Please let no

In the Country of Big Game 131

passengers come on platform at Simba; yard full of lions." On the arrival of the train, the lions retreated and the flagman was able to descend.

At the station of Makindu, a Goanese boy was surprised by a lion, which chased him as a cat does a mouse, while the hunted fugitive, like the mouse, sought for some perch, or hole where the big cat could not follow him. Just as the lion was close at his heels, the boy came upon an empty iron water reservoir, with a comparatively small aperture, into which he bolted, just in time to hear the lion thump up against his iron fortress.

Growling angrily at his discomfiture, the monster man-eater reached in one of his terrible paws, intending to pick the boy out of the iron shell as one extracts the meat from a nut. The boy drew himself up in the furthest corner, as the distended claws scraped fiercely on the iron plate, and the beast, frantic with rage and hunger, turned sidewise to give his enormous forearm its greatest reach.

The iron talons came nearer and nearer, until only an inch and a half — an inch — yes, a hair's breadth of sounding iron was left between them and the boy's bare knees. One more savage thrust and the distended claw touched and ripped the quivering skin, but took no hold. The blood oozed from the tiny cuts, and its smell roused the lion to great frenzy. Again and again these lethal claws rang and tore on the reverberant iron; again and again the angry jaws and terrible eyes filled the narrow mouth of the reservoir; but all in vain. Then the boy retaliated with the only weapon at hand — a box of matches.

One of these he lit when the great claws again sought for his life, and, watching his opportunity, dropped it on the shaggy paw. There was a flash of burning hair, a savage growl from the puzzled lion, and a sudden withdrawal of the slightly burned forefoot, which was immediately followed by another attempt with the other paw. Another blazing match discouraged investigation for a moment or two, but the lion was hungry and the boy resolute, and so the contest went on until morning came, when the foiled man-eater went back to the jungle, sore and supperless.

There is a more remarkable story, related as sober fact, but one which impresses an American reader as being not unworthy of the " nature fakirs " who have lately been impaled on the critical pen of our truth-loving Ex-President. It is told succinctly by Sir Charles Elliott, one of His Majesty's commissioners of the Protectorate, who heard it " from the lips of an excellent man who appeared to believe it himself and resented incredulity in others." Told briefly: This gentleman was marching up from the coast with a caravan of laden donkeys, which on

In the Country of Big Game 133

one day made remarkable speed with the exception of the hindermost, which lagged behind in spite of every inducement to keep up with his companions. On arriving in camp, the men were horrified to find that the supposed donkey was a great lion, which, during the previous night, had killed and eaten a donkey, ears, hoofs and all, and was so gorged and torpid that he could scarcely move. In the uncertain light of dawn he had been saddled and laden with the burden carried by his victim, and so driven along behind the donkeys, who were so alarmed that they kept ahead of their natural enemy the whole day.

It is doubtless true that, as the game is wholly preserved south of the railroad line and the lions are promptly hunted down by local and visiting sportsmen, they have begun to recognize the difference between a white hunter armed with the modern breech-loader and the native archer or spearman whom they formerly despised. Nevertheless, lions are found in great numbers back in the scrub and forests, where there are thousands of haunts which no white man's foot has ever trod; and there they are still lords of the jungle and devourers of men until some modern Nimrod learns of their ravages and hunts them down in their terrible fastnesses.

Such a hunter is Da Silva of Nakuru station, a Portuguese guide, who holds the highest record as a lion-slayer, being credited with seventeen lions killed in one day. Herr Bast, military commandant at Moschi on the German frontier, has a record of five lions in one day. An African record, however, is made — and closed — very quickly when men devote the greater portion of their lives to jungle travel and exploration.

As there is so much big game hunting in British East Africa, there is no trouble in finding a man or a firm, either at Mombasa or Nairobi, to procure all the necessary porters, tents, ammunition and food for a party going into the wilds. There are several mercantile firms which make a business of supplying hunting parties, and there are men who will take charge of everything at so much per month.

A hunting party with porters and attendants is called a Safari.

The battery for each member, to be sufficient for all needs, should consist of a .450 express, a .303 sporting rifle, British model, and a 12-bore shot gun; and I should think that sufficient ammunition for a three-months' trip would be two hundred and fifty rounds of .450 (fifty hard and two hundred soft), 300 rounds of .303 (one hundred hard and two hundred soft), and five hundred 12-bore shot cartridges of, say, the 6 and 8 sizes, sufficient for a three-months' trip.

The hunter's kit should include a good pith hat,

GERMAN HUNTERS AT MOSCHI AFTER A BUFFALO HUNT. HERR BAST SECOND FROM LEFT.

a couple of suits of khaki, leather gaiters or a couple of pairs of puttees, wash-leather gloves to protect the hands from the sun, and two pairs of boots with hemp soles; long Norwegian boots will also be found very useful. The usual underclothing worn in America in the Fall is all that is required if the shooting is to be done in the highlands, as the temperature there corresponds to our October. A good warm overcoat will be much appreciated up-country, in the cool of the evenings, and a light mackintosh for wet weather ought also to be included.

The caravan for one sportsman — if he intends going far from the railway — is usually made up as follows, though the exact numbers depend upon many considerations:

1 Headman	50 rupees per month	
1 Cook	35 " " "	
1 Gun-bearer	35 " " "	
1 " Boy " (personal servant)	20 " " "	
2 Askaris (armed porters)	12 " " "	each
30 Porters	10 " " "	each

The sportsman is obliged to provide each porter with a jersey, blanket and water bottle, while the gun-bearer and "boy" get a pair of boots in addition. A cotton shelter tent and a cooking pot must also be furnished for every five men.

The food for the caravan is mostly rice, of which the Headman gets three pounds per day; the cook, gun-bearer, "boy" and askaris, two and a quarter pounds, and the ordinary porters one and one-half pounds per day.

The ordinary porters will carry their sixty-pound loads day in and day out without complaint, so long as they are well fed; but stint them of their rice, and they at once become sulky mutineers. In addition to carrying the loads, they pitch and strike camp, procure firewood and water, and build grass huts if a stay of more than a day is intended to be made at one place. On the whole, the Swahili porter is one of the jolliest and most willing fellows in the world, and I have nothing but praise for him.

For the white travellers, there are plenty of chickens, which can be bought for eight cents apiece anywhere throughout the country. In a good hunting party there is no want of delicious viands made from antelope steak, for there are hundreds of Grant gazelles, Thomson gazelles, kongoni (Jackson's hartebeeste), Chandler's reed-buck, and the little paa, which forms a very toothsome morsel to the hungry hunter. The natives will eat all the *membra disjecta* of any of the wild game killed. They are especially fond of the entrails of the animals, which they roast over fires without removing the offal.

Zebra steak is palatable to the white man and there are in East Africa wild boars in abundance. Elephant's steak looks something like corned-beef,

In the Country of Big Game

but it is very tough. The flavour is not very good. It always reminded me of a combination of stewed cobblestones and sawdust. When a band of German hunters with whom I was travelling shot over ten tons of elephant meat in the Kilimanjaro region, the natives came for two hundred miles, and almost every ounce of available meat was voraciously devoured. The natives draw the line at eating the dead lions, and the Mohammedan portion of the Safari will eschew the pig in all its forms. My Swahili tent "boys" absolutely refused to eat anything cooked in pig lard when they discovered the picture of a pig on the Chicago tins.

In the wilder districts around Mount Elgon there is plenty of honey to be had from the wild natives of Bukedi.' Native sheep and goats will be found in nearly all the villages, even in the wildest parts. The natives, however, do not like to sell any of their domestic cattle, because such animals are used for the purchase of wives and are supposed to be a sign of wealth.

There is a 'rickshaw line being established, for 1909, across Uganda nearly 200 miles from Entebbe to Lake Albert Nyanza. All the country abounds in game and there are plenty of wild guinea fowl and plantain-eaters, besides abundance of partridges and pigeons. Among the game animals in Uganda are the Speke's tragelap (a water-loving animal of a dark mouse-brown or chestnut colour), the Palla antelope, Baker's roan antelope, the white-eared kob of Unyoro, the steinbuck, and the Duyker antelope of the unwooded plains. There are plenty of lions and hippopotami and even okapi have been seen. This strange animal, seemingly coming in between a zebra and a giraffe, is eaten by the natives. These are the lands of the Big Game of Africa. Here the remnants of the Tertiary age have made their last stand. They are on the losing side, against white men and repeating rifles. They are two hundred thousand years behind the times: and they must go.

GAME IN THE NAIVASHA COUNTRY.

CHAPTER VIII

SOME TRIBES AND CUSTOMS

ON our trip along the Uganda Railway and around the shores of Lake Victoria Nyanza we came in contact with the most interesting tribes of East Central Africa. The first and most important tribe is the Masai, the famous tribe of blood-drinking warriors and nomadic shepherds.

Their central home is on the East African highlands near Lake Naivasha, a beautiful sheet of blue water over which white cranes are flying. One can see zebras and antelopes feeding not far from the water, and with field glass one can watch the ugly black heads of hippopotami bobbing up and down like giant fishing corks upon the surface. The shores are swampy, and lined with masses of reeds. Just back of them the ground rises into rich pastures, where the numerous game are protected from sportsmen by the reservation laws.

The climate is delightful. The region is practically on the equator, but the altitude is such that blankets are needed at night and it is never excessively hot during the day. Naivasha is a little higher up in the air than the top of Mount Washington, and the climate of the whole Rift Valley is said to be suitable for white men.

This is one of the strongholds of the Masai race, who have always been noted as warriors and stock raisers. Not a few of them carry spears and shields. They have many little towns nearby, and their settlements are scattered throughout the Rift Valley.

They live in huts about four feet high, six feet wide and nine feet long. The huts look like great bake ovens. They are made of branches woven together and plastered with mud. Sometimes they are smeared over with cow-dung, and that material often forms the floors. When it rains, skins are laid over the roofs to protect them.

The houses are usually built in a circle about an enclosure, in which the cattle are kept at night. The sheep and goats are allowed to run in and out of the houses. Some of the towns have fences of thorns around them to keep out the wild beasts.

These Masai are a fierce-looking people. The men are tall and straight, and they walk as though they owned the earth. When they have their war paint on, they use a decoration of ostrich feathers which surrounds their faces, and is supposed to carry terror to the souls of their enemies. The men are usually bare to the waist, and not infrequently have a bullock hide wrapped around them.

The Masai women are as vain as peacocks and are loaded with ornaments. Some of them have great rings of brass wire coiled around the neck in connecting circles, wire after wire being used until the whole extends out as far as the shoulders. They have brass wire woven about their arms from the wrists to the elbows, and from the elbows to the shoulders, and also great coils of similar wire fastened by strings to the lobes of their ears. Aside from this they wear but little. A skin wrapped around the body and falling to the knees or below is usually their only clothing. Sometimes this garment is fastened over the shoulders, sometimes under the arms, and sometimes about the waist.

The Masai are by no means pure negroes. Their noses are often straight and their lips are not thick. As to their hair, it is difficult to make out whether it is woolly or not. The women shave it close to their scalps, using razors of iron, flint, or glass, and then they polish their heads with grease so that they fairly shine in the sun. Even the babies are shaved. Many of the men carry with them tweezers of iron to pull the hairs from their chins, cheeks and nostrils, and they keep themselves shaved until they are old enough to be warriors. This comes about the time they reach manhood. They then let the hair of their heads grow and plait it into pigtails. A common way of wearing these pigtails is down over the forehead. They are sometimes soaked with oil and red clay in connection with a similar anointing of the rest of the body.

The warrior often wears a lion's head and mane in addition to the circle of ostrich feathers about the face. His weapons are a sword and a club. He also has a spear with a very long blade and an oval shield bearing figures which indicate his clan.

These people buy their wives. Girls are looked upon as purchasable commodities and are paid for in goats and cattle. After the cattle are handed over, the girl goes to her husband, and she may not come back to her father's house thereafter, unless she be accompanied by her husband.

A Masai may marry as many wives as he can pay for; and if he be a rich man he will have a hut for each one. If not, he may keep two or three wives in one hut. The first wife is always considered the chief wife, and is supposed to rule the establishment, although the favourite sometimes supersedes her.

Marriages of warriors, however, are not supposed to take place until the Masai citizen-soldier becomes an elder — that is, until he reaches the age of from twenty-seven to thirty, when his campaigning days are over and he is ready to settle down. The warriors and the young girls of the tribe live together up to that time in a separate establishment managed by the young men's mothers, apart from the rest of the people.

In order to marry, an El moran or soldier has to ask permission of the elders of the tribe. If this is given, he straightway buys his wife, and if she is a fine-looking girl she will cost him two cows, two bullocks, two sheep and some goat skins. This payment, which may be lowered in special cases, goes to the nearest relative of the woman he has selected.

Divorces may be had for laziness and bad temper on the part of the wife, and in such cases a part of the marriage fee is sometimes returned. A widow cannot marry again. If her husband dies the woman goes back to her mother; or to her brother, if the mother is dead.

The Masai girls have an easy, indolent youth. They are required to do nothing until they are married. Before that they play with the warriors, spending their time in dancing, singing and idleness. The unmarried girl does not do her own cooking. This condition continues for a long time after marriage and even until the babies of the family are fairly well grown.

As soon as that is accomplished, however, the hard-working period begins. Almost all of the menial labour of the tribe is done by the old women.

They build the mud houses. When the villages are moved from place to place, these withered dames take the part of donkeys and bullocks in carrying the burdens. They erect the new huts, and they are, as a rule, mere hewers of wood and drawers of water.

The Masai do practically no farming. They are a nation of stock raisers, and own herds of cattle, sheep and goats, which they drive about from pasture to pasture. The cattle are of the humped variety, like the sacred cows of India, many of them being fat, sleek and fine looking. Some of the animals are branded, and not a few have rude bells of iron so that they may be traced if they stray. Usually the cattle are watched by half-naked boys, who drive them about with sticks from place to place.

Every morning and evening the cows are brought into the village to be milked, and nearly every town of mud huts has its cow house. The women do the milking. This is contrary to the custom in some other parts of Africa, where it is thought that the cows will go dry if any female touches them. The milk is caught in gourds, which are afterward cleaned with handfuls of burnt grass.

The calves are brought alongside their mothers at milking time, and the cows will not let down their milk unless they are present. If a calf dies it is

Photograph by Peter Dutkewich, copyright, 1900, by Underwood & Underwood, N. Y.

MEDICINE MEN OF THE MASAI IN CONSULTATION.

Some Tribes and Customs 145

skinned and stuffed and then placed under the cow's nose at milking time.

The people always drink their milk fresh, but the method of cleaning the gourds gives it a smoky flavour.

The Masai are also blood drinkers. Their country has practically no salt, and they keep in health by blood drinking. They consume all the blood of the animals they kill, and sometimes bleed their cattle in the neck and then tie the wounds up so that they grow well again. Sometimes a strap is tied around an animal's throat and an arrow is shot into the jugular vein. As the blood gushes forth it is caught in the gourds and is drunk warm.

Their cooking is usually done in pots of burnt clay, varying from eight to twenty inches in height. The larger pots are not placed over the fire, but at the side of it, and are turned around now and then in order that they be evenly heated.

The nomadic Masai are now quiet and are becoming semi-civilized. They are paying the annual hut taxes of about three rupees each to the government. Three rupees means $1.00 in American money. It means but little until one remembers that it takes many a native a month to earn that amount.

When the English took possession of East Africa about 1885, each village was independent and almost constantly at war with neighbouring villages. The citizens of one settlement knew nothing of those of the other settlements. A man dared not venture more than ten miles from his house, and he had but little knowledge of the country outside that radius. There were no roads whatever excepting trails which wound this way and that over the land. The only meeting places were the markets, which were held at fixed points on certain days of the week or month.

It is a rule throughout Africa that warfare and fighting must be suspended on market days, and no one dares bring arms to a market or fight there. If he should engage in fighting and be killed his relatives cannot claim blood money.

Captain Hinde, one of the British officers, said to an American traveller: "When we took possession of the Kenia province we had to fight our way in. As soon as we had subdued the people, we made them work at making roads as a penalty for their insurrection. We connected all the villages by roadways and gave each town so much to take care of. As a result we now have in that province alone four hundred miles of good wagon roads, each ten feet in width. We have also made it the law that every road shall be considered as having all the rights of a market place. This means that no native can assault another while walking upon them, and that all feuds must be buried while travelling over the roads. Many of these roads connect with villages which were formerly at war with each other, and the result is that they have become peaceful and that the citizens can now travel safely from one town to another. They are really changing their natures and are going through a process of travel-education. As I have already said, five years ago they never left home; now thousands of them travel over the roads down to the sea coast, and we have something like eighteen hundred natives of Kenia at Mombasa."

The pastoral nomadic Masai will not dig, but they are paid for herding stock, and some of the other tribes are doing actual work on the farms and on the railroad. They are beginning to have wants, and as these increase they will work to supply them. Many of those who formerly went naked now desire more or less clothing. Cotton goods are becoming popular, and it is interesting to know that the American white cotton sheeting brings the highest of prices among the natives. It outsells the Indian and English goods and in some places it even passes for money.

Another article from America that is in great demand in Central Africa is coal oil. The natives buy it to light their huts, and the big chiefs almost universally own one or more kerosene lamps. Other foreign articles much desired are umbrellas, knives, and hardware of various kinds.

There is another branch of the Masai that are not nomadic but are pastoral and agricultural; I mean the Wataveta, who live in the Taveta forest and whom I have described elsewhere in the book.

Another extremely interesting race we met with are the Baziba. Baziba lies in German East Africa, just south of Uganda, on the western side of Lake Victoria. It is bounded on the east by the lake and it includes a part of the Kagera River, which many believe to be the source of the Nile. That river rises in the highlands not far from Lake Tanganyika and flows in a winding course through German East Africa, emptying into Lake Victoria almost on the boundary between the two countries. The Kagera is quite wide at its mouth and it can be navigated for about seventy miles.

The Baziba are clad in grass clothing. The men have grass or fibre cloaks which they wear around their shoulders. The women have skirts of grass fastened to a ring at the top through which the neck goes. The unmarried girls have little fringes of grass or raffia fibre, not over eight inches long, which they wear around their waists. In addition to this the girls may have a bracelet or two and some anklets of wire, but otherwise they are bare.

Some Tribes and Customs 149

This matter of nudity, however, is entirely governed by custom. On the hither side of Lake Victoria, among the Kavirondo, thousands go naked from one year's end to the other, but in their manners they are just as decent and quite as modest as our own people at home. In Uganda, the women are clad from their chests to their feet in robes of bark cloth; and it is impolite for a man to lift up his gown above the middle of the calf. Nevertheless, the Baganda are said to be much less virtuous than the naked Kavirondo, and I venture the opinion that they do not rank higher in that respect than the grass-clad Bazibas.

Indeed of all the inhabitants around Lake Victoria these Bazibas are the most rigid moralists, and offences against the marriage tie are punished severely. The Baziba man and woman who attempt to live together without being married take their lives in their hands. They are liable to be tied hand and foot and thrown into the lake; or, if they dwell in the interior, to be carried to the nearest swamp and buried alive under the flags.

Marriages take place on about the same conditions as in other parts of Africa, the girls being sold by their parents. Just now the usual price for a bride is ten thousand cowry shells, or a little over $3.00. This is for a well rounded, handsome maiden of about fifteen. The price from that age falls rapidly, and an older woman or a widow often brings less than $1.75.

Bukoba, one of their most interesting towns, is the northernmost station in German East Africa. It is beautifully situated, lying on a moon-shaped bay environed by low hills. At the south are grass-grown bluffs ending in palisades of granite which rise straight up from the water to a height of two hundred feet. Right under these bluffs is the landing place, and it was a little outside of them that our steamship came to anchor.

We were carried to the shore in native canoes of wonderful workmanship. Each boat was about thirty feet long, three feet wide and two feet deep. It had a keel made out of the trunk of a tree and the sides were of hewn boards about a fourth of an inch thick and one foot in width, running almost the full length of the boat. The boards were sewn together and fastened to the keel by threads of fibre or bark. There were also larger boats, some even fifty feet long, made in the same way, and used for navigating the lake. The boats are very leaky and require constant bailing.

We strolled into the town of Bukoba to look at the stores and the market. These are near the fort, the village proper being some distance away. The chief business street consists of a dozen or more

Some Tribes and Customs 151

little booths, each occupied by a Hindu merchant, who sits or stands in it, surrounded by his goods. The black, grass-clad customers make their purchases by means of cowry shells.

The chief things sold are coloured and uncoloured cottons, the favourites, as I have said, being American sheetings. Another popular article of merchandise is wire, of copper, iron and brass. This is used by the natives as jewelry, and it is almost as valuable as gold and silver are in our country. The wire is brought here in great kegs, and coils of it are hung up in front of the stores. It is of all thicknesses, from the size of a human hair to the diameter of one's little finger. The thicker wire is hammered out into armlets, anklets and collars, and the finer is woven and plaited into similar ornaments. Some of the wire jewelry is heavy, and a very common anklet worn by the women looks as though it might have been torn from our woven wire fences and twisted together.

In the market square, near these stores, were many black pedlars. They squatted on the ground, with their wares piled about them. Here a woman sold sweet potatoes, there one offered little piles of entrails of sheep or goats, and farther on were others selling peanuts and white ants. The white ants had been roasted, and were displayed upon bits of banana leaves and were sold at so many shells per pile.

The cowry shell is the chief currency of this part of Africa, and travellers say that it is in common use throughout the regions about Lake Tanganyika and the Congo valley. The shells are brought here from the coast of India and are exchanged for rupees at the rate of one thousand to the rupee. A rupee is worth about thirty-three cents, and as the shells are put up in strings of one hundred each, a string of shells is worth just about three cents of our money. Seven dollars' worth is a good load for a man, and ten cents would weigh about as much as sixteen of our silver dollars.

This makes commerce difficult, and the Germans are trying to introduce a new coinage based on the Indian rupee. The chief difficulty is to make the coin small enough. The present issue includes coins known as hellers, one hundred to the rupee, so that one heller is worth one-third of a cent in our money.

In the interior we found an even more primitive life. The largest huts had only two apartments about three feet wide and six feet long, which were used for sleeping. In the centre of the hut was a fire, upon which, in an earthen pot, some food was constantly steaming. There was neither stove nor chimney and the smoke filled the hut. Under con-

Photograph by Peter Dutkewich, copyright, 1909, by Underwood & Underwood, N. Y.

A GROUP OF WISE-MEN AMONG THE NANDI.

Some Tribes and Customs 153

ditions of such discomfort we were always glad to find refuge in the open air.

In those parts of the country remote from the white man's influence matches are unknown, and fire is gotten by twisting a stick in a hole made in a block of wood until the friction brings a light. Years of practice are required to produce fire in this way. Very few white men have ever been able to accomplish it.

Referring again to the marriage customs of Central Africa, we observed among the Nandi tribes on the highlands beyond Mau that the richest men have from ten to forty wives. The price for a good wife of fourteen is six cows. Girls are often betrothed as early as seven and they are married at eleven. The cows are paid on instalments, and if no child is born within a year after the marriage the husband may stop payment.

It is among these Nandi, as among the Masai, that the unmarried girls dwell with the young unmarried men in the bachelor quarters until they are old enough to get married. This revolting custom has injured the children; and it is being prohibited by the German and British governments.

Among the Buvumas the standard price of a wife is two cows and five goats. The father of the bride keeps one of the cows and a goat, the balance of the dowry being given to the nearest relatives.

The Uganda women wear bark cloth and cover the whole person. They have great blankets which they wrap around them, binding them in at the breast and waist. They more nearly approach the American standard of decency in clothing than any other tribe in Africa.

The Kikuyu tribe wear skins. They do a great deal of the manual labour of East Africa and have the most hopeful future.

The simple native girls of Central Africa resemble their sisters of more civilized lands in their desire to heighten their personal charms. Our American belles adore dimples, and it is said that their dimples are sometimes artificially made. They adorn their white faces with black patches of court plaster, and also comb their hair in outlandish shapes.

The same effort to beautify oneself goes on throughout Africa, save that the standards of beauty are different. Among the Banyoro, who live north of Uganda, the women knock out the six front teeth of the lower jaw and the young men do the same. The Jaluo women have a similar custom. On the south side of Victoria Nyanza there are tribes where the women file their teeth sharp like a saw, and the Buvumas knock out two of the incisors, the price for such an operation being four cowry shells or a fraction of a cent.

Most of the African women scar their bodies as

DANCE OF YOUNG MEN OF THE KIKUYU TRIBE IN HONOUR OF THEIR COMING OF AGE.

a means of adornment. I have seen girls with Persian shawl patterns on their breasts, and others with great welts on their foreheads and cheeks. The latter marks also indicate the tribes to which they belong. In the Sudan there are scores of such tribal marks, and each tribe has its own way of scarring. Mutilation of the ears is common throughout Central Africa. The Swahilis enlarge the holes in the lobes until they become mere straps which will inclose a glass tumbler. The women have holes all around the rims of their ears, which they fill with rolls of paper and pieces of wood.

In German East Africa it is the custom in some localities to wear great rings and plugs in both the upper and the lower lip. Such ornaments elongate the upper lip so that it extends several inches out over the mouth. The result is both ludicrous and deforming.

The ebony belles of the black continent have many and marvellous methods in the dressing of the hair. Though they have to conquer the kink and the screw curl which is natural to them, they nevertheless have many creations which surpass the wonder of the marcel wave, the mighty pompadour and other oddities formed with the aid of the rat, the curling-tongs or the hair-pin. The Sudanese dress their hair in long even curls, so that it hangs out like the snakes of Medusa. The Zulus put it up in mighty towers, which often extend a full foot above the crown of the head; and down in Natal a bridegroom goes out to court his sweetheart with a pair of real cowhorns tied upright on his head, so naturally that they look as if they grew there.

Along the eastern coast of Africa there are many natives who braid the hair in little windrows over the scalp. The Baganda and the Masai shave the head. Many of the native women of Omdurman, in the Sudan, shave not only their head, but every part of the body, and it is a common custom among many tribes for both men and women to have themselves shaved from head to foot before marriage. Among some peoples the hair is pulled out.

The Batoro, a tribe which inhabits the country between Lakes Albert and Albert Edward, shave and oil their brides before the wedding. The girl's head is scraped off by the village barber, and her own sister uses the razor over the rest of the body. After this she is smeared from crown to toe-nail with butter and castor oil, the stuff being well rubbed into the skin.

Some of the older African villages are nothing but cemeteries, and there are little towns each hut of which contains one or more dead bodies and nothing else. The people are superstitious and want to be buried in the same places in which they lived. The Wayanika and Wakamba tribes have the same

Some Tribes and Customs 157

superstitions and family customs as those already mentioned among the larger clans.

In Mr. Dutkewich's diary, you will find a great deal about the Kavirondo and Kikuyu tribes in addition to the foregoing customs which I have noted.

CHAPTER IX

ACROSS THE SERENGETI PLAIN

HAVING made the journey to Victoria Nyanza and lingered among the tribes of the upper plateau of British East Africa, we decided to make a trip from the railway into German East Africa. In the month of June, 1908, Mr. Dutkewich and myself made an expedition from Voi across the Serengeti Plain to Mount Kilimanjaro, one hundred miles away. The British frontier is at Taveta, seventy-five miles from the railway station, and the German settlements are twenty-five miles beyond that, among the rich green foothills of Marangu and Moschi. A fairly good wagon road has been constructed by the two governments and there is a transport service every week of donkeys or camels.

The whole country here is about two thousand feet above the sea; the days are warm and the nights are cool. Across the plain for fifty miles there are no springs or streams. On the whole journey we met just two white men, the British tax collector

Across the Serengeti Plain

at Mtate, among the Wataita tribe, and a German planter, named Koerfer, at the plantations of Burra.

We took twenty-five men of the Taita tribe and hired sixteen donkeys from an Italian firm that runs a transport system from Voi to Moschi. The march at first is through interesting scenery, out beyond the station and past the American Fibre Company's plant, then through shrubby forests in sight of the beautiful Taita Mountains and the Burra Range. We camped the first night ten miles from the railway, on the banks of the Voi River.

I shall not soon forget the pitch-darkness and the silence that might be felt in the African forest. Pigeons, partridges, guinea fowls and gazelles were seen on every side before we made our camp, and we bagged a guinea fowl and two partridges for the cooking pot. As the night fell we put the donkeys into a zareba, a little round enclosure fenced with the thorns of the Mimosa tree that grows along the road-side. We made big fires and got pure drinking water from the clear running river.

After the evening meal the men sat around the fire, telling stories of other Safaris they had made with English and German hunters. Their soft language in the quiet twilight had a restful influence after the hot journey of the afternoon. We retired early, for we were to make an early start next day. At midnight I took a walk around the camp. Some of the porters were asleep, some were still talking by the fire. I detailed two to keep the fire going all the night against the coming of wild beasts. Always I could hear in the conversation the word " Shimba " — which means the lion, for that fierce beast enthralls the imagination of the simple natives and enchains their minds with its alluring horror.

We slept until four o'clock and heard no voice nor sound. We started the caravan a little after four and the moon was shining so clearly that it almost seemed like day. As yet everything was as quiet as the dim aisles of a cathedral. The caravan started. Mr. Dutkewich took the wagons across the river, while I went down to a ford and waited for the dawn, hoping to find an antelope and bring it home for breakfast. We had started without food, drinking only a cup of coffee.

I sat down beside the river with my tent boy Salim. In a short time the jungle began to awaken. First I heard the chirp of an insect, then the squawk of a parrot, the snarl of a leopard, the moaning wail of a hyena and last of all, and only a hundred feet away, the ominous growl of a lion.

I asked the boy " What is it? " He answered " Shimba, Bwana " (the lion, master). I was thoroughly aroused. I had heard how dangerous the lion is when he is wounded. I had never met a wild lion before, and had only a .303 rifle with me.

GAME SHOT BY THE AUTHOR AND MR. DUTKEWICH ON THE SERENGETI PLAIN.

Again I asked the boy: "What kind of a lion?" I was merely talking to keep my courage up. The boy replied: "I think, master, lady lion with two chicks." A lioness with two cubs; that is, the most dangerous antagonist one can find in the whole of Africa.

There was an old wooden bridge near me, and I resolved to creep up under the bridge where I could get a better shot, and if I missed, escape the terrible claws of the lion when it leaped. As the boy and I kept advancing toward the bridge, the growls became more angry when the savage beast saw that some unknown foe was approaching. It began to retreat, however, and as soon as I got under the bridge, I took a good aim and fired at its head. With a fierce yell the animal leaped back toward the jungle, snarling like a huge cat; and I expected every moment that it would leap upon me. It was evidently too startled to make a stand, and, not being able to see its enemy, was frightened; for it kept snarling and retreating, and finally disappeared in the jungle. There were two or three of the beasts. The boy, whose sight was much keener than mine, saw the cubs, although they were not evident to me at all.

I was glad when the daylight arrived; and I left my cover under the bridge and proceeded after the caravan. From five to seven in the morning the plain through which we went was filled with the songs of wild birds, the drumming of partridges, the voices of the fields and jungles.

The grass was heavily laden with dew. The heavy rains had just ceased and the whole country was an overflowing sea of verdure. In two months it would be all sere and brown, with not one green spray in the whole wide prairie. We travelled twenty-five miles the first day, and the second night we camped at the Burra plantation, where a German company is developing the land and planting great fields of rubber and coffee.

We were invited to the hospitable home of the German manager, Mr. Koerfer. His wife had been a nun at the Mission, whose white buildings shone out bold and clear against the hills of Taita two miles away. There is an Indian store at Burra and some native shops.

I was interested in the natives, who are the Wa-taita tribe. They carry bows and arrows, and live on corn and bananas and what game they can hunt. But the peculiar thing about them is that their farms are nearly all on the very tops of the mountains. Ten or fifteen years ago the war-like Masai who dwell on the adjoining plains destroyed the Taita villages, and drove the frightened natives to the highest hills. The English government has now stopped the maraudings of the Masai, but the Wataita have not yet become quite reassured; and we oftentimes saw their fires at night upon the mountains. The fires look like beacon lights along a dark shoreland at night.

Mr. Koerfer, our kindly host, is a German and he has interesting ideas about disciplining the natives. For example: he had them trained to come to his house whenever he sounded a whistle. One night my little dog strayed out from my camp and I could not find it in the dark. Mr. Koerfer sounded the whistle, although it was nearly midnight, and all the natives within a mile came running together. Even the women came at the sound of the whistle. We searched long, but in vain. I went out in the moonlight later in the night, and in the long grass, a hundred yards from the house, I could make out the motion of some huge beast. Our host told us not to go far from the house after dark, but I hung around some time to try and make out what this wild creature could be. While thus engaged, my friend came out and advised me to be careful and come back on the verandah, because the field was infested with leopards.

In the morning, I went down through the field, and at an open space near where I saw the animal in the night, I found my little dog all eaten but his tail. He was a little round, fat native dog, and the leopard must have mistaken him for a frankfurter sausage — not an unusual mistake, and one that has been made before and since.

When we started from Burra we had to cross the Taru desert, which extends for fifty miles to the Lumi River. Although a desert with no springs or streams, the wild Taru was blossoming like fairyland when we crossed it after the rains.

On the slopes of the far distant Parri Mountains the land looked desolate and burned, but in the meadows toward the Serengeti Plain the grass waved luxuriantly, together with pink and white lilies that starred the prairie lands in all directions. The acacia trees, growing like huge umbrellas, looked like an orchard, so straight and regular did they grow in rows.

In the open plains, where there were few if any trees, wild animals were thickly clustered. The giraffe scudded away, as did herds of elands whose glossy hides gleamed like silk in the sunlight; red hartebeeste, sable antelope, mpalas, the tiny paa, and herds of zebra studded the undulating plains. Small groups of well behaved, genteel ostriches walked daintily in the long grass; and once or twice we came upon a rhinoceros under an acacia tree flicking his tail and leering at us with suspicious eyes.

One morning I was bringing up the rear of the caravan, the rest of the party having gone a mile

MR. DUTKEWICH AND HIS CARRIERS IN THE TARU DESERT.

Across the Serengeti Plain 165

and a half ahead, when I observed a huge rhinoceros not more than fifty or sixty feet from me. For the second time I was taken aback in the presence of wild game. Being alone and having a light rifle, I did not care to tackle the "rhino" in that lonely corner of the fields. Accordingly I crept away to the windward of him and let my scent drift down toward him. As soon as the animal felt the scent he started after me with a lunging lope about as fast as a horse would trot. Meanwhile I started back to get behind him, about as fast as a motor car would go at sixty miles an hour. The "rhino" galloped on and was finally bowled over by the other hunters who had heavy rifles.

In crossing this desert we had to carry water in big tin cans upon the donkey wagon. Before starting I gave one of my Swahili boys particular directions to fill the tin cans from a spring beside the river. He filled six five-gallon tin cans and we started in good heart.

The first afternoon out on the desert I noticed that the water was full of bubbles and very bad to the taste. I called the boy who had filled the cans and said to him: "Boy, what is wrong with this water?" He said: "Safi maji, bwana " — "clean water, master." When I inquired still further from the boy about the water he said he was quite sure it was very clean. "I put the soap in it myself," he exclaimed with great emphasis. Thus we had soap suds all the way across the dry Taru.

We had the most difficulty with the donkeys. The poor little animals were willing beasts, but they were attacked by tsetse flies and two of them died during the first three days' tramp. A few days later we lost two more by lions. Our tent was 200 feet from the zereba where we kept the donkeys; and one night we had kindled a fire at the door and set two men to watch it. They fell asleep; the fire went out. At about two o'clock in the morning we heard a dreadful uproar, but we did not dare to leave our tent in the darkness as the whole plain was swarming with hyenas, leopards and lions. In the morning, however, we found that two of our best donkeys had been dragged out of the enclosure and had been left in the jungle half-eaten by lions.

As we advanced farther from the settlements the lions became more bold, and we heard from the natives a continual story of their atrocities. An Arab merchant ahead of us had two of his donkeys devoured, and when we had crossed the plain and reached the Lumi River we were met at the fords of the river by a delegation of young Wataveta hunters. They told us a terrific tale of how they had hunted a man-eating lion and how one of their number, named Martini, eighteen years old, the son

WATAVETA WARRIORS READY FOR A LION HUNT.

of their chief, Melikanoi, had stood in front of the great beast with his spear; and how when the lion had jumped upon him he thrust his spear clean through its heart and, leaping aside like lightning, fell under his ox hide shield to save himself from the cruel claws. The fierce beast rolled on the ground in agony and a second warrior came forward to stab it to death, but it reached out its awful paw and grasping the hunter disembowelled him. Martini, however, was safe, and he was the pride and joy of the tribe. So, when we had rested at the Lumi River, we prepared for a visit among the agricultural Masai or Wakwafi tribe who are called the Wataveta.

CHAPTER X

IN THE TAVETA FOREST

JUST beyond the Lumi River, and on the borders of German East Africa, we came upon an old abandoned mission. The mission buildings are situated on a little hill overlooking part of the Serengeti Plains with a beautiful view of the great cone of Mount Kilimanjaro to the South-West. Directly to the south are the blue Parri Mountains. To the east lies the famous Taveta Forest; the beauties of which have been described by Dr. Carl Peters, Mr. Joseph Thomson, Sir Harry Johnston, and others.

We found in the old mission one of the most delightful characters that I met in all of Africa, Count Coudenhove, an Austrian nobleman, who has lived in and near these Kilimanjaro forests for fifteen years. The Count speaks English perfectly and was therefore a first rate comrade. He knew the languages of all the Masai and Wakwafi tribes, and he knew a great deal of the habits of the baboons and colobus monkeys, the hyenas, leopards, lions and antelope that range through the jungle and the plain.

A quarter of a mile beyond the mission lies the village of Taveta. Here there are several Hindu stores and a number of the houses of the Taveta tribe. On a knoll outside the village is the home of the English Commissioner. The incumbent of the position, when we were there, was a renowned hunter and delightful gentleman, Mr. Hyde-Baker, nephew of Sir Samuel Baker, who discovered some of the sources of the Nile. Mr. Baker has hunted a great deal in the Congo forests to fill the museum of Baron Rothschild at Paris. He has killed two hundred lions, nearly as many elephants, enough of other wild animals to fill a museum, and he is the only white man who has ever seen a live okapi. (The okapi is an animal new to science, found in the dense, dark jungles of the Ituri forest at the head waters of the Congo River.)

Mr. Baker had about a dozen Sudanese and Somali soldiers at the fort, which is located a few miles from the frontier line where the road enters German territory, going through to the great Province of Moschi. It is greatly to the credit of this young Englishman that, situated here on the German Boundary line and in a very difficult and delicate position, he is quite as popular with the German officials as he is with the men of his own race. All the white men that we met in the two hundred miles from Mombasa to Taveta were loud in their praise of Mr. Baker. They said to us in effect: "If you have any difficulties, if you need good men from the tribes to carry your stuff, if you want advice and kindly hospitality, apply to Hyde-Baker of Taveta."

We made our camp beside the road a few hundred yards from the English fort, at a place where there was a shelter-shed built by the English government for the convenience of teamsters making Safari from the railway at Voi to the German post at Moschi. We always put up our tent at a little distance from the rest houses, perhaps a hundred feet, because they are often infested by "spirillum ticks" whose bite produces the spirillum fever, one of the most fatal diseases in Africa. Our tent boys and carriers slept in the shed and our donkeys grazed in the open fields about us. We bought rice from the Hindu merchants and chickens from the natives. The price of chickens was eight cents apiece, and that of rice was about five cents a pound. This was the staple of our food. We had tea, coffee and cocoa, sugar, butter and canned goods, brought from Mombasa. Also the Greek baker of Mombasa, Mr. Papyanos, had prepared for us several bags of hard biscuit whose indurated surface could not be pierced by insects on the journey.

When we became acquainted with Mr. Hyde-

Baker, we found him a splendid, genial English gentleman, who was a first class sportsman and who knew how to "play the game." There was a great friendship between Count Coudenhove and Mr. Baker and we often met them together at Mr. Baker's house.

On one occasion when I was there Baker was told by the chiefs of the tribes that there were elephants in the river two hours' march from the fort. We went along to see the fun. We found two huge bull elephants in the river badly wounded by the spears of the natives. The animals were trumpeting and in an ugly and desperate mood. Creeping up to within a few feet of the huge pachyderms, Baker let go with his heavy express rifle and got the biggest one through the brain. The elephant fell over on his side like a big house settling in the mud, and Baker turned his attention to the second one. Two or three shots proved ineffectual, because the brain of the elephant is small compared to the size of the body, but finally, with a well placed bullet under the ear, the second elephant was killed. There were about a thousand dollars' worth of ivory tusks and more than three tons of meat. One might imagine that the meat was wasted; but not so. The natives came for a hundred miles and within three or four days scarcely a pound of the meat from the giant animals was left.

I had some elephant steak. I boiled it from Monday morning until Friday night, and then I chewed it from Friday night until Monday morning. By that time I had enough elephant steak to last me all summer. The natives consider elephant steak very good. Elephant's feet are a great delicacy. They bury the foot in the ground; then they kindle a fire over it and let the fire burn for two or three days. By the end of that time the meat is very tasteful, and can almost be scooped out with a spoon. This is a great delicacy, even to white men who may have had many a dish of pig's knuckles and other delicious viands of civilization.

Mr. Baker showed me the pelt and the terrible teeth of the lion killed by young Martini two weeks before our visit. The other hunter, who was killed by the lion was brought to Mr. Baker's house. Baker had a pharmacopœia and often treated the ordinary diseases of the natives with great success. He had been around the world in many capacities, as a sailor, a soldier, a hunter, a traveller. Accordingly they brought the poor disembowelled Taveta man to his house. But all the kindly English Commissioner could do was insufficient to heal the terrible wounds, and the man died in a few hours.

Mr. Dutkewich and I determined to spend a week or two in the Taveta Forest and make photographs

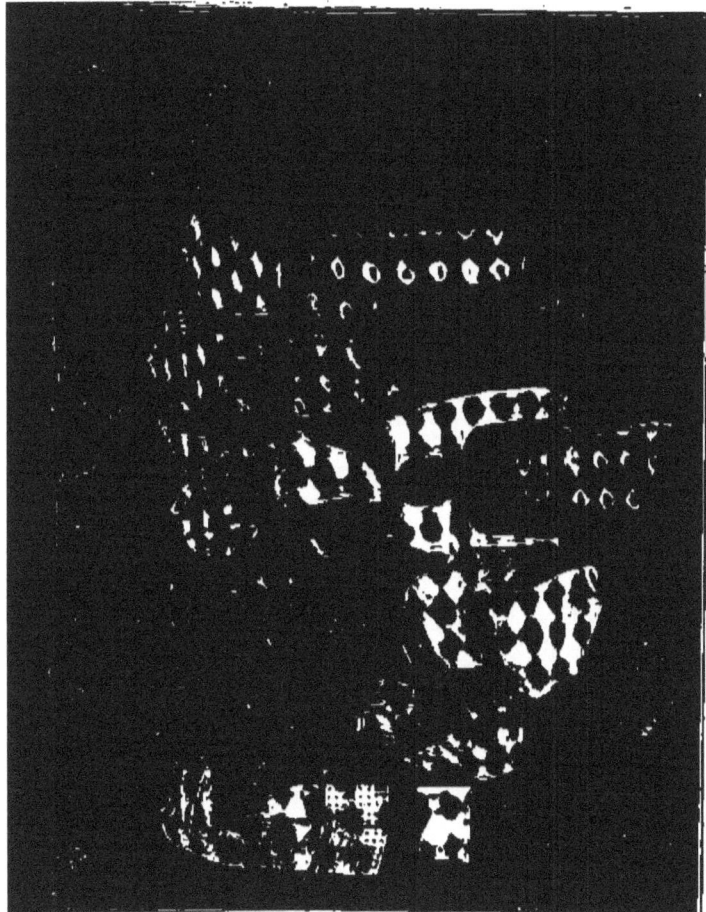

A MISSION AMONG THE WAPARE

In the Taveta Forest

and moving pictures of Martini and the interesting Wataveta tribe.

We were fortunate enough to have with us in our excursion Count Coudenhove. The Count told us many interesting and comparatively unknown things about the tribes. The Waparri, who dwell in the mountains near by, he says, are a mild folk who have some very simple habits; almost as primitive as their fellow primates the baboons. For example, when the food supply of the Waparri is low, infanticide among them is common. The mother takes the child to the brink of one of the many precipices with which the country abounds; leaves it on the edge of the rocks asleep, and when the little one awakes it turns and rolls off its perilous cradle into the depths beneath. If the upper teeth of a baby come in before the under teeth the fact is considered unlucky and the child is often killed. If there are twins, one of the babies is usually done away with.

On the way to the Taveta Forest the Count also told me a story of a baboon family and of a love affair and an elopement in the monkey tribe. It seems that this particular family, numbering about twenty in all, came to Count Coudenhove's tent when he was in the Parri Forest. They came at the same hour every morning. He noticed a quarrel between an old broken-handed baboon and a young dude with fine fur. The trouble was over a fair young baboon lady. The dude was always getting thrashed. At last the whole family united and kicked the dude out of the tribe. He came down alone to eat at Coudenhove's camp every morning for ten days; but on the eleventh day he came and behold the young lady was with him. She had eloped with the dude. So you see that human nature is the same the wide world over.

There are many old bachelors among the various communities of monkeys. They have been put out either for bad conduct, or because some old Sultan of these monkey Moslems has become jealous of their attentions to one of his many wives. To return to the tribe after being expelled is certain death.

Another interesting point the Count told me about the baboons is that they march through the forests like a company of men — the big, strong males first, then the females carrying the children, and last of all the little monkey boys and girls.

We saw many baboons on the outskirts of the Taveta villages. They subsist on maize and other foodstuffs stolen from the gardens of their more highly developed fellow primates, the black men. Throughout all the inhabited regions of the Kilimanjaro country baboons are strangely abundant. They are seldom molested by the natives and so have small fear of man. They often stopped until we came within twenty yards of them, and then the larger members of the male sex would show their teeth and grunt. They are frequently driven from the plantations by the natives like a troop of truant boys, and they retreat with swollen cheek pouches, dragging with them part of the spoils.

A traveller tells of killing a baboon in the Chaga country. It was one of a troupe who were rifling a maize plantation. Its companions, instead of running away, surrounded the corpse and snarled at the hunter. With the approach of several men the baboons ran away. Out of curiosity the hunter cooked and ate part of the baboon next day, gaining in this way some lawful idea of cannibalism. He declared that the flavour of the creature's flesh was quite beyond criticism.

I found a leopard's cub one day, voraciously devouring the body of a dead baboon. I got a boy of the tribe to help me and with a long chain we caught the savage young brute. It snarled viciously, but did not attempt to attack us. I could understand afterwards the horror of the monkeys when, coming down from their perches on the high trees, and picking up bananas or heads of corn, they came upon the track of a leopard. I often saw them rushing back to the tree, yelling in terror, never stopping until they were fifty or sixty feet from the ground.

With entertaining stories the Count beguiled us until we reached the home of Melikanoi, the father of young Martini, who had slain the lion with his spear. The Taveta Forest we found to be a most delightful and arcadian place. The Lumi River turns and winds through a wilderness of trees, bananas and gardens on its way to Lake Jipe. The houses of the natives are built back from the pathway and are embowered amid tall trees and gorgeous flowers. The home of the chief was surrounded by a palisaded wall, and there was also a palisaded zereba connecting it with two or three houses adjoining it. These latter houses were the homes of the principal advisers of the clan.

In some of the houses we saw the women feeding grass to the cattle inside. Many of the cattle are never allowed out into the sunlight, and they lose their eyesight and also their power to walk. The cattle are kept thus in the house for fear of wild beasts and of the nomadic Masai, who are akin to the Taveta, but do not hesitate to make war upon them and steal their cattle.

As we approached the chief's house the following salutation took place between him and Count Coudenhove.

The Count: Hodi — Good day.
The Chief: Karibu — Come in and sit down.
The Count: Sitarahe — Do not disturb yourself.

This is the common salutation throughout all this part of Africa.

The chief came out attended by his principal followers, and we were each given a little stool to sit down upon. Then curdled milk was brought in a gourd and we drank some of the delicious Masai milk, — a kind of kumyss. The young warriors came out, dressed in colobus-monkey fur, their bodies gleaming with groundnut oil and Kilimanjaro ochre. Each had a head-dress set with ostrich feathers, the white ones being a sign of royalty or great achievement. Melikanoi had a long garment around him like an Arab burnous, and over the burnous a yellow blanket fell in graceful folds. Upon it in a red pattern was the figure of a lion.

The chief did not wear a turban like the Arabs, but a high head dress made of colobus monkey fur and shaped like a cornucopia. He seated himself amid his elders with great dignity, and the scene was one never to be forgotten. In an open space in the forest we talked to this untutored barbarian. While wanting the polish and education of the white man, he retained the dignity and calmness which the white man has lost in his scramble for commercial supremacy. There was no rush, there was no fluster. Everything was done decently and in order. We were treated as if we too were kings from a distant friendly land. Our audience with Melikanoi was with reference to making photographs and moving pictures of his people in national costume and gala attire. We agreed to give the chief the value of three fat oxen, which amounted to about $35.00. I noticed that when the money was distributed each man, woman and child who took part in the dances given for our benefit received exactly the same amount.

Count Coudenhove, who conducted the diplomatic *pour parlers* very delicately and graciously, told me meanwhile that the Wataveta are almost a perfect communistic republic in the woods. When all the arrangements were made, twenty young men and sixty women and girls presented themselves to the chief for the dance of " Welcome to the returning Warriors." The Taveta dance as we saw it is a weird and interesting sight. A row of armed men dressed in colobus monkey furs, with gleaming spears and plumes of ostrich feathers stand on one side of the open green. Opposite to them a bevy of the most beautiful girls of the village, arrayed with gorgeous beads, their bodies glistening with groundnut oil and Kilimanjaro ochre, are arranged. A big drum sounds from the end of the lines and the two columns move up together.

First the women sing a weird chant and wave their bodies back and forth in graceful contours. Then the warriors start a march, each brandishing his gleaming spear. The young fellow who leads the dance throws up his spear and jumps after it to catch it in mid air, singing as he does so a martial pæan like the ancient Greeks. Thus the two lines move up together and the men and women join in a sort of waltz movement. Then they retreat to their former positions; and advance again as before. This is repeated ten or a dozen times before they get tired and sit down in the shade.

After the dances were over we walked through the forest to a place, where, in a sunny corner of the woods, there was a little mound on which we saw a human skull. Upon inquiry I found that this was the skull of the head of a family. When a man dies among the Wataveta he is buried in his house or near the house in a sitting posture. The grave is opened when putrefaction stops, and the head is taken out and put in a nice, quiet corner, and covered with a jar shaped like a hat. Sacrifices are sometimes made of beer and bananas to the departed spirit of a man, or milk, honey and sugar to the departed spirit of a woman.

As to religion, the Wataveta show the influence of the Mohametan Swahili and Arabs from the coast. Polygamy is common. The wife costs one bull, one cow, seven goats and six jars of beer. The *modus operandi* of marriage is as follows:— The young man's father goes to the young woman's father and says: — "My son wants to marry your daughter." The other answers: — "All right, if the young people wish it." Then the young folk talk the matter over and, if they agree, the young man's father makes beer of bananas or maize in his house. The family of the girl come and drink for six days. After the sixth day the bull and the cow are taken to the home of the girl's father. Then in a few days the seven goats. The girl's uncle asks the young couple if they want to get married. They reply in the affirmative. This is the marriage ceremony.

As for the honeymoon, it is spent in the home of the parents of the bridegroom. The old folk go away for a whole month and leave the young people in the house. The bride is not allowed to leave the house during the month. At the end of that time the two mothers go and cut wood for the building of a new house, the home of the young couple. There is no chance for a man to marry a wife without conforming to these hard and fast customs.

When the pains of childbirth come upon a woman in the tribe, she tells her husband, and he fetches her mother. If the mother finds she needs assistance, she calls in her neighbours, elderly women who act as mid-wives. The patient is put in a sitting position on the grass and, when the child is born, the old women cut the umbilical cord with a

Photograph by Peter Dutkewich, copyright, 1900, by Underwood & Underwood, N. Y.

PLAYING THE GAME OF "BAO."

flint knife and cauterize the wound with ashes of wood.

The husband is put out of the house for the time being. He must, however, kill a goat and give the young mother the blood to drink, and the fat to eat. Then a soup is made, which is coloured red from the bark of a tree that grows near the villages. If a man fails to kill the goat and prepare the soup when his wife presents him with an heir, it is a matter of great reproach to him, and she can even have him divorced for this neglect.

The economics of the Wataveta are apparently communistic. The chief's income is from his own private estates. All tribute monies and gifts from travellers are divided in equal ratio among all the families. The same is true of the division of meat killed by the hunters.

Like nearly every race on the globe, the Wataveta will gamble. Their favourite game is called " Bao." The trunk of a tree is cut into a square block and little compartments are hewn out. These compartments are filled with pebbles, and the game is to move the pebbles back and forth as pawns are used on a chess board. I saw them thus playing for bananas and sugar cane and even for their bows and spears. The youngsters of the tribe were watching their elders and picking up those lessons that childhood always learns from older folk.

It was a pleasant month that we spent with the quaint folk of the Taveta Forest. I often met young Martini, the hero of the lion hunt. He was a dignified, refined and self-respecting lad. The men who were associated with him reminded me of the simple Hebrew heroes told of in the Books of Genesis and Kings. As for the modest hunter himself, he might have been young Esau chasing the wild-roe over Judah's hills, or the Shepherd King who with his own hands slew a lion and a bear.

CHAPTER XI

THE PROVINCE OF MOSCHI

FROM Taveta to Moschi the distance is about thirty miles. We made it in one day's Safari. It is through the rolling foothills of the Kilimanjaro Range of mountains. On our way we saw, as usual, herds of kongoni in the distance, ostriches flitting about among the long grass, and an occasional jackal, showing the presence of lions. The view in front of us became more and more picturesque as we approached Marangu, the first of the German settlements in the province of Moschi.

In the morning light across valley and plain we saw a foreground of trees and beyond deep ravines of vegetation flecked with shadows of clouds; a misty middle-ground of mountainside lost among the fogs; and then, high in the sky, apparently right above our heads, the great cone of the Kibo, the highest peak of Kilimanjaro, and the grandest mountain in the whole continent of Africa.

I cannot express the wonder and the glory of that great gleaming cone of whiteness towering above our heads; it was so different from all other mountains I had ever seen. Cut off in part by the clouds that so often hang around the middle slopes of it, the Kilimanjaro Mountain seems to be a white Mer de Glace hung down from the sky. We knew it was not cloud land by its bright immovable whiteness. For miles and miles along the weary journey our eyes kept constantly rising from the plain to gaze on this eternal whiteness, rising from a sea of eternal green.

We came to the settlement called Marangu, which is up among the foothills between four and five thousand feet above the level of the sea. There are some German missionaries of the Lutheran church located here. Here also are the coffee plantation of Mr. Patterson, a canny Scot, and the farms of two European gentlemen, one from the Caucasus and the other from Riga in Russia. Besides these there were the Italian family Monchardi, father and sons, who have made a fortune in the transport business. They run donkeys and camels across the wagon road from Marangu and Moschi to Taveta and Voi. These names sound unfamiliar to the reader, but they are all thoroughly located and full of local colour to the present colonists and pioneers. Monchardi has made a fortune at Marangu, and Patterson will be a Lord of the Manor if he keeps improving his coffee farms for ten years.

The Province of Moschi

From Marangu to Moschi there is a road through woods and dells, past the Kilima mission of the Catholic church. I was entertained at this mission over night by Father Balthazar, a young priest from Alsace. The gardens are at an elevation of four thousand feet, and yet so near the equator are they that all kinds of flowers and fruits, delightful to the eye and grateful to the taste, will grow. The buildings lie a little way off the main road, upon a tongue of land surrounded by the hills. The gardens are in the nuns' quarters, and here potatoes, lettuce, parsley, and celery grow alongside of Tangerine oranges, lemons, apples and tropical fruits. A kindly Brother, Carre by name, who had built the fine halls of the mission, took me out in the evening twilight to see the gardens and the buildings. The gardens are a little Vale of Tempe. The green gorges below us are an Austrian Tyrol, and away out on the plains of Moschi for a hundred miles one sees green woods and rich farm fields being cultivated by a thousand colonists who have come here during the last two years.

On Sunday morning I went to the Mass at the Catholic chapel. It was a rainy day but there were twelve hundred present. The singing was very spirited and the people seemed to join in a wholehearted way with the simple service of Father Balthazar. The good padre afterwards told me that his parish numbered twenty-five hundred of the wild Wachaga tribe that inhabit the platforms of the Kilimanjaro.

I left the Kilima mission and walked on toward the town and fort of Moschi. The road is one made partly by the Wachaga tribes and partly by the German government. On the way, we met many of the simple people moving back and forth from one farm to another, carrying bunches of bananas or stalks of sugar cane. The streams we crossed were all cold and pure, running from the melting ice of the great white crown of Kibo. At one of these streams I came across a party of men of the Wachaga tribe, under the direction of a young German engineer, building a bridge, and this suggested to me the fine possibilities the Germans are developing in the Moschi district.

By many winding paths, along the edge of sounding streams, across deep ravines and through umbrageous forests, we made our way until at nightfall we descended from the higher slopes down to the village of Moschi, three thousand eight hundred feet above the Indian Ocean. Moschi is a fort of the German colony. Commissioner Zencke was in charge of the civil department, and Sergt. Major Bast was in charge of the soldiery. There were about two hundred native soldiers or ascaris in the command. Herr Wolfe was the Municipal Secre-

The Province of Moschi

tary, and these three men treated us with great cordiality. We camped a quarter of a mile outside the town on a high platform of the hills, near the kraal of one of the native kings, Sulima.

At Moschi there is a good hotel, kept by a Greek, named Papyanos. Here we met each night the German officers, and any of the white men who came in from time to time from the plantations of the province. We learned from them that Moschi is a fertile province, three hundred miles long, and one hundred and fifty miles wide, and that all its fertility comes from the melting snow of Kilimanjaro. When the Germans made a treaty with England in 1890, the Kaiser insisted upon Germany being given the whole Kilimanjaro region. It was one of the great diplomatic successes of Germany; for the colony promises to be one of the richest and most fruitful of all the German territory in Africa.

A railway is being built from Tanga on the coast to Moschi, at the foot of Kilimanjaro. The whole distance is about two hundred and twenty-five miles, of which a hundred and twenty-five miles have been finished to the village of Mombo. Every three days the German mails are sent by carrier through the jungle and the forest to Mombo, and thence to Europe. Both the German and English mail systems in Eastern Central Africa are remarkable for their completeness. The English government will send a letter for two cents from London to Mombasa, six thousand miles by sea; thence six hundred miles by train to Victoria Nyanza; thence two hundred miles by steamer to Entebbe; thence two hundred miles by jinricksha to Albert Nyanza; and thence four hundred miles by carrier into the heart of Bahr-El-Gazal. The German government will send a letter from Hamburg to Dar-es-Salaam, seven thousand miles; thence by train to Taborah, two hundred miles; thence by carrier four hundred miles to Ujiji on Lake Tanganyika; thence two hundred miles by boat across Tanganyika; and thence again two hundred miles by carriers to Lake Kivu. And this is only one example of the myriad ways in which England, Germany, France and Belgium are developing, with lightning speed, the whole of the heart of Africa.

I found the Germans very enthusiastic about their colony. In the day time I talked with Papyanos in the hotel about Greek history, the battles of Leuctra, Marathon, and Thermopylæ; at night, I conversed with the German officers on the beauties of Moschi, and the splendid future for German colonization in German East Africa. Recently the German Reichstag voted thirty-five million dollars for the completion of railways in Africa. Already work had been begun between Taborah and Lake Tanganyika. In two years the country between Moschi and Meru

The Province of Moschi

Mountain, called Warusha, has been settled by seven hundred colonists, and thousands more are soon expected.

The colonists thus far have been Germans, Boers and a few Russians. The Germans complain that the Boers will not cultivate the soil, but live by grazing their cattle and by hunting. The latter pursuit threatens to destroy all the wild animals in the colony of Moschi. The Boers have also come in conflict with the Masai herdsmen; and while I was there a Boer farmer was killed and burned by this tribe of blood-drinking shepherds.

I met a Russian Jew who was the leading farmer of Warusha, and found him a very intelligent agriculturalist. He is raising cotton and rubber, coffee and cocoa, and is going to be one of the rich men of the colony. I told him I was glad to meet a Jewish man who took an intelligent interest in farming, and he replied, that the Jews had been great farmers in antiquity, before they were oppressed and crowded to the wall.

Seated on the verandah of the Greek hotel at Moschi, one looks to the southwest and sees rising out of the plain ninety miles away the symmetrical cone-like form of Mt. Meru, twelve thousand feet high. Occasionally we saw a drift of snow on the highest points. Mt. Meru dominates the plain, and, next to Kilimanjaro, is the highest point in German territory. Across this plain are the homes of two hundred and fifty thousand natives. There are forty thousand huts, and each hut pays about a dollar a year to the German tax collector, the same as in English territory. The German government protects one tribe from another, opens up roads, and gives the natives a chance to trade the produce of their little farms with the white men, and with the Hindus, who are coming into the colonies in search of land or commerce. The leading tribes are the Masai, the Wachaga, the Waparri, the Wameru, the Warusha, the Wambukwa, the Wambulu, the Wataturu, the Warumbu, and the Wakahe, the latter an offshoot of the Masai.

Of these tribelets, all will work except the pastoral Masai. The Masai here as in British East Africa are nomadic shepherds. They carry their loads on donkeys. The women do all the work, as is common among all the tribes. Among the Masai moreover the pariah class called Ol Kononis make spears from the iron in their own mountains. All the tribes except the Masai keep their cows in the house. The Masai are so warlike that they are not afraid of any of their neighbours, molesting either them or their cattle.

I entered the hut of one of the Wachaga. It was in shape like a hayrick. It was thatched with palm leaves and grass and apparently absolutely impervious to rain. The only opening for light and air was a little oblong space three feet by four which is closed with a door of wicker work. The woman who lived in this hut was a widow. She had a farm of about two acres. Her only son, a bright-looking Wachaga boy who was doing some work for the missionaries, was her sole support. She worked on the farm, and the boy made some money at the mission. They appeared to me like a family of very respectable and admirable people.

The German missionary, Dr. Fassman, introduced me and we went through the little doorway into the house. An aisle runs across the house and on one side of the aisle I observed two compartments for the animals. In one compartment was a big goat and a small kid, and, in the other, a small cow and a still smaller calf. On the other side of the aisle were three little compartments, the one nearest the door having two or three stools. The one in the centre was the bedroom. It had skins on the floor and a little charcoal fire was burning at the foot of the bed. The third compartment held the family cooking utensils.

The Germans are making more progress in their colonies than I had supposed. It is true that they have not finished their railways to Moschi, to Tanganyika and to Victoria Nyanza, and that for the present at least they must send a great deal of their commerce by the English steamboats on Victoria Nyanza to the Uganda railway at Port Florence and so down to Mombasa. But they are learning their lesson. They are ambitious, they are vigilant, they are men of pronounced ability. Their citizens are among the best colonists of the world.

German East Africa is more than twice the size of the German Empire. It has three hundred and eighty-five thousand square miles of territory, and eight millions of black men. The most fertile province is that surrounding Taborah. The natives in this part of the territory are called the Usukuma and number three and a half millions. They are strong and willing to work along with the German colonists; and are wealthy in lands and cattle. There is no fever in their country, and much water; the forests have much valuable wood and the grazing lands in the plains are six thousand feet above the sea.

Taborah is equi-distant from the coast, from Tanganyika and from Victoria Nyanza; and the German government proposes to have a railway with one branch going from Taborah to Mwanza on Victoria Nyanza, and another branch to Ujiji on Tanganyika.

This land is one of the newest of the white man's dreams. A land of wild things; a land of streams that trickle and rivulets that play, and over it and as the cause of it all the fructile mother with the pure white crown, the splendid summit of the Kibo. Although full sixteen thousand feet above the village of Moschi, the Kibo on a clear day seemed to be a white coronet set just behind the swelling foothills and the Wachaga villages. Thirty or forty streams run from the melting glaciers of the Kibo and make the fruitful plains. It is a land of wild beasts now, but a land of milk and honey for the white men yet to be. Coffee and cocoa, rubber and cotton, will ripen in the valleys in the constant sun. On the hillsides will flourish all the plants of the temperate zones, from towering, giant trees through orchard blossoms to the blown roses and pied windflowers of the German Fatherland.

CHAPTER XII

AN AMERICAN ASCENT OF KILIMANJARO

AFTER a delightful week with the Germans and the colonists of Moschi we made ready for an ascent of Kilimanjaro. We consulted with Sultan Sulima, and he procured for us sixteen of his strongest young men to carry our loads up the mountains. The chief guide was the famous Souho, who five months before had guided an expedition led by Dr. Ahlbory. They had reached the edge of the crater of Kibo, but on the way down had lost several of their men by the terrible cold on the bare, storm-swept slopes of the upper mountain. We took an abundant supply of chocolate, dried goats' meat, and rice; also medicine, and four blankets each.

With the good wishes of the Sultan and his people we started up the mountain, July 6th, 1908. We had thirteen carriers and two tent men, all Wachagas, and our big headman, Mohamet, who was a Swahili from Zanzibar.

At first we were amid teeming tropic gardens on the hillside. The goats and flocks were feeding

SULTAN SULIMA AND HIS WIVES.

Ascent of Kilimanjaro

around the huts, and the boys whistled and the birds sung in the soft air.

The good fellows who carried our burdens had forty pounds each and we let them rest whenever they wished. Very beautiful birds were found as we came toward the higher slopes, resembling humming birds and sun birds. These little creatures may be noticed hovering around the long tubular flowers of certain labiate plants, and on their feathers pollen is conveyed long distances. Nature thus uses them as she does certain insects for purposes of fertilization.

The spoor of eland, elephant and leopard were found, but none of lions. At an elevation of between six thousand and seven thousand feet, long drooping creepers, lianas and moss hung from the trees. Great tree ferns were seen in graceful fronds along the valley. A brook followed our path most of the way. It was an artificial canal cut by the natives from the glaciers to their gardens. Rain came weeping from the clouds at two o'clock and we encamped at about nine thousand feet above the sea. Here we found the remains of an old camp, and our men cut down trees and brought in fire wood. I felt very much as if I were in the Adirondack Mountains. Soon three great fires were burning, and Mr. Dutkewich and I had a lordly lunch of hot tea and hard biscuits.

I kept a diary of each day of our trip and difficulties on Mt. Kilimanjaro; and perhaps I cannot do better than to quote here directly from it:

"*July 6th, 1908, 4 P. M.*: As I write this, the men are seated about the fire or bringing in the wood. Our tents and beds are all arranged and Peter Dutkewich has gone into the forest with a guide to look for game. We are in an open space surrounded by trees, one of which is a species of cedar.

"*July 7th, 1908:* It rained terribly all night, and we put most of the Wachaga porters in our tent. It was rather distressing to the olfactory nerves, but Peter Dutkewich is so Russian in his democracy that he must needs put the dusky crowd all under cover of a single tent. I was glad for them, poor fellows, protected only with a cotton rag from either nakedness or the bleak wind. We had a blanket for each of the porters, but did not realize at first how bitterly cold the ascent was going to be. At 4 A. M. a leopard visited us but did not fancy our scent.

"We broke camp at 8.45 and ascended through steep and bushy country to the Muè stream. Trees began to look spindling, the bush and briar and thorn cut our hands and impeded our porters. Spoor of elephant disappeared, but marks of wild boar, eland and leopard were plentiful. The kudu, a beautiful antelope, ascends the mountain to fourteen thousand feet, and the wild buffalo comes nearly as high, probably attracted by the sweet perennial pasture. The gorgeous scarlet of the turaco lapped through the forest aisles and we heard the chatter of the hyrax, a kind of squirrel whose voice in the trees sounds almost human.

"By noon we were through the heavy, dripping woods and out in a series of brown fields. We saw much evidence of boar and eland, and sighted a paa, about as large as a small lamb.

"In the afternoon, the sky was hung with dense curtains of purple-gray cloud, and the plain below lay in monotonous blue shadow, only away to the west, behind the pyramid of Meru, the heavens exhibited one clear, cloudless belt, which the descending sun turned to refulgent gold, and, against this relief, as on some antique illumination of decorative design, the peak of Meru and the jagged hill tops at its base stood out in a simple tone of indigo.

"There was no end to the beauty and the wonder of the wild flowers. Small pink irises studded the ground in vast numbers, and the crimson gladioli gleamed out brightly from the tufted grass. Along the pretty streams which flowed from the snowy crest of the mountain, through deep ravines, our path was gaily lit by the brilliant red-leaf shoots of the protea shrub.

"At one place where we crossed the stream the banks were shelving, and above the little ford the water fell in dainty cascades. About this spot the scenery lost much of its accustomed asperity. Strange sessile thistles grew here, and fairy-like lobelias. Other remarkable plants were the bright ultramarine flowers, and a peculiar arborescent plant, named Senecio Johnstoni, looking somewhat like a banana, but in reality consisting of a tall, black, smooth trunk, with a crown of broad leaves and yellow blossoms.

"Tufts of chevril and patches of vivid green moss overhung the gleaming water, which itself was lovely in its pellucid clearness. At an altitude of twelve thousand feet bees and wasps were still to be seen — their very presence seeming to account for the vivid colours of the flora. The fields were sprinkled with beautiful flowers, red and pink, blue and purple. Heather and gorse appeared. There were plenty of signs of game in this upland plateau. We were now up thirteen thousand feet.

"We set up our tent in a hollow at the timber line, among long dry grass, with plenty of small cedar and cypress trees which could be used for fire wood. We made the Wachaga build a shelter and thatch it with grass close to us in case of wild beasts or rain, and also three fires against the cold.

"Yesterday at 5 P. M., Ther. 54° Fahr., we felt

ON MOUNT KILIMANJARO AT 8,000 FEET ELEVATION.

the cold keenly in the woods, and slept little, with all our woollen clothes and four blankets apiece; we gave our mackintoshes to the black porters. To-night, we are looking at a misty sun. This afternoon, we saw a wonderfully clear view of the foothills of Kilimanjaro. We could look upon an unbroken stretch of green ridges, fields and plains; the Catholic mission at Kilima; the houses of Marangu; the Lutheran mission at Moschi, and that town itself.

"A formation of clouds, the most peculiar I have ever seen, formed an archway under which we saw the near hills and far away plains, framed as in a picture. At 5 P. M. we were comfortably settled in the highest camp of Africa, and P. D. (Peter Dutkewich) had gone to shoot wild boar.

"*July 8th, 1908:* Written in our camp above the clouds, at an elevation of thirteen thousand feet.

"Last evening P. D. returned from boar-hunting, having twice fallen into native traps about eight feet deep. These traps are deep holes, being wide at the top and so narrow at the bottom that the animal cannot use its legs when once it falls in. The natives cover the hole so cleverly that, in the growing dusk, it was impossible to detect the natural ground from that covered by the trap. Hence Dutkewich fell into the snare.

"Between five and six last night the clouds

parted, the mist drifted down into the valley and Kilimanjaro, the grandest peak in a whole continent, showed its white forehead. From our cots in the tent we could see this glowing wonder of eternal snow amid the eternal green. On the west gleamed the waning sun in a bed of old rose and amber, amid the scarred rocks of Mount Meru, eighty miles away. To the east the piled-up clouds were below us. At one place they were like castles in the air; at another like cities of jasper amid walls of gold; ending in one high mountain peak which leaned close against the Southern Cross and seemed to be the throne of God himself. Then slowly, softly, faded the pink and amber and chrysoprase, and the light left hill and forest and cloud and far off fortifications and missions of the white man; and the sky paled and then became aglow with the splendour of the moonlight, and all around was darkness over the land except where the proud Kilimanjaro on her silver throne shone silent and alone, the queen of all the Afric land.

"We retired about 7 o'clock and were well wrapped, but we shivered all night, having come from 86° to 22° in two days. I was clothed thus: four pairs of socks, one pair of trousers, one pair of puttee leggings, one jersey-woollen, one woollen blue shirt, one negligee shirt, a suit of underwear, a khaki coat, a mackintosh, a skating cap and two

Ascent of Kilimanjaro

blankets, and yet I was 'acold.' Shall put on a pair of boots up to my knees to-night."

"We shall probably make the final attempt to reach the summit to-morrow. The height of Kibo is nearly twenty thousand feet. There is a ridge running from Mwenzi Mountain to Kibo. The saddle is sixteen thousand feet. Mwenzi and Kibo are the twin peaks that form the Kilimanjaro. We will get our guides up to the saddle and leave the rest of the men here. We hope by moonlight to walk all night and reach a point near the top of Kibo by daylight. Meanwhile we rest awhile. P. D. makes pictures and I collect all the flora I can for a picture. There are thousands of wild flowers on this plateau, Scotch heather, violets and immortelles.

"*July 9th, 1908:* Clear and bright this morning. We made pictures from the top of the hill above our camp. At 9 A. M. I started up to the snow line with my guide Souho. He did not seem to mind the rarefied air; but when we had risen a thousand feet I got dizzy; from that time onward for two thousand feet the dizziness continued, till up at the snow line, sixteen thousand feet, I became fearfully nauseated. My guide was as polite as Lord Chesterfield and kindly as the finest gentleman of the world could be. So I owe much to the bare-footed natives of this country, who patiently for eight cents a day bear the white man's burden. On the wild, desolate uplands I thought of what the Scotchman said of the Kyles of Bute: 'The works o' God is hellish.' For athwart the landscape are rocks, hills and mountains thrown in dreadful confusion, the wreckage of a former world.

"To-night trouble and mutiny developed in camp. The Wachaga did not bring posho (corn) enough for more than a few days, whilst we had paid them to bring food for ten days. We began giving two heads of corn by the hand of Mohamet, our Swahili man. They all brought the corn to our door, and laid it down, declaring they would not go further with us. We made it three heads, but still discontent. Peter threatened that we would have the discontented flogged and he went out to get a whip. This brought the discontented to their senses.

"*July 11th, 1908:* To-day foggy all day. I went up to fourteen thousand feet to try my weakened system. Was all O. K. except a bit of indigestion pain. Breathe easier after a number of days in high altitudes. The small boy, Moji (waters), hunts rats. The rats are striped like chipmunks. They are very tame and clean.

"The man we call 'Moses,' an old bald headed fellow, has a fine name, Michili. He came back to-night from the foot of the mountain with a dress

THE EXPEDITION AT 15,000 FEET ELEVATION.

Ascent of Kilimanjaro

coat and we gave him a chicken which died on the way up. We have eaten up the goat and chickens sent us by Salima, King of the Wachagas. Food question alleviated by the arrival of more maize brought by 'Moses' and four men.

"They keep this posho money to buy wives. A wife costs ten goats. One of the boys said to me, 'Ver hard on Wachaga to get wife, but when he get her she can make do plant corn, she make wash and cook and make do work for him. Ingreza (English) man very much money to spend. She wife no can wash, no plant corn, herd goats or cook. All money, much merkani (cloth), heap money, big dinner. She eat much posho. She no can cook dinner. She only make " Safari " and look. Porr, porr Ingreza man.'

"*July 12, 1908:* We ascended in the afternoon with two guides and five men to cave at foot of Kibo. It was at first through dry grass, then through scrub and heather, on to one solitary cactus and huge rocks and stones in great cosmic confusion. Bright yellow euryops flowers studded the occasional patches of bare earth. Beyond rise Kibo and Mwenzi and on the plateau a few volcanic hills, just *membra disjecta* of the Creation.

"On upper plateau we made kinetoscope pictures; some stereos and a few fine 4 x 5's also. Came to cave. Men cold. Passed two corpses of young men who died of exposure, a short time ago. The vultures had pecked out their eyes, the leopards had taken a leg from each. Nothing beautiful now save the beauty that comes from the sublimity of death. Made fire in cave. Guides looked weird, like some play of a theatre. Slept a little, but feet cold in spite of heavy boots and several German army blankets.

"*July 13th, 1908:* At 6.30 A. M., after a cup of cocoa, a potato and some cold goat's meat, we started for the glaciers of Mount Kibo, highest and grandest of all African mountains, nineteen thousand eight hundred feet. Mwenzi, the nineteen thousand feet neighbouring peak across the plateau to the east, showed its scarred, serrated head wrapped in a cap of white clouds. The moon was going out. The sun was filling this theatre of wonder, making a gallery and museum of things magnificent and grand.

"Just when we reached the edge of the snow at 16,000 feet, our guides looked at the ice, picked up a few handfuls of the gleaming wonder, then ran away, exclaiming: 'Oh, masters, this is magic: this is water turned to burning wood.' So the ascent was made more difficult; for they carried away all our food.

"By nine o'clock we made some panoramic views of the country at a height of seventeen thousand

Ascent of Kilimanjaro

feet above the sea. About this height I began to breathe so hard I had nausea, which continued all day. P. D. carried cameras and plates. On we went over a scarified river where formerly the glacier was a burning coal, a river of lava, when the earth was just beginning. For, before the eland and the elephant took shelter in her sacred heights, — reigned Kibo, Queen of Africa, Kibo, queen of white water, now crowned with gold in the sunrise and sunset. Clothed with ermine always, mysterious, inaccessible, unapproachable, Sovereign now of snow; once of fire. Her glorious crown flashes back the ruby and the diamond to the sun; and in her diadem of snow were the purple of the jacinth, the blue of the amethystine fire, the brilliance of the emerald, the soft shining of the opal.

"By 11 A. M. I noticed, at eighteen thousand feet, even stalwart Peter Dutkewich beginning to weaken in the 'breathing apparatus.' At noon we were well nigh on the roof of Africa, photographing, from the very glacial throne of Kibo, the Mighty, plains that stretch away towards Nairobi on the northeast, the great German steppe of Moschi, with the blue Parri Mountains in the far, fair, shining horizon, sixty or seventy miles away. At 1.30 we seemed to touch the very sky, we could not walk ten yards without stopping to breathe. I was excessively nauseated. At nineteen thousand two hundred feet we were struck by a snow storm. It chilled us to the marrow of our bones. .

"We decided to return to camp and try the ascent next day. We put a small American flag up in the snow at nineteen thousand two hundred feet, the highest point yet reached by English-speaking men in Africa, although the peak was ascended by Dr. Hans Meyer, a German, in 1889.

"We came in safety almost to the cave when P. D. (Peter Dutkewich) fell on an old glacial rock and fractured several ribs.

"We hastened to bring him down from the mountain and got lost in the rain and the clouds. We found our way to camp by the dead bodies of the men who died on Dr. Ahlbory's expedition. Arrived at camp at 10 P. M. Got P. D. to bed. Slept fairly well but still *cold*.

"*July 14th, 1908:* We are getting ready to move P. D. Men are around the camp fires, drying out their garments, only one cotton rag, not difficult; one is trying to dry my stockings. But it rains, and when one side is dry the good fellow turns it so that the dry side is rained upon and he makes no progress in the drying process. The air is very wet in this camp, which is just among the clouds. I question if there are any people in all Africa so highly situated as we are. Perhaps few are more uncomfortable. Rain, mist and fog, morning, noon

MR. MACQUEEN AT 19,200 FEET ELEVATION.

and night. We shall get away to-morrow and then shake our fists at the worst the cruel Kibo can do to us. I read on my German map: 'Kibo, 6,010 meters; Mwenzi 5,353 meters.' Ah, those careful, scientific Germans!

"*July 5th, 1908:* We had a most awful time to-night. All had gone well with Peter Dutkewich till 6 P. M., when he gave signs of fainting and of heart failure. He had a fierce chill and called me to put a fire near him. We built a fire in the door of our tent; it suffocated him. Put it out and then the natives showed me how to arrange coals in three pans, one at his feet, one at his middle and one at his head. This I did every twenty minutes for fourteen hours. His pulse would go sixteen and then stop four beats. Temperature 102°. Rained and nearly put out the fire. My feelings as I thought fire was going out I cannot describe. It did not go out, and by 6 A. M. he slept an hour.

"He awoke and told me to make a stretcher. I cut two long poles of cedar in the forest and then put two cross poles at each end, about two and a half feet long. First we rolled a blanket-waterproof around each of the long poles. These we secured by ropes and then we tied on the cross poles as they do in the army. Afterwards we put two good thick blankets in this improvised stretcher, and, placing P. D. on it, we threw four heavy ones over him, also a waterproof received from the German Bureau.

"At 7.30 A. M. eight of the men took up the stretcher and the march down the mountain began. It was raining, and the long grass wet us, and the cold dawn chilled us to the bone. When we had gone an hour, I saw three of our men cowering and shivering in the grass. Mohamet would not leave them behind. I had no heart to desert the poor, wretched, fever-stricken men. So I returned to where they lay and carried one on my back for a mile. The others could walk. I found my strength giving out, but ate chocolate and gave some to the sick men. Was revived.

"Looking ahead I noticed that the stretcher with P. D. had been carried across the fields and that the carriers had entered the woods. For fear that I should lose Dutkewich in the forest, I left the sick man with two of his comrades to take care of him. I plunged through a thicket of trees and lianas and by calling to the men who were carrying Dutkewich I found the party had emerged upon a field.

"We took the wounded man up to a knoll in the open space, and laid him down while I sent back after the shivering men left out in the grass. The strong men came through the wood without the sick comrade whom I had carried on my back. I gave them chocolate, as they could hardly stand upon their feet. The strongest one I sent back for the lost comrade. He soon returned and told me that he could not find him. The horror of the situation began to break upon me. This man was going to die; he was only half a mile away, and yet I could neither go for him myself nor send a man strong enough to bring him.

"Souho, the guide, I had sent on through the forest in the darkness of the night with a letter to Dr. Ahlbory, beseeching him to come and save us, if he could. We were making half a mile an hour; would we ever reach the German station? Or would half of us be alive when we did?

"So we kept moving slowly and painfully through the forest, over fallen trees, under the great tree-ferns, crossed the little streams that were coming from the glacial heights. The forest was one long, dank vista of gloom. At 4 P. M. we met Souho, the guide, who had carried the letter through to the German fort and returned bringing us two askaris and six new men to carry our stretcher.

"Sent Souho back for the sick man; and he saved him, carrying him in next day on his back. The Germans sent also a hammock and a tent; and Herr Wolfe sent two bottles of champagne. I went ahead to look for a place to camp; got too far and was lost. Soon darkness came on in the gloom of the forest.

"I got back in time to see P. D. lying on sloping ground, slipping off the stretcher, and in great pain. Small fire had been made under the root of a great tree. Rain soon came on and wiped out the fire. Tent was not put up and we were all in great misery. Men with tent lost in the darkness. Thought if the rain stopped we would go on in the moonlight. Rain did not stop.

"Sat down beside P. D. in the mud. Gave him one bottle of champagne. Revived him greatly. An Askari gave me three thin blankets. Peter had four or five blankets over him, but the pain of his poor broken ribs was intense all night, and the unfortunate position of the stretcher, which I could not move, caused him to slip down constantly hurting him. Wet to my thighs for twelve hours.

"Night came very dark; no moonlight. Soon the rain became a torrent and for fifteen hours we lay there in the mud. The poor Wachaga men were almost as badly off as ourselves, some were worse, and poor Mapandi, a carrier whom I had noticed shivering with fever for the last day or two, stiffened, grew cold and died beside me in the mud. We prayed for dawn. Again and again it seemed to brighten, but it was only the clouds getting thin near the face of the moon.

Ascent of Kilimanjaro 211

"*July 17th, 1908:* At eight o'clock this morning, I looked around upon the wretched camp; another man had died. Dutkewich was quiet and I thought at first he was dead. I had now been wet and chilled twenty-seven hours, no food, no fire, no warmth. A few chocolates left; I divided them with the men. Even the new carriers sent us by the Germans seemed utterly demoralized. We started the stretcher; it still poured rain, the men had no food. At 9.30 Mohamet, our Swahili man, deserted and ran away. He could stand the strain no longer.

"I resolved to go for white help. Gave P. D. half a bottle of whiskey, and started down ahead to find the doctor in case some mistake had been made. Met a boy carrying hammock. Offered him three rupees to get me to Lutheran mission. On I went; fell in the stream fainting. Took a little champagne from the second bottle sent me by Herr Wolfe. Got out of the stream; dragged myself onto my feet and began to repeat in German the words: 'I will give any man five hundred marks who will bring my friend down from the hill to-day.' Left Dutkewich at 9 o'clock, met Dr. Ahlbory and Mr. Mauck, one of the German officials from the boma, at 11. At first I could not speak, but sat down on a fallen tree, quite overcome.

"After a few minutes I recovered and was able to show the doctor the spot where Dutkewich was when I left him. The Germans went on and found Dutkewich entirely deserted, except for one of the askaris. The askari was helping him to stand upon his feet; another of the Wachagas had died. Dutkewich threw a blanket over him, as he crawled up toward the stretcher, trembling with cold and exposure. Shortly afterwards the stronger men came out of the woods where they had been hiding and took the blanket from the dying man, Kasungu. Then Kasungu died. The doctor gave Dutkewich hot tea and rum, with food. Upon examination he found three ribs crushed in over the heart. I was taken to the German Lutheran mission where I was treated with great kindness by the missionary, Dr. Fassman and his wife. Mr. Dutkewich was brought down to the German Hospital where he had to lie for ten weeks. He wrote me later that the German Dr. Ahlbory treated him as if he had been a brother and that all the white residents of Moschi had helped and cheered him in his long and dangerous illness. Thus ends a really tragic incident that came near wiping out our expedition."

There are a few particulars of the ascent that I have not mentioned. At the height of fourteen thousand feet I saw the kudu antelope. At the same place I made a note of a brown Stonechat

Ascent of Kilimanjaro 213

bird who sang to us a cheery note and kept us company amid the chilling mists. Moreover, in our camp at over 13,000 feet, there were many field rats of which I have read no mention in the books of other travellers, and which might well be named *Rodentis Macqueeniensis*. These mountain rats were very tame and came almost up to the table to eat. They were striped like chipmunks but had tails like rats.

I quote again some leaves from my diary:

"*July 19th, Sunday: Lutheran Mission, Moschi, 4800 ft.* It was a calm and restful day to me after an exciting week. Dr. Fassman and I had breakfasted together. Then to church. Two hundred clean, well-dressed Wachaga went to service. Seemed glad to go to the House of God. Singing good and vespers sounded sweetly in the quiet Sabbath hush. In the afternoon I looked for signs of my camp followers from the mountain, but they came not. Slept again. In the evening looked over the scene. Very striking one. Sun sets over Mount Meru, 12,000 feet in elevation. Plain is very green after the rain. Small volcanoes on the plains and the Parri mountains in a blue haze on the horizon. Streams flow, birds sing before they repair to rest. The Wachaga cattle graze peacefully. Glorious are the streams of light: tints of brightness, blues, mauves, — opalescent, glistening.

Garden smells of wild flowers. Chirp of insects. Great Kibo covered up in mist. I hear songs of praise from German church. The whole scene sings itself into my memory for ever. Limes, pears, nasturtiums, bananas, the pawpaw. Respectful attitudes of the people. Mission folk look better than other natives.

"Sun comes out. Sinks and it is night. In no romance of olden travel was this scene ever surpassed. A railway to Tanga will make this Moschi province one of the great lands of the future."

The great beasts of the Tertiary Age still haunt the Kilimanjaro regions. Hippopotamuses abound in the lakes and swamps. The crocodile is beside the still waters; the lion sends his roar across the plain at night like the booming of distant thunder, the leopard, hyena, cheetah and jackal prowl in all the secluded places. It is the world as it was before the flood.

Kilimanjaro was discovered on the 11th of May, 1848, by Dr. Rebman, a German missionary. When the devout explorer first saw the gleaming cone of snow, rising almost on the Equator, he fell upon his knees and recited the fourteenth Psalm, overawed by the unexpected beauty and majesty of the spectacle. A book was written to prove that there could be no snow near the Equator and the missionary was not believed till 1860. It was said

Ascent of Kilimanjaro

that he had seen a mirage. In 1862 Baron Von der Decken, a Hanoverian, reached a height of 10,500 feet upon the mountain. In 1871, Rev. Charles New reached a height of 14,500 feet. He returned in 1873, but was robbed by Mandara, the chief of Moschi, and died of a broken heart before he reached the coast.

In 1883, Mr. Joseph Thomson tried the ascent, but he also was robbed by Mandara and reached only 9,000 feet. Mandara was the father of Sulima who entertained me so kindly on the ascent of Kilimanjaro. Thomson, however, collected twenty plants new to science. In 1889, Dr. Hans Meyer, a German, ascended to the very summit of the mountain, 19,800 feet.

In 1885, Sir Harry Johnston, the famous English traveller and writer, notwithstanding the sinister opposition of Mandara, ascended to a height of 16,800 feet. Sir Harry made a fine collection of the flora and fauna of the region and wrote a most interesting book about it. Mr. Dutkewich and I were the first Americans to try the ascent and the only men who ever tried it in rainy weather. We were greatly aided by Sultan Salima, the successor of Mandara, and reached a height of 19,200 feet. We would have climbed to the summit but for the accident to Mr. Dutkewich. We did the best we could.

Kilimanjaro is not so difficult to climb as the mountains of Switzerland, because there are few crevasses, and the snow line is not reached until one is at an elevation of 16,000 feet. Moreover we had the help of the native chiefs, whereas Thomson and Johnston were opposed by Mandara.

CHAPTER XIII

PHASES OF JUNGLE LIFE

AS soon as Mr. Dutkewich was out of danger I was obliged to leave him and to proceed alone across the plains back to Nairobi, and thence to Victoria Nyanza, Uganda and the headwaters of the Nile. I took one of the tent-boys, Osmanie, and three Wachaga porters. We started on our journey in an afternoon of light and shade, through banana plantations and then on to a long road, winding by the foot of mountains, and looking into deep gorges.

At 4 P. M. we came to the Catholic Mission at Kilima. It lies a little off the road down an avenue of hedges and on a tongue of land, surrounded by the hills. Gardens are in the nuns' quarters and here lettuce, parsley, potatoes and celery grow, alongside of tangerines, oranges, lemons and tropical fruits.

Padre Balthazar, the rector, has a church of twelve hundred members. I went to mass at 8 A. M.

A thousand people came. Responses were hearty and apparently sincere. The service was during a heavy rain.

Rain ceased at noon and I came on and lunched with Mr. Monchardi at Marangu. There were several Italian gentlemen at his home. In fact the Greeks and Italians of a sturdy class are the very foremost of the pioneers in Africa.

The house had an air of homely plenty. It was red-roofed, with white pillars arranged in a sort of old mission style. Monchardi's sons often kill lions which attack their donkeys on the road to Voi. The youngest son had slain two lions before breakfast one morning during the very week that I was there.

On Sunday afternoon I reached the coffee farm of Mr. Patterson, the only Scotchman in the Colony. I made a picture of his house. His farm is one of the finest in the colony. He is exporting Kilimanjaro coffee to England. The flavour of this coffee is as fine as the best Mocha and Java brands. There were also thousands of Para rubber trees. The place is in the very centre of the Edenic Kilimanjaro platform at Marangu. But Patterson longed for Scotland even in this grand Scenic Theatre.

Next day we made Safari from Marangu to Taveta. Mr. Hyde-Baker sent me refreshments and some meat and invited me to lunch with him and Count Coudenhove. Hyde-Baker and Coudenhove know all the jungle lore from the Zambesi to the Nile. Baker knows every haunt of game in the wide country. Coudenhove speaks the language like a native, and told me many recondite legends and unique habits of the Waparri, the Wachaga, the Wataveta. I spent a few days with these two fascinating African explorers.

The last evening of my stay, Count Coudenhove came and dined with me. We were leading the simple life; but it was good. Good was it to be away from the madding crowd; good to hear the bird-songs and listen to the humming of intoxicated bees: good to see the great plain stretch away to be lost in misty mountains; good to see at sunset the white crown of Kibo. The green afternoon faded; twilight approached like a wolf: the moon came fumbling the shadows, checkering the underbrush with silver, and we looked up into the immensities where even the lightning wearies and subsides. We talked till midnight — brothers of the soul.

The Count came with me next morning to the Lumi River, where I bade him farewell as if I had known him always.

My tent-boy, Osmanie, was one-half Taveta and one-half Masai. He did not like the English language. All words that ended with a consonant he ended with a vowel, as bed, beda; tin, tini; soup, soupi; food, foodi.

He had nice words for animals: dudu, the ant; buni, the ostrich; kongoni, the Hartebeest, etc. One tribe calls the ant, " Maji, a moto," — " Water on fire."

One of my men, Kungungu, was a stupid boy. On the road one morning he fell and broke a dozen of my camera plates. He said that he had a pain in his breast bone. I quickly transferred it to the fleshy part of his hind quarters with the palm of my hand. He said: — " Thank you, Little Master, that will do me good." Then the good fellow walked twenty miles. Bata was the dude of the party. A small chap with a beard and some Arab traces, he carried best and walked fastest. Next to him was a stately lad; ears cut so that one side of each ear seemed half-way down his cheek. Ornaments were in his ears, from which, pendent, there was a brass chain fastened to a ring around his neck. He had other chains and rings on his neck and also on his ankles and above the calf below the knee.

We camped at Mbuni, among antelopes, lions and ostriches; a good camp, and I slept the sound slumber of the out-of-doors. Towards morning it rained a little and I brought the men inside my tent. Count Coudenhove has written me that in February, 1909, he and his brother killed a huge lioness in this camping place.

We started next day at 7 A. M. and got to our destination, Makatao, at 2 P. M. My two best men went to look for water, but returned saying: " Lion drank it all." I rested and read " Nanon " by Dumas.

We made a Safari of twenty-five miles to Burra and then six miles to Mtate. Poor Kungungu was so lazy that we called him Punda, the donkey. I had brackish water carried in tins. When I got fresh water from the forest streams at Burra, I tell you it tasted delicious.

We had a beautiful dawn the last day in the jungle, radiant light and lovely bird-songs. The Taita hills glowed with emerald green to their summits, seven thousand feet above the sea. We walked fifteen miles to Voi. The trees were brown and seared, where two months before they had been bright with blossoms; the river Voi was almost dry. I said farewell to the carriers with regret. They had taken me across the scorching desert, carrying their burdens without complaint. The average load was fifty pounds to each man and they would carry thirty miles a day and be quite cheerful when they came to camp at night.

I took the train to Nairobi. There I met Mr. Harry Edgell. With him for a week I studied the taming of wild animals. He said in a long interview:

"Professor Crossar-Ewart, of Edinburgh University, declares that the zebra is equine, and results prove that the hybrid from an Arab horse and zebra mare is fertile, whereas the foals from a Muscat donkey and a zebra mare, and from a zebra horse and a donkey mare are mules, or zebrule."

"Of zebra there are three kinds. That of Southern Africa is the Burchell's zebra, striped head and body, but with white legs. In size it is from twelve to thirteen hands and of heavy build, with low withers."

"The second is the common zebra or Chapman's variety, which is striped right down to the hoofs. It is estimated that in British East Africa alone there are eight hundred thousand of this variety. They are rarely to be found exceeding thirteen hands." With this variety many experiments have been made by Mr. Edgell, who asserts that the wild animal trained will only work at his own pace. The withers of these need to be developed before an animal of much service can be obtained. From observations, a pair of Chapman zebras, perfectly trained to double harness, became wild beasts on crossing a lion's spoor. They went raving mad; and one kicked clear and broke loose, but so persistently fed round the enclosure in which the other animals were kept that she was driven in and was subsequently exported to Hamburg for Hagenback.

Mr. Edgell, in taming these zebras, had no trained domestic animal wherewith to break the wild ones. He did not find them vicious, but constantly on the defensive, and his success was achieved solely by patiently pacifying the animals. Other men who have made experiments with zebras have used rougher methods, and broken their hearts. These little beasts are very quick to use their teeth and all four feet, but their usual procedure is to lie down and refuse to budge.

One, that was trained in German East Africa and subsequently exported, was a perfect hurdler. Practically all have good quarters. Experiments have been made to find out whether or not these animals are immune from the tsetse fly. Of twelve known experiments not one has been lost. But in captivity the majority of those that die do so from a worm which attacks the smaller intestine, *ascaris megalocephela*.

"I made an experiment," said Mr. Edgell, "by breeding three foals from selected young mares and a fine vigorous five-year-old stallion. I did this because of the natural deterioration of the zebra, owing to the old stallion getting control of the herd. The foals reared, on attaining maturity, did not come up to the expected size. But their ears were smaller and there was evidence of improved shoulder.

"One of the foals was exported from British East Africa into German East Africa, where this domestication of the zebra meets with intelligent government assistance. There are to be seen at Dar-es-Salaam and Tanga trained zebras as mounts for non-commissioned officers; besides healthy zebroid and zebrules — the former term is used for an equine cross, consequently fertile; the latter asinine and therefore mule."

The finest result Mr. Edgell has ever seen was from a zebra mare and a shetland pony in the Berlin Zoölogische Garten. When zebras were required for experiment in India, instead of obtaining them direct from East Africa, they were purchased in Hamburg from Hagenback though these animals originally were caught wild near Kilimanjaro and exported through Mombasa.

"I do not see," continued Mr. Edgell, "a big future for the present wild Chapman zebra, though I am convinced that by selection and careful breeding an all round useful animal can be obtained in the third generation."

"The third variety of zebra, of which we hold the monopoly over the Germans, and which bids fair to become a great enterprise, is the Grèvy variety. This animal has never yet been the subject

ZEBRAS TAMED AND TRAINED TO HARNESS.

of an experiment, owing to its inaccessibility. It belongs in North East Africa exclusively, averages about fourteen hands, — and is very closely striped down to the feet, with a white belly. In build this zebra resembles a Clydesdale horse and his hoofs prove him to be as hard as the Chapman zebra is soft."

In this zebra Mr. Edgell sees his goal, viz.: The production of a transport animal, both for Africa and India. In East Africa horses have not been satisfactory, owing to East Coast fever and tsetse fly. But fever has not been seen among the zebras. Mr. Edgell has had a great deal of difficulty in obtaining any kind of assistance from the government in making his experiments in British East Africa. Such experiments as have been previously made at Naivasha and elsewhere with government funds or by private enterprise have been failures, the experimenters expecting the success of the work in six months, and having started with the wrong variety of zebra.

Mr. Edgell has also been seeking permission to experiment with other wild animals, especially eland and buffalo.

"The eland is the largest of all antelopes, easily domesticated, and immune from the pests of the country, ticks and flies. It remains to be proved whether this animal, when domesticated, retains these qualities. Should it do so, it will prove an excellent milker and have great draught power. In double harness a pair trotted thirteen miles without a break. The eland is sure footed and, though not fast, keeps a steady pace uphill and down dale. The eland has the kidney of a sheep and in other ways resembles the sheep."

" Now buffalo are bovine, and should cross readily with the native domestic humped cow. Young buffalo kept in captivity should produce a heavy trek-ox, which may or may not prove immune from the pests of the country."

" The simplest and easiest way to catch wild zebras is to drive a mob into an angle, secreting an enclosure.

" Another way is with wedge-shaped pits at recognized drinking places. Still another way is to use strong, green hide nooses pegged down and resting in pegs about seven inches from the ground. Many of these are placed in a track and the herd chased over them. By this means some are caught by the feet when they are easily secured with lariats."

" I hope myself to catch some with boleadors and a fleet horse such as I used in Argentine. Experiments have proved that the zebra is easier trained if handled at once on capture. I was on my way from Kilimanjaro to the St. Louis Exposition with thirty zebras to train them there for Hagenback, but the S. S. *Kurfurst* was unfortunately wrecked off Sagrey on the coast of Portugal. I worked hard to save the zebras but only succeeded in saving seven out of the thirty. And with them and the many other wild animals and birds I was knocking about in Lisbon and elsewhere for one month before I made Hamburg. Finally we got on an old Slowman cork ship, and had a fearful time in the North Sea; the zebra cages being tossed about on deck like cork. This spoiled my American plans which may work out later."

During the eight months that I spent in Central Africa I made a study of the imitation of animals. I have consulted several books on the subject, especially that of Drummond.

I found out some new forms myself and I give here the results of my reading and personal observations. Imitation is not the exception in nature, but rather the rule, involving more or less every part of the animal kingdom. It is found on every hand by the traveller through the African jungle, and in fact through any tropical forest. Here are found extraordinary resemblances of creatures to other creatures or plants and inanimate objects; and one sees here hundreds of thousands of creatures whose lives are the most ingenious fraud and colossal deception. All animals and insects, on the principle of being mistaken for something which is safe from attack and annoyance, have come to resemble the objects among which they live — sticks, moss, leaves, the bark of a tree, etc.

Although there are some exceptions to the rule, yet it cannot be denied that many insects and animals are coloured in such a way that detection of them is difficult. Certain species of butterflies, when resting with folded wings closely resemble the dead foliage on which they have alighted.

Colour in animals serves two purposes, that of protection, the object of which is to make the animal less conspicuous; and that of warning, which serves to make it conspicuous. Certain families of butterflies are inedible, owing to the presence in their bodies of acrid juices. These butterflies are distinguished by their brilliant colouring and curious marking, so that they are readily distinguished by their enemies, and given a wide berth. Those living danger signals fly leisurely about the forests without the slightest fear, knowing that the monkeys, birds, spiders and lizards, seeing them, beware. Wasps, bees, and other stinging insects have for this same reason been made as brilliant in colouring as possible and can be recognized by their enemies at a glance. It may be safely taken as a rule that all brilliantly coloured insects belong to these two classes — they are either "bad-stingers" or "bad-eaters." An interesting fact in this connection is that these gaily coloured insects are imitated in outward apparel by others not protected by unwholesome juices, who, in imitating them in colouring, share their immunity from danger. That this imitation is certain is proved in many ways, one being that quite frequently one of the sexes is protectively coloured and not the other.

The brilliant colouring of snakes is often attributed by naturalists to " warning," but the details of colouring have never been thoroughly worked out. The question arises whether, if the vivid colouring is meant to warn off enemies, these same conspicuous colours would not also warn off the animals on which these snakes prey, and, while the brilliantly coloured skin would be of advantage to the snake when being hunted, whether it would not at the same time be of equal disadvantage in hunting prey.

The Puff-adder, which is one of the most beautiful of the tropical reptiles, is essentially a forest animal, and, when lying among withered leaves in the shade of the trees by the side of a stream, is with difficulty distinguished from the forest bed. When lying on the ground it commands nearly its whole body, and when any part is touched, it doubles the head backward with amazing swiftness, and attacks its victim. In this way it forms a trap which is entirely unperceived until it closes with alarming rapidity upon its prey.

Even more marvellous is that kind of imitation where disguise of *form* is added to that of *colour*. An example of the mimetic insect is that of the family of Phasmidae, which lives among the long grass which grows in patches through the forest to the height of eight or ten feet. During the greater part of the year the sun dries the grass into a straw colour and the insects are coloured to match the grass. Each change in appearance is closely imitated by the insects, even to the extent of developing antennæ to represent blades of grass, which are 'from one to two inches in length, standing out from the end of the body on each side to represent blades of grass at the end of the stalk. The insect closely grasps the grass stalk, compresses its body against the stem, holding itself in position by the two fore-limbs which are so extended as to form a long line with the body, and appear to be a part of the stalk. It is absolutely rigid, and in colour, shape and every particular is like a blade of grass. It changes in colour and appearance with the season, the colours varying from gold to a brilliant red.

After the rainy season, when the grass with its new bright colouring springs up, these straw coloured insects disappear and new ones, coloured green as the new grass, appear in their places. Whether these are the same insects in a new colouring to match the new grass, or another generation of insects is not known.

This family also possesses the power to imitate death, though even in life they are not much more than mere skeletons, and are of such extreme thinness that squeezing them with a great deal of force between the thumb and forefinger has absolutely no impression on them, and decapitation seems to be the only method of putting them to death.

Another class of insects imitate twigs, sticks and the smaller branches of shrubs, and with these the imitation is even more perfect, the insects copying down to the smallest detail the bark, producing to perfection the mould spots and the node intervals, the very attitudes of the insect carrying out the deception in the most perfect manner. A great number of this species are called "walkingstick insects" from their singular resemblance to twigs and branches. They are sometimes a foot long and their colourings, form and arrangement of head, legs and antennæ give them an appearance identical with dead sticks. A small branch or twig cut from a tree and laid by the side of one of these would challenge the closest observation.

Still another form is that representing leaves. These for the most part belong to the Mantis and Locust tribes and are found in nearly all colours, forms and sizes, imitating foliage in its many stages of growth and decay. There is, in fact, no growth in nature which is not imitated in some form — lichens, mosses, mould, bark, thorns, all have their living counterparts.

Among the larger animals which, one might suppose, would be independent of imitation, the harmony of colour and environment is no less striking.

In the treeless portions of the deserts, where the climate is hot and dry and the rainfall not abundant, all birds, reptiles, and insects are dull in colour, while in the thick jungle where the sun cannot penetrate, the colouring of animals is uniformly dark, and again among those which live in forests where the sun penetrates through the foliage the animal is usually striped or spotted. The hartebeests, which are red in colour, bear a great resemblance both in colour and shape to ant-heaps, so that at a distance it is almost impossible to distinguish them from the ant-heaps; giraffes, with their long necks, at a distance greatly resemble trees, their heads and horns closely resembling broken branches, while the colouring of this animal assimilates well with the dull shades of bushes and trees in the locations which it frequents.

The zebra, when seen away from his natural environment, seems an extremely striking and conspicuous object, but when seen in his natural surroundings, the black and white blend and harmonize into a soft and inconspicuous gray, giving an effect not unlike the shadows of the branches of shrubs.

The leopard, which abounds in the African jungle gives the same sense of indistinctness as the zebra; the hippopotamus spends most of his time in the deep waters of the river, finding this the best means of protection; the alligator, concealed by his mud-coloured hide, is with difficulty distinguished from the fallen logs lying along the banks of the river.

It is a well known fact that when in danger wild game is absolutely motionless, and even the largest animals are seen with difficulty at close range, as in this way they are often taken for a part of the landscape, and are protected from their enemies.

CHAPTER XIV

NAIROBI — CAPITAL OF EAST AFRICAN PROTECTORATE

NAIROBI is the capital of England's equatorial colony; and the English pioneers think that, in time, it will be one of the finest cities in Africa. The town is not half a decade old. Three years ago it had five houses; to-day it has a population of fifteen thousand. Streets have been laid out over an area ten miles in circumference; hundreds of buildings erected in iron, wood and stone; churches, banks, hotels, racecourses, golfing and tennis grounds, clubs and suburban villas are scattered across the veldt.

This smart little town lies at the western end of those vast plains that rise to an altitude nearly as great as that of Mount Washington. It is just about half way between Mombasa on the coast and Port Florence on Victoria Nyanza. To the north, one hundred miles away, Mount Kenia washes her white forehead in the clouds eighteen thousand feet above the Indian Ocean; and on a bright summer day, from a hill below the town, the traveller may

Nairobi

get a glimpse of the twin peaks of Kilimanjaro, lying southeast in the German territory, nearly one hundred and fifty miles away.

Although almost on the Equator, the torrid sun is conquered by the altitude and the white race can live and work upon these African plains all the year around. In fact this is a white man's land; and with a little care the Caucasian race will thrive upon thousands of square miles of its rolling green.

After a twenty hours' ride from Mombasa on the Uganda Railway, we left the Athi plains, which, for a hundred miles before you reach Nairobi, are literally covered with game. There are fifty thousand square miles of game preserves in the East African Protectorate; and it is estimated that fully ten million wild animals are living to-day upon these verdant meadows. The country is a great empire of undeveloped possibilities; and Nairobi will, in time, be the centre of great trades and industries. Hitherto in the history of the world big cities have grown, as a rule, either on the sea-board or on the edge of rivers. Nairobi will be an exception to these rules of the past; because it will never be possible to have a vast metropolis either in the steaming climate of Mombasa or the malarial sedges of the Victoria Nyanza.

As yet, Nairobi is like one of our newly settled western towns. It has not graduated from galvanized iron and tin roofs. The great forests of Mount Kenia have not yet been exploited. There are no saw mills or planing mills worthy of the name and nearly all the lumber comes from America and Norway. Hence, the buildings are mostly in the pioneering style of tin and iron, which come in great sheets from Belgium and Great Britain. There are indeed a number of good stone buildings rapidly rising in every part of the town: the Norfolk Hotel, the Bank of India, Limited, and the new Post Office are types of buildings characteristic of a fine English town. Outside of the town there are pretty villas and neat farm-houses, typical of an English colony. The Indian market, the chief retail business section, is an aggregation of one-story iron booths, open at the front, in which sit solemn Hindoos, surrounded by their wares.

The Government treasury is merely a wooden shed, with a tin roof, in front of which a negro policeman stands, gun in hand, guarding the door. The office of the Land-Surveyor, the Police Headquarters and the Supreme Court Buildings are very much the same.

In the surrounding country, from two to ten miles out, there are native villages of the Somali, Kikuyu, Masai, and Nandi tribes. The Nairobi of to-day is full of cow pastures. Every place of importance is a mile from any other place of importance, and the

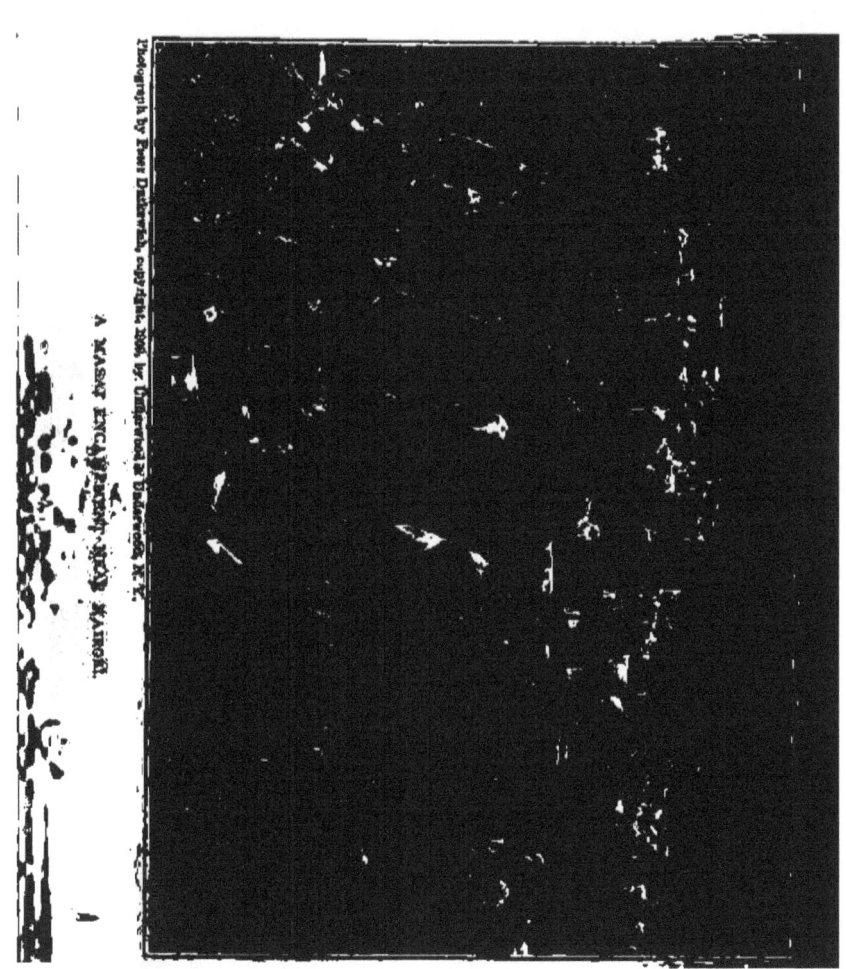

A MASAI ENCAMPMENT NEAR NAIROBI.

Photograph by Paul Dukervich, copyright 1909, by Underwood & Underwood, N.Y.

Nairobi

patches between are grazing lands. The houses run from the Railway station out into the prairies for an indefinite distance.

The chief ways of getting about are on foot, on horseback or in jin-rickshaws — the last being the most popular. The rickshaws are like those of Japan and they have been made in America. They are pushed and pulled by two black men to each vehicle, one pulling the shafts and the other pushing behind. These men are clothed in a single cotton rag, which serves neither for purposes of warmth nor decency. It is merely a concession to the prejudices of the English law-makers of the place.

Along the streets are rows of eucalyptus trees which have grown rapidly and shade the roads with their dreamy foliage. The unpaved ways are masses of dust, but the bright equatorial sun enlivens the whole scene and the crisp, bracing air gives to the traveller a stimulus like wine.

There are about a thousand Europeans in an area of twenty-two miles. Of the remaining fourteen thousand, one third are East Indians and two thirds are a conglomeration of African tribes.

The surrounding country is the home of the Wakamba and Kikuyu tribes, and from my hotel every morning I watched a long line of these greasy natives passing by on their way to the Department of Labour. They work on the roads and at Public works and receive five cents to eight cents a day. The cost of living is seventy-five cents a month. Many of them wear dirty, greasy cloths, about a yard wide and two yards long. These they hang about their shoulders and let fall down on each side. The law is that everyone, coming into Nairobi, must wear some kind of clothing. In the early morning, when the air is still cold, many of them are clad in red blankets — and they go about with their long legs bare to the thigh.

Some have the lobes of the ear so stretched that I actually saw a man with a condensed milk can in one ear and a jar of Liebig's Extract of Beef in the other.

The natives do all the manual labour of Nairobi. I noticed hundreds of them, loaded with brass and iron ornaments, carrying loads of dirt on their heads and wood on their backs, pushing and pulling carts and wagons through the streets.

A large number of the business men are East Indians. This is also true of Mombasa and of all the settlements I visited in German and British East Africa. The Hindoos have made their way on every travelled route and their little stores may be found in the remotest African village. They have trading stations upon Lakes Victoria and Tanganyika. An enterprising lot, they can live on almost nothing and hence they undersell the whites, who retaliate by agitating for the removal of all Asiatics. They handle cotton of light colours and gorgeous patterns. They sell wire for jewelry, and all the knick-knacks that the African loves. They also deal in European goods and one can buy from them almost anything the average man would need.

In Nairobi there is a long street devoted to the Hindoo trade. These Indian merchants dress in a quaint costume consisting of a long, black coat, buttoned up to the throat, and trousers of bright-coloured calico, cut very tight. On the head is a flat skull-cap of velvet, embroidered with gold, and the feet are bare or protected by light slippers.

As to the white population, they are the real rulers of the community. They dress well and spend a good deal of time in the open air. They have already introduced into this part of the Black Continent the golf and tennis of old England. Then there are the sportsmen and the distinguished visitors from abroad. There is a scattering element of second sons of noble English families who have come here to invest their money and build up the country. These are usually men of some considerable means — so the prices of large tracts of land are high and the farm estates vary from five thousand to one hundred thousand acres. In addition to these there are land speculators, who are chiefly young men from England and South Africa.

They dress in riding boots, wear big helmet hats and dash about on ponies, reminding one of what might have been seen in Virginia and Carolina in the pioneering days.

There are not many European women in Nairobi. Some of the Government officials have their wives with them, and now and then comes a titled lady with her friends, to hunt. There were three women in Nairobi last year who had, themselves, shot lions. There are English doctors, dentists and lawyers, two photographic firms, several real estate offices and a number of men who advertise themselves as Safari outfitters. These men supply the hunters with tents, provisions and all things necessary for a shooting trip. They will hire porters to carry the tents and chop boxes (boxes containing sixty pounds of tinned meat). They (the porters) will chase the lions out of the jungles, assist in setting the camp, make a corral for the animals, if any animals are taken, and they are useful in a dozen different ways.

One of the functions of the porters is to scare up rhinoceroses and, when the hunters wish to catch a young "rhino," they cautiously approach where the mother and the young one are feeding. One of the cleverest of the porters will then be hired for a special duty, and given twenty or thirty rupees extra to perform it. The hunters approach very cautiously the mother "rhino," where she is feeding with her young. They have a wagon and huge bags made of burlap. The porter selected to startle the mother "rhino" goes and stands to the windward of her, about two hundred yards away. She is sure to charge upon him, and the boy then runs perhaps a hundred yards — waits until the "rhino" approaches, and, when the enraged beast makes a lunge for him, he cleverly side-steps, after the manner of a toreador in the bull ring. Meanwhile the hunters, with a big burlap sack, rush upon the young one, thrust the sack over its head, hustle it on to the wagon and drive away as fast as they can. A young "rhino" is worth seven thousand dollars in Bostock's menagerie.

Among the interesting men I met in Nairobi one well known through the American press is Mr. William N. McMillan of Missouri. In one of the wildest parts of the Dark Continent Mr. McMillan has his farm, where antelopes and zebras, gnus, lions and leopards are as thick as domestic cattle in our Western prairies. It is one of the great game preserves of the world.

Mr. McMillan is about thirty-five years old, tall, dark, fine-looking, a man of culture as well as a man of enterprise and great wealth. It is said he spends sixty thousand dollars a year on his farm in improvements. The name of the farm is Juja, and it is about thirty-four miles from Nairobi. The Juja farm is bounded by three rivers and surrounded by a wire fence. Inside this fence there are " rhinos " and " hippos " unnumbered, and one day last summer Mrs. McMillan's favourite terrier tried to swim across a little stream near the house but was eaten by a crocodile. A day or two later a " rhino " attacked the men working in the lettuce garden and every now and then a hippopotamus breaks in and has a meal of sweet potatoes. The amount these animals eat is not so great, but they wallow and crush and ruin a garden or a farm field.

Mrs. McMillan is one of the most charming hostesses in all of East Africa. In the bungalow, which is painted green and white, with wide halls and cool verandahs, many a saddle-tired hunter just in from the chase has experienced the delightful hospitality of these two amiable Americans.

Here, surrounded by beautiful engravings and books and all the charm that wealth wedded to good taste can give a home, Mr. Roosevelt was entertained before he started on his famous hunting tour.

Mr. McMillan has a hundred milch cows, each one of which gives a gallon of milk a day — rich and creamy, testifying to the butter producing qualities of the grass lands of this great plateau. He has all the modern appliances that an up-to-date

American dairy would have. Outside there are piggeries and chicken-runs and the stables are protected against mosquitoes. The draft animals are Bombay mules and East Indian oxen. There are about six hundred cattle and seven hundred labouring men on this interesting farm. The workers are Hindoos, Somalis, Masai and other native Africans. The pay for each man is about $1.33 a month. Of course they are given their food and lodging extra — which costs about 75 cents a month. Some of the Swahili boys used as cooks about the house get as high as $13 a month. I asked Mr. McMillan if he could live all his life in Africa and feel perfectly happy, away from the great centres of the world. He replied, "I could not be happy anywhere else; I will probably never leave Africa. There is a disease that we have down here called Africanitis, and I feel sure that I have caught it. I spend a good deal of my time in civilized countries, but I shall always return here."

Mr. McMillan is renowned the length and breadth of Equatorial Africa on account of his kindly, approachable disposition, and he must have been a man after the ex-President's own heart.

There are droves of zebras all around Nairobi and one of the most interesting men I met there was Mr. Harry Edgell, the famous tamer of zebras of whom I have previously spoken. Edgell is a young

Englishman about thirty years of age, a typical pioneer and a man like McMillan with Africanitis. No office in the English Government would tempt Edgell away from Africa, if he could get a good chance at catching and taming the wild animals of this new land.

Another citizen of Nairobi whom I found an extremely interesting man was Mr. Bailey, recently of the local legislature. Mr. Bailey of Nairobi and Lord Delamere of Njoro have so stoutly maintained the right of the English colonists to limit the game preserves, which are now eight times the area of Massachusetts, that they have had a collision with Governor Sadler. From what I could learn about Governor Sadler, I should esteem him to be a conservative man and one inclined to be extremely kind to the native races. But, of course, the reserving of so much land for the wild game and the granting to the natives of reserves large enough to accommodate the increase of population for a hundred years to come, has raised a storm among the pioneers. Mr. Bailey and Lord Delamere were the spokesmen of the more radical of the pioneers. They went to the Government House last year with certain requests to the Governor, and some of the more ebullitionary of their followers cried out to the Governor, " Resign! Resign! Flannel foot," as they did in Boston in the good old

days. Whereupon the Governor promptly expelled Mr. Bailey and Lord Delamere from the Legislative Council.

The ejected councillors appealed to the Government at London, but the Home Government supported Governor Sadler. Mr. Bailey and Lord Delamere are considered the patriotic leaders of the colony and the end is not yet.

This is another illustration of the immensely individualistic character of the Anglo-Saxon. Here is a colony of three thousand Englishmen, trying to raise a revolution in a land inhabited by five million blacks, against a Government directing the destiny of four hundred million human beings. I met Mr. Bailey one day at the station in Nairobi and he gave me a little idea of his side of the question.

"There are," said Mr. Bailey, "one hundred and fifty-three million acres of good land in the Protectorate. At the present time only two million acres are under cultivation of any kind. Allowing the natives fifty million acres for their reserves, and cutting out the game, it would give one hundred million acres to English farmers from the home country. Now, what we contend for is that, since this colony costs the English Government a million dollars a year in your money, the average citizen of England should have a better chance at the developing of the country and the making this plateau a home for Europeans. Coffee and tobacco and even cotton will grow in the neighbourhood of Nairobi and on the wide plains. And what we want to do in East Africa is gradually to bring in the smaller farmer, who, on a homestead of one hundred and sixty to six hundred and forty acres, can make a respectable living. The cost of land is from thirty cents to one dollar and fifty cents an acre, and homesteads of one hundred and sixty acres, with the right to preempt four hundred and eighty acres more, can be purchased by instalments spread over sixteen years. There is no reason why we cannot have a colony of from one hundred thousand to one million Europeans here inside of fifty years.

"The settlers are not given the advantage of proximity to the railway — instead of that the game preserves run for hundreds of miles alongside of the railway, and it is estimated that there are ten million wild animals in this Protectorate. Now, there can be no doubt that where so many wild animals graze, European settlers could raise an enormous number of domestic animals."

I quote this interview from memory, but it gives, I think, a fair idea of what Mr. Bailey and his compatriots in the East African Protectorate have in mind.

One day at the Railway Station of Nairobi I

saw a man with long hair who, I was told, was Lord Delamere. Lord Delamere's farm is at Njoro on the Uganda Railway. The estate is seven thousand feet above the sea and the Equator runs through it. On this estate there are a thousand acres under cultivation. His Lordship has eight thousand native sheep, and six hundred imported merinos, seventeen thousand head of native cattle and eight hundred oxen. He is experimenting in the interbreeding of native cattle and sheep with English varieties.

Among the regular visitors to Nairobi one often sees Lord Hindlip, who has written several books on Africa and now owns over a hundred thousand acres in the East African Protectorate. There is an East African Syndicate that has three hundred and twenty thousand acres.

But, wandering about this Equatorial capital, I can see that as yet it is no place for poor Americans, and the poor Englishmen who can do well here are the exceptions. The land seems to be good and can be bought comparatively cheap — but everything is far from the markets and all the imports are high. Labour is extremely reasonable, but it is difficult to control the workers, and the conditions thus far render life hard for the ordinary English or American farmer who have but little money and must rely on their energy and brains. An English or American farmer with five or ten thousand dollars of capital could, I think, make a very good living in the vicinity of Nairobi. There is no reason why this should not some day be a white man's country, settled by white men, and where the white race can live and thrive. There is no fever above fifty-five hundred feet and at eight thousand feet ice is seen in the early morning. A great part of the highlands has a good rainfall, a little heavier than that of New England — between forty and fifty inches a year. At Nairobi the temperature varies from 49 degrees to 86 degrees, Fahrenheit, in the shade. The Hindoos have gardens in the outskirts of the town, cultivating practically the same vegetables as those grown by the market gardeners of Massachusetts or Maryland. Nearer the coast cotton is yielding four hundred pounds of lint to the acre. The Algerian fathers at the Catholic Mission outside of Nairobi are growing a first rate variety of coffee. The greatest obstacles at the present time are the insect pests and animal diseases. But these will ultimately be conquered by advancing science, and upon these vast, upland Equatorial prairies, now supporting millions of zebras, antelopes and other wild animals, there will be the farms of a million white men teeming with sheep and with cattle.

Nairobi has three weeklies, and all claim to be

prosperous. They are good-sized journals selling for from two to three annas, or from four to six cents each. They have regular telegrams from the Reuter agency, which gives them the big news of the world, and they furnish full reports of the local cricket, polo, tennis and golf matches.

As to the advertisements, the most of them come from the local merchants and some are odd in the extreme. One that appeared last summer was signed by a well-known American circus manager, and stated that he desired to buy a white rhinoceros, giant hog, some wild dogs, a white-tailed mongoose, and a bongo. Another advertisement was that of the " Homestead dairy " showing the improvements made along farming lines. There are many land sales advertised; also machinery, American wagons, and all sorts of agricultural implements.

One of these newspapers of Nairobi is edited by an American. It is known as the Globe Trotter, and has a good circulation. The editor's name is David Garrick Longworth. He is certainly enterprising, and partakes of Roosevelt's character in his love for wild game. He came out here originally to buy lions, giraffes and rhinoceri for Barnum & Bailey's circus, and he still " takes a whack " at the wild beasts during the intervals of his editorial writings. Mr. Longworth has done some newspaper work in the United States, and edited a newspaper at Cairo, Egypt, just before he came here.

Another paper of note is the Star of East Africa. This is owned by Mr. Low, the brother of A. Maurice Low, the well-known Washington correspondent of the Boston Globe. The Star is very American in its methods, and it delights in sensations. One week it published a supplement consisting of a pamphlet of sixty-four pages on the outside of which was printed in large type the words, "What the British government is doing for British East Africa." Upon opening the pamphlet the other pages were found to be blank.

The hotels, of which there are half a dozen in the town, are fairly comfortable. We stayed at the Norfolk at the upper end of the town. It is a low one-story building, with a wide porch in front, separated from the dirt street by a picket fence, and shaded by eucalyptus trees, through which the wind seems to be ever sighing and moaning. The charges are three dollars and thirty-three cents a day, including meals, but our own servant had to make the bed and attend to our wants.

A German sportsman next door had a little lion cub, about as big as a Newfoundland dog, tied in a box outside of his window. During a part of the day he let the baby lion out, and tied him by a rope

A WATERFALL NEAR NAIROBI.

Nairobi

to one of the pillars of the porch. The animal seemed harmless, but his teeth were sharp. A full grown lion came into the town one night while I was there.

The heavy hauling in this part of East Africa is mostly done by the sacred humped cattle of India. Some of these beasts are hitched to American wagons brought from Wisconsin. Indeed American goods are slowly making their way into these wilds. American sowers and planters are sold by the East Indians. The drug stores carry our patent medicines, and every market has more or less American cottons. The wood cutters are using American axes, but they complain of the flat or oval holes made for the handles. They say that a round hole would be better, as the natives who do the woodcutting are clumsy and the handles snap off at the axe. If round holes were used heavier handles could be put in and the natives could make them themselves.

Nairobi promises to become one of the important railroad centres of this part of the world. It is the chief station between the Indian Ocean and lake Victoria, and a road is now proposed from the capital to Mt. Kenia. By and by another road may connect with the German Railway from Tanga to Kilimanjaro.

The Mount Kenia line will open up a rich agricultural region which is thickly populated by tribes more than ordinarily industrious.

The railroad shops and the headquarters of the management are at Nairobi. The telegraphic rates are comparatively low. Away out here in the wilds of Africa one can send messages far more cheaply than in the United States. This is so, notwithstanding the difficulty which the linemen have to keep the wires in shape. The natives steal the wire from the poles and make bracelets, anklets and earrings of it. They use it for trading, and in some districts it will pass for money. During the Nandi rebellion, forty miles of wire were carried away and never recovered, and in one of the provinces adjoining Uganda, above Lake Victoria, the natives are so crazy after the copper wire there used that it is almost impossible to keep the lines up.

Another serious danger to the telegraph system is the big game. The giraffes reach up and play with the bracelets and pull the wires this way and that. At Naivasha the hippopotami have once or twice butted down the poles, and I understand they have been doing considerable damage to the lines along the coast near the Tana river. In the heart of Uganda the monkeys have a way of swinging the wires and twisting them together which stops the transmission of messages. But nothing daunts the white man's progress. East Africa is only one more theatre for the transcendent achievements of the Anglo-Saxon race.

CHAPTER XV

PORT FLORENCE

THE Kavirondo people on the Eastern shores of Lake Victoria on the western edge of British East Africa are all more or less naked. This is in the heart of the continent, with the Equator only a day to the north, but so high is the elevation above the sea level that the climate is not unpleasant. Port Florence is on Kavirondo Gulf on the shores of Victoria Nyanza nearest Mombasa. It is the terminus of the Uganda Railway, although the line is in reality continued in a steamboat line to Entebbe the capital of Uganda.

Hippopotami may be seen swimming about the shores, near the station, while in the background are pasture-covered plains spotted with droves of cattle, antelope and gnu, and the thatched huts of natives.

On the plains are sparse, tropical trees, and over them the hills rise to the Mau escarpment, beyond which is the Rift Valley; and still more to the east

THE RAILROAD STATION AT PORT FLORENCE.

STEAMER AT PORT FLORENCE.

are the level highlands of British East Africa, extending to near the Indian Ocean at Mombasa. The distance to the ocean is five hundred and eighty-four miles.

Port Florence will be one of the great cities of East Central Africa. When the Cape to Cairo Railway is finished there will probably be a branch from here, running through Uganda, to connect with it; and all the vast commerce of the lake will flow through this point, down the Uganda Railway, to the sea. At present the trade is greatly increasing in ivory, hides, grain and rubber from German East Africa, the upper Congo and the lands to the north. The cars come down to a wooden wharf extending out into the gulf. On the lake are numerous small steamers, which were brought thither in pieces and put together. They bring freight from all parts of the inland sea to the railway. There is a comfortable government bungalow, and there are the stores of a few Hindoo traders. The only Europeans here as yet are the soldiers of the King's Rifles, government officials and railway employes; but this is a stupendous advance over the conditions which Emin Pasha and Stanley found only two decades ago.

The old market place at Kisumu, a quarter of a mile from the station, was one of the most romantic centres of those strange Wakavirondo. I visited it with my fellow traveller to Uganda, Prof. Palazzo of the University of Rome. The natives were almost entirely naked. They are all dark brown, with intelligent features, woolly hair and negro lips and noses. They are of the Bantu race and among the best formed of the peoples of Africa.

Travelling through their villages is like walking through miles of living statuary. Their figures are ebony and look as if they might have been cut from black marble. They stand firmly on their black feet, heads thrown back; and they often burst out laughing. They are all naked, except for beads and anklets, and they seem to be the perfection of manhood.

The Professor points out to me a black Adonis in the crowd. Around the biceps of this man there was a coil of wire, and a pound of the same material on his right wrist. He was smoking a pipe, that hung down from his white teeth. Another had two brass rings on each thumb, bands of telegraph wire around his wrists and wide coils of wire above and below the biceps of the left arm. There were wire bands about his neck, circles of wire under each knee and great anklets of twisted wire on each side of his feet, where the skin was calloused. The ankles of still a third man were loaded with twisted wire — several pounds on each leg, and on the right leg extending to the middle of the calf. They

saw us watching them and laughed gaily at us—
they were just bright children of the sunlight.

As for hair, the first man had short wool and
the others had their hair twisted like the snakes of
Medusa. These black marble figures were not absolutely naked, for they had on behind an apron
of deerskin as large as a pocket handkerchief. The
skin is tanned with the fur on and it is used only as
an ornament and is of no use as far as decency is
concerned. Some have more jewelry and others
have cotton waist clothes. There is no trouble in
getting the men to pose. They think as a rule that
the use of clothes is decidedly foolish. Their wise
men say that it contributes to immorality.

The women are not nearly so well formed as the
men, and are shorter. The younger girls have bead
belts and the older ones sometimes have a tassel of
fibre attached to a girdle. This tassel is fastened at
the small of the back and looks at a distance like
the tail of an animal. This last is said to be an
article of dress indispensable to a married woman.
Some of the women wear little aprons of fibre about
six inches long. It is very hard to get these women
to wear cloth-protection—as they want none of
these foreign customs.

The land is thickly populated and the people are
good-natured and quiet. One can go anywhere
among the Kavirondo without danger. The girls

marry very early and are often betrothed at the age of six years, but in such cases the girl stays with her parents for about five more years. As is generally the case in Central Africa, all marriages are matters of sale. The parents sell the girls for a price and a man can buy a good wife for forty hoes, twenty goats and a cow. In early betrothals the suitor pays part down and the rest in instalments. If the father finally refuses to give the girl up after payment is made, the suitor gets his friends together, captures the girl and carries her away.

A man usually takes a wife from another village than that in which he lives, and her gentlemen friends often resist the invasion of a suitor and fight the suitor's party with sticks, but the girl usually allows herself to be captured. Old maids are not popular and the Kavirondo girls are as anxious to get married as members of the fair sex are at home. Indeed, if there is no bid made for her, she will often proffer herself in marriage and make overtures to that end, — giving a reduced price. There are however not very many on the mark-down counter.

The man who gets the first girl in a family has the right to dispose of the other girls as he decides. Polygamy is common and thus a man may often have several sisters among his wives.

As to the morals of these Kavirondo girls, they

are much better in regard to morals than the maidens of neighbouring Uganda, who are almost all clothed. Virtue stands high and infractions are severely punished. Divorces are uncommon, but a man may divorce his wives if he wishes to. If a man and his wife quarrel, and she leaves the house and he shuts the door after her, it is considered equivalent to a divorce, and the woman thereupon goes back to her people.

As for the Kavirondo villages back in the country, we found no difficulty in entering the houses. There are many little settlements, with paths from village to village. A dozen huts form a good-sized settlement. The houses have mud walls, and cone-shaped roofs, thatched with grass. The doors are so low that it is necessary to crawl inside, and many houses are not over seven feet from the floor to the top of the roof. The roof usually extends over the sides, making a verandah, and is there supported by poles. The huts are usually built around an open space and are joined together by fences of rough limbs and roots, forming a stockade in which to keep the animals during the night. Some villages are made up of a number of such enclosures, — each collection of huts belonging to one family. One of the huts is for the polygamous husband and one for each of his wives.

Inside, the floor is of mud, with a few skins scattered over it, upon which the people sleep. Goats and chickens are often kept in the houses all night, and driven out in the morning. The only furniture is a few pots. The cooking is done in clay vessels over a fire in the centre and is served in small baskets, the men eating first and the women taking what is left. Each family has its own mill outside the hut, made of a large stone with a hole in the centre. The women grind Indian corn with a second stone a little smaller than the hole. Sometimes the grit of the stone gets into the flour and this is apt to give the people very severe dyspepsia.

The Kavirondo are a pastoral people, and flocks of sheep and goats are found everywhere, and frequently there are seen droves of humped cattle. The animals are fat. Every drove has usually a flock of white birds about it, some of the birds being on the ground and others on the backs of the cattle, eating the insects that they find there. They are the rhinoceros birds which feed on the flies and insects that attack those beasts and which warn them by their flying and fluttering of the approach of danger.

The women do the milking, but it is said they are not allowed to drink it. They mix it with flour into a soup.

The country is very rich, and, although the trees have been cut down as far as the mountains, the

Port Florence

ground is covered with luxuriant grass. Near the villages are patches of cultivation, where the natives raise Indian corn, peanuts and a millet-like sorghum. They are everywhere digging in the black soil.

Along the Uganda Railway in the neighbourhood of the Lake, large tracts of land have been taken by Europeans and it is being ditched and drained with the intention of making it into a cotton plantation. It is too hot for white men to do steady out-of-door work, but the plantations could be handled by the native labour. The whites who take care of themselves are reasonably healthy; this is especially so of those who live on the uplands, the low lying country being malarious and productive of fever and the dreaded sleeping sickness. A large number of Hindoos have farms near Port Florence.

After the accident at Kilimanjaro, I was forced to make part of the journey alone and I spent two months on the Victoria Nyanza and in Uganda. These travels and observations will appear in the chapters concerning Uganda and the upper Nile.

Meanwhile, Mr. Dutkewich was kept in the hospital at Moschi, by his broken ribs, for three months. In November of last year he proceeded through the Kenia country and spent several months studying the Kavirondo, Masai and Kikuyu tribes, and hunting hippopotamuses and crocodiles in

Kavirondo Gulf. The result of his studies and observations during November and December of last year, and January and February, 1909, I have embodied in the next two chapters. These chapters are a rescript of Mr. Dutkewich's diary which he has kindly allowed me to use in this connection. Mr. Dutkewich has had to learn English as a foreign tongue; I have kept his own words as nearly as possible, in order to retain the vigour and vividness of his descriptions.

CHAPTER XVI

THE MOUNT KENIA DISTRICT

(From Mr. Dutkewich's Diary)

"NOV. 25: I am encamped in the midst of a beautiful country at the head waters of the Guaso Nyiro, the paradise for big game shooters. On each side of the river there is a thick, thorny jungle, giving cover for wild beasts. Even the tall trees are full of toothpick-like thorns. In the dry season oftentimes the numerous water pools dry up in the plains and the wild beasts come here to drink. The jungle is then sheltering lions, leopards, and hyenas in great numbers whose growling and howling as darkness sets in is anything but pleasant. The lion roars like thunder; often it seems as if the very trees were shaking for fear; he frightens herds of zebras to a tumult while the lioness stalks its prey against the wind, noiselessly, and with terrific leap and growl brings it down. To camp here means to hear at night the music of a perfect wilderness. In the daytime it is as quiet in this jungle as in a church on Sunday, but at night the terrific roaring of lions and miserable, laugh-like howling of hyenas make one wish for a safer place to sleep.

"*Nov. 28th:* Came to Masai settlement yesterday, Masai mothers are seen butter making and enjoying the warmth of the early morning sun. Common house flies swarm around them wherever they go. Masai women don't understand the use of soap, — they seldom wash themselves, — only, perhaps, when wading some stream. They dress in sheep skins, and adorn themselves with brass or iron wire ornaments. The food they eat consists of cow's or goat's milk mixed with ox blood and beef or mutton. They live a long life.

"Another industry seen in this village tableau is the drying of tobacco. Like all other work it is done by the women. Both sexes smoke tobacco and each family cultivates it, just for their own use, outside the village enclosure. A group of men are in the background pulverizing iron ore for red paint which they use for beautifying their cheeks and foreheads.

"*Dec. 1st:* Nights are cold in Africa, especially in this village forty-eight hundred feet above the sea level. Sleeping in the huts on skins and without covers is rather hard. These folk at daybreak are stiff with cold. As soon as the sun rises they come out to bask themselves for an hour or so — the pet cows follow their example. Against a grain storage hut one sees a man supporting a long stick with several small baskets attached to it. In each one is a quail caged. These quails are used for decoying others into traps when erected outside in the gardens. The Masai eat wild quail.

"There seems to be a great mortality among the children, or else mothers do not bear many because comparatively few are seen.

"*Dec. 5th:* Scene at sunrise in a Masai zareba at the foot of Mount Kenia. The zareba is built of thorny shrub to protect the cattle from lions, leopards, hyenas, and other carnivorous beasts. The Masai live in these flat roofed dwellings built of tree branches and then plastered over with mud mixed with dry grass and cows' dung. There is only one opening to go in, and a perfect darkness reigns inside to keep out the millions of flies that swarm in every Masai zareba. Here one may say that cattle, sheep, goats, a few dogs, and human beings live together like one big family, displaying a good deal of affection for one another. At sun down, from all points of the compass, men with their herds and flocks return from pasture and fill the zareba as compact as sardines in a tin.

"*Dec. 7th:* Placed camp at the lower timber line at the West side of Mount Kenia, whence numerous streams flow to the plains, feeding the great river

Guaso Nyiro, which empties itself into the Indian Ocean. Took a picture, as the sun rose, of the snow-clad peak; for later in the day this virgin forest is constantly hidden by clouds. Elephants, rhinoceroses, wild buffalos, bush-bucks, colobus monkeys, leopards and several species of birds live in this jungle. The men of the plains dread it, thinking that the forest is infested with evil spirits. Being nine thousand feet above the sea the cold at night and the torrential rains keep the superstitious aborigines out of it.

"Just as the sun rises the Masai shepherds let their herds of cattle, goats, and sheep walk out of the zareba into the open plain to bask themselves in the warm sun after the chills in the night, for night is rather cold on these highlands of East Africa. All the men, women and children sun themselves too. About 7.30 A. M. the herds move on to feed in the plains while women folk go to the zareba for their daily routine of work. This plain is situated to the South West of Mount Kenia and is within fifteen miles of the lower timber line, the home of the El-Moran (Masai warriors).

"Had successful hunting to-day at the head waters of the Guaso Nyiro, British East Africa. In the afternoon, within one half an hour of my camp, I came upon a very large male water-buck. Upon seeing me at first the animal made a dash into the

Photograph by Peter Dutkewich, copyright, 1909, by Underwood & Underwood, N. Y.

MASAI WARRIORS ON THE TRAIL OF GAME.

thicket, but, as it almost got out of my sight, I fired a guess shot, and as it afterwards turned out, the bullet went through the hind-quarters crippling it. I thought at first that I had missed it, and, in order to get another shot at the animal, I rushed through the bush into an opening where, to my great surprise, I saw my water-buck standing under a giant tree, crippled. A second bullet through the heart blotted out its existence. When I fired the first shot my headman, a Zanzibari, named Mohamet, ran away for fear of the animal's horns. It took fourteen men to fetch the water-buck to the camp. I should compare it in size to a full grown elk.

"*Dec. 12th:* It is pleasant to watch the jolly little Masai maidens gorgeously adorned with brass wire. They are daughters of chiefs. Every morning these girls walk ten to twelve miles through a bush country to Naivasha station, to sell milk. They are as swift as gazelles and not afraid of anything, always chattering as they go along and happy like the birds in freedom. As I met them on the trail they ran into the bush and hid. Having had two El Morans (Masai warriors) with me I soon got the little ones out from their hiding place and levelled the camera on them. A handful of beads as a present for the trouble made them laugh and wonder what all this was for. They had never seen a camera before. The whole performance seemed so funny to them. Anyhow the little girls had a round laugh at me when let go.

"*Dec. 13th:* A hunter's camp in the jungle of Guaso Nyiro is well protected by a thorny zareba on all sides, since at night lions and hyenas prowl about and make sleep uncomfortable. Even the opening for a gate is closed with the big thorny top of a tree. The native men sleep near the tent at a camp fire, the hunter on a camp bed, with guns loaded and handy in case a lion should jump inside of the zareba to snatch a man.

"It is now night. The hunter is having his dinner consisting of curry and rice, antelope steak, with sweet potatoes and a cup of tea. The cook does many 'stunts.' He is the head man over the porters, acts as an interpreter and as a go-between when dealing with native chiefs. He has an inborn dread of lions and of all huge wild beasts. The Kikuyu porters sit around him and hug the camp kitchen whenever the smell of food is about.

"The men were glad to break up the camp because the howling of hyenas at dawn and midnight shakes their nerves. Several times the hunter had to fire shots into the darkness to make sleep possible.

"*Dec. 15th:* In the dense forest of Mount Kenia. Only a very few white men have ever plunged into its thicket. Compass is the only guide here, for there is no human being in the virgin forest, only elephant tracks pointing in all directions.

"The lofty trees, junipers rising from undergrowth of bamboo, overgrown by lianas and other intangling parasitic plants, showing the weird and gloomy aisles, fill the heart of an explorer with the solitude of this great primeval forest, where even the elephant roams about in comparative safety from the ivory hunter.

"The aborigines shun it for fear of death, and dislike of exposure to the cold and rain. They believe that the forest is inhabited by pigmies and spirits. One morning I thought I heard human voices and fired a shot to attract them, but of no avail. It might have been a group of hyraxes.

"Warm cattle blood mixed with fresh milk is used by the Masai and other warlike tribes of East Africa. Women hold the steer, while an old chief and the medicine man draw the blood by shooting an arrow into the animal's jugular vein. The blood is collected in a gourd and immediately mixed with fresh milk and drunk on the spot by a wolf-like hungry herd. Strange to say, all the childless widows are strictly kept away, while the others fill their stomachs with this precious food.

"The El Morans, or warriors, unmarried men, kill the beef in the thicket and eat it by themselves. No woman dares to approach the spot.

"*Dec. 20th:* Still camping in a vast region of well-timbered and well-watered country with soil black as coal and yet practically uninhabited. This wilderness is the top land of British East Africa. In the not very distant future white settlers may change the aspect into a New Zealand landscape dotted with farmsteads and occasional townships. Forty miles from this place as the crow flies the Uganda Railway crosses the Naivasha Masai land. There the white men have already taken up farming land, but as yet they have no market for their produce and railway freights are high, so that with an inadequate capital their progress is naturally slow.

" The land laws, and the conditions under which land may be acquired in British East Africa, are so framed, at present, that only white settlers of independent means can thrive in this vast country. Australia, Tasmania, New Zealand, Canada, and South Africa weren't peopled at the start by the well-to-do class of farmers and miners who placed the first cornerstone to the foundation of the self-supporting, great new white men's countries.

" On Mount Kinancop-Donio Ngorinito, from an altitude of thirteen thousand five hundred feet, we look at the Kinancop escarpment, a perfect wilderness dreaded by the natives because of the frosty nights and cold rains. In time to come,

Photograph by Peter Dutkewich, copyright, 1909, by Underwood & Underwood, N. Y.

ON THE ROAD FROM NAIROBI TO MOUNT KENIA.

The Mount Kenia District

thousands of white squatters will raise wool and send frozen mutton and beef into the London market.

"This upland is traversed only by occasional caravans and herds of elephants. The air is perfectly clear, and so is the water in the numerous streams that nourish the great plains. This is the crest of the African Continent. It is a continuous line of escarpment for hundreds of miles from the North to the South. The climate is cool, good for whites, but too cold for the semi-naked natives. The latter dread this region. Their lungs cannot stand the cold, rarified air at such high altitudes.

"*Dec. 29th:* We camped over night out on the open plains. At three o'clock next morning we had to get up and build a huge camp fire for we were stiff with cold, the whole country around was clad in a snow-white mantle of frost. Not until the sun melted off the pathway could we continue our journey to the lake Naivasha.

"Looking over the slopes, overgrown with impenetrable bamboo, on the Kinancop escarpment into the Naivasha country and the Mau escarpment, at the foot of which lies lake Naivasha, we see in the plains below the homes of the pastoral Masai, the greatest fighting race in East Africa. In former years it was considered very unsafe to cross these plains on the way to Victoria Nyanza. To-day, with the Uganda Railway and the English and

Boer settlers, the travelling is safe, the land is well stocked and fine farms are springing up all over the plateau.

"*Jan. 5th:* At Kenia Falls camp near the great pool and the rocky walls that encircle it. The vegetation is very rich. The mist of the Falls moistens the ground. A bridge near me leads to Fort Hall, thirty miles away. Fort Hall is the government and military headquarters for Mount Kenia province, the richest in agriculture of all the provinces of the Protectorate. It has excellent climate, fertile soil, and an industrious people, the Wakikuyu. About thirty white officials and four hundred native chiefs govern a tribe of half a million natives.

"The natives never descend to the water's edge for fear of crocodiles. Descending, myself, I saw more fish than crocodiles. I found the undergrowth, trees and rocks very dense. There were many baboons in the trees, shouting at me. They reminded me of a group of baboons a mile further down that I mistook for Kikuyu natives. I had left camp to shoot antelope for dinner, and, after an hour's useless search, I sighted what I thought was a company of people leisurely walking down the track, with children jumping in the grass in a playful way. They must have been a thousand yards away. After a little while they all disappeared in a hollow. I could not understand what those people were doing in such a wild place, so I made a bee line for the point where I saw them last.

"I approached the spot cautiously from behind a bush, and to my great astonishment discovered that they were not people at all but big baboons, with their little ones, enjoying a family picnic in the open air. Just for fun I fired a shot in their direction, not intending to hit any one, but merely to see the result. The monkeys not seeing me, not knowing whence the terrible noise of the shot came, were panic-stricken and scattered in all directions. The little ones screamed for their mothers, and in vain tried to run fast through the tall grass. The poor mothers urged them on, trying to pick out their own children and to make for the big trees in the ravine. The fathers, mounted on ant hills in search of the enemy, said bad words in monkey language. Upon exposing myself to their view they dashed away to the jungle, with the rest of the tribe, climbing tall trees, whence they showered all sorts of abuse upon me, telling me I had no business interfering with their outing.

"This territory is exceptionally well-timbered and very rich in streams, more so than even the slopes of Kilimanjaro. In East Africa and Australia every stream is called a river, and since Kilimanjaro and Mount Kenia are the highest mountains in Africa and covered with perpetual snow they give rise to many streams, which may very properly be called little rivers. They meet many obstructions in the form of rocks, boulders and fallen trees, and sometimes lose themselves altogether in the great swamps.

"The great Kenia Falls are one hundred and fifty feet high and more than one hundred feet wide. They might properly be called the Niagara of British East Africa. In East Africa the great highland plains during the dry season present a very scorched appearance and a foaming volume like this inspires one with profound satisfaction.

"The Falls of Thika are in the Kikuyu country, Mount Kenia district. A big pool like a lake receives the water of the falls and feeds the Thika river on its weary march through vast plains inhabited only by countless numbers of wild animals. The pool is surrounded by almost perpendicular walls overgrown with green jungles in which baboons glory in a life of perfect freedom. At times, however, the poor monkeys are disturbed by bloodthirsty leopards, or crocodiles, while they are drinking the sweet waters of this immense reservoir.

"The waters of Thika come from a primeval forest, twelve thousand nine hundred feet high. From the sun-dried plains the sight of the green vegetation surrounding the falls is a welcome sight to the traveller, and coming upon this precious sweet-flowing river is like reaching a heaven on earth.

"Above the falls there is an open country where antelopes and zebras roam about in great numbers, while in the dense woods close to the water's edge the rhinoceros, the lion, leopard and hyena, and troupes of monkeys find shelter. Men avoid such places as these for fear of the carnivorous animals.

"This Thika river, and several others from the eastern slopes of Kenia, nourish men and beasts through the dry season clear down to the coast of the Indian ocean. The Thika is one of the tributaries of the famous Tana river. It is one of the largest streams flowing through British East Africa. In the dry season, when all its rivals on the plains are dried up, animals and men congregate on its banks. It is not difficult to trace its course because the thick green vegetation by the river side is clearly contrasted with the yellow colour of the sun scorched plains.

"Where the river is deep and its banks are swampy, crocodiles and hippopotami live. The natives dread the crocodile because it has a peculiar penchant for monkeys and men. I had great difficulty in making the poor fellows follow to the water's side.

"Leave for Kavirondo country on Victoria Nyanza."

CHAPTER XVII

THE KAVIRONDO PEOPLE

(From Mr. Dutkewich's Diary)

"JAN. *11th, 1909:* Came to this Kavirondo village on the shore of the Victoria Nyanza, six days' journey from Port Florence. It is surrounded by huge boulders. In the morning one observes the little ones and old folk basking in the sun. Two maidens, going after water, carry clay vessels upon their heads. One sees poles placed in an upright position with numerous basket-like cages attached. In each of them there is a quail. Later on in the day these poles are erected in the open field to decoy others into the snares. The pet-pet-pet chirrups of the captive quails please the passing white traveller in this distant land, informing him of a big village in the vicinity, where he may purchase food for his men.

" The wild quail are caught and eaten by these people. In the main street are small grain storehuts, inside the line of houses. The whole village is surrounded by hedges of evergreens covered with pink and white blossoms.

The Kavirondo People 277

"The types of womanhood in a Kavirondo village are interesting. One hard-working mother has her baby at the breast. Another a maiden, wearing a screen, is ready to be given away in marriage in exchange for one or two domestic animals and brass wire. A man in this country may have as many wives as he can afford to buy. He looks upon women as created for him, to do his work and bear him children. Some big chiefs possess as many as fifty wives, and of course are fathers of any number of children.

"*Jan. 12th:* Made photographs of women cultivating the ground. I noticed that they stood upon their own shadows at midday, because they are right under the Equator. The fierce rays of the sun have hardly any effect upon their dark skins, while if a white woman were so exposed she would certainly die of sun stroke. Every married woman wears a tail of palm leaves or grass behind, and no man, not even the husband, dares to touch it under the penalty of sacrificing a domestic animal for her food to smooth over the insult. The tail is sometimes made of papyrus plant fibre, the same as the small screen used for cover at the front. The Kavirondo never part with their long pipe and smoke it whether at work or ease.

"Kavirondo plow-women are happy at the plow. Work they must in the field, for men generally look after the cattle, sheep, and goats. Children take care of themselves, but if very small the mothers keep them under some shady tree close by in the field.

"They gather two crops a year under the Equator; and consequently, as seen by their strong well developed bodies, they suffer no lack of food. Sweet potatoes they grow in great abundance — it seems to be their staple food — their bread. A certain kind of millet, too, ground into flour and cooked in the form of a paste is eaten in great quantities.

"They are quite unconscious of their nudity; their husbands also prefer nature's garb.

"*Jan. 14th:* Adorned with a crown of ostrich feathers and smeared with grease and lamp black to look blacker than his skin really is, a Kavirondo bridegroom rode through the village to-day, naked on a cow, which he is to present his bride. The belles of the village accompany him to the house of his future wife. Women as a rule smear themselves with hippopotamus fat, all over, before putting on a fine finish of lamp black. An unmarried man has no standing among these people, and, therefore, when the day comes for him to step into the bonds of matrimony he is overcome with pride and happiness.

"Saw the great young King of the Ya-Luo

The Kavirondo People

adorned with an immense crown of black ostrich feathers, and two long colobus monkey tails hanging down from his shoulders and waist to denote his position. He commands an army of thousands of fierce-looking savages, armed with long dagger-pointed spears, protected with oval shaped shields, bent back on the sides to hide the flanks of the warrior. He wears a fantastic headdress, beautified with white ostrich feathers. His tribe represents one of the largest of the black-skinned nations of mid-Africa; also one of the most industrious. The Kavirondo and Wakikuyu have a future; while the Masai will probably die out by the advent of the white man's civilization. The Ya-Luo live chiefly by agriculture. They eat any kind of meat, even the crocodiles. The young warriors eat lion and leopard to make them courageous in war.

"These Victoria Nyanza aborigines have a superb war dance. The king is at the head of the dancers. A long tail hanging down on his arm denotes his rank. Two withered witches lead the crowd of semi-naked women and fantastically clad warriors. They have remarkable head gears of ostrich feathers, eagle wings, baboon skins, shako-like hats and what not! They dance around the circle of the village — the women leading the cavalcade. All sing and yell at the top of their voices. Soon, as the women fall out of the dance, the men start to rush savagely to and fro, exhibiting their valour by sham attacks upon an imaginary foe, to the great delight of the fair sex.

"These are the most picturesque warriors in British East Africa, inhabiting the country North East of the Victoria Nyanza and numbering over half a million people. Before the rule of the British they used to be very war-like but now their energy is mostly given to the cultivation of the soil and to cattle raising. Those that live close to the great lake spend a lot of their time in fishing, and in hunting the big hippopotami of whose meat the Kavirondo are so fond. Fish is cured or smoked and used as an article of barter for sweet potatoes, peas, pumpkins and pottery.

"Savage, blood-thirsty, in war paint, armed with sharp, long spears the women used to follow their men in a sudden attack before daybreak upon some neighbouring tribe, and if successful they gathered the dead bodies of the slain to feast upon. To encourage the men they danced and yelled in front of them with ferocious madness. The men would then begin to tremble all over with savage excitement, and, crazed by the thirst of blood, they would rush out furiously, jumping high up in the air with spear and shield in hand, raising a war yell, and by it attempting to drive the fear of death into the hearts of the enemy. The women at that moment becom-

THE PECULIAR HEAD-DRESSES OF THE KAVIRONDO WARRIORS.

ing very desperate would howl like a pack of hungry hyenas for the carcasses of their slain foes. They are cannibals. After the fight the women would bake the dead upon red hot stones for the warriors to feast upon.

"There are some splendid types of Kavirondo maidens and women in Equatorial Africa. They represent the most beautifully formed women among all the tribes inhabiting the shores of the Victoria Nyanza. The maidens after marriage discard the small screen they wear in the front, but keep the short tail behind. Sometimes we see a dainty belle wearing a crown made of wild boar teeth smeared from head to feet with lamp black mixed with hippopotamus fat to look blacker than she really is.

"In the civilized world the fair sex put rice powder upon the face to look white, while in mid-Africa coal black women powder themselves with a black mixture to look blacker than they are. Different countries, different tastes, — but to the same point — to look beautiful.

"A big strong Kavirondo young man the other day brought in a few goats on a string as a price for any one of several unmarried young women.

"Women are sold, or bartered away, for cows, sheep and goats in this land of naked barbarians. The prices vary as the women's beauty does. If exceptionally well made and pretty in the face, a maiden may fetch to her parents as many as ten milking cows. A common one, five goats will buy her. A young man never gets a wife for nothing in mid-Africa. If he is very poor he engages himself as porter to caravans, carries heavy loads over rough countries, underfeeds himself — all that to save enough money to buy cows or goats to exchange them for a wife or two.

"Women are a wealth to men in Africa. They do all the work while the husband loafs about and if he is not a chief decorates himself all over as if he were one. Here these women walk through the papyrus swamps in the early morning, coming after drinkable water in the open lake. Sometimes a crocodile snaps one of them away to feast upon her at the bottom of the lake.

"A husband of twelve wives takes life easy under the Equator. Early in the morning he goes out to bask himself in the warm sun and watch his wives at work. He takes pride in having so many good working wives and chats with them encouragingly.

"An afternoon sociable pipe-smoke under the Equatorial sun is enjoyed by the well-made and pretty faced Kavirondo fair sex. These women have no idea that dress has ever been invented for women; it actually seems to them that all their sisters on earth wear as much dress as they do, that's to say, only a tiny screen in front. They are very innocent of this comparative nudity, and are said to be the most moral women under the African sun. Some of them have beautiful forms and pass as the belles of the tribe. The very prettiest of them might be bought for from four to ten milking cows. These women are not given away to their husbands, but are sold, in cold blood by their own fathers and mothers as so much valuable property.

"A cure was administered to-day by the village witch, with her assistants, to a poor woman who was suddenly attacked with stomach cramps caused by excess in eating of a relation's dead body. The scarcity of wild animal life, the enormous density of the population and their fondness for meat may account for the horrible custom of devouring their own dead. When camping in their villages, I sometimes heard, in the middle of the night, yells of pain as if some one were dying. Next day I would be told that a native had died; but the dead man was gone; no funeral; no burial place anywhere. They had devoured his body as soon as he was dead. They hide their repulsive custom of eating their own dead; don't do it openly in broad day light.

"*Jan. 16th:* To-day some medicine women were instructing the maidens in the sexual initiation ceremony dance. These sorceresses are childless women, wandering from village to village and living on their wits. They are feared because of their witchcraft, and their power to hypnotize the superstitious into fits. These women are supposed to foretell one's future by examining the entrails of a goat. The chiefs consult them as to rains and the right time to cultivate the fields.

"Shot another big water buck. He jumped out of a swamp. I sent a bullet after him. He fled and I pursued him and found him under a big acacia tree. Another bullet ended his pain. He was as big as an elk. A fine feast for the boys! They will eat it down to the marrow of the bones. Plenty of food and sleep, and a big camp fire — that's what pleases them the most. When it comes to lion-shooting they all prefer to stay in the camp. 'Shimba' (the lion) drives the fear of death into their humble souls, especially when the said lion happens to break the stillness of the Equatorial night by his dreadful roaring.

"Feed these big boys well on meat and grain and they will follow you, Mr. Hunter, to the very Hell's Gate, but whatever you do — don't talk 'shimba' to them!

"Kavirondo women pull in the fishing nets made entirely of papyrus stalks, and the men on rafts out on the lake watch to protect them from the hippopotami. The top knots of the papyrus stalks make a compact net, through which fish cannot escape. They eat all and everything they catch. If the fish is only half an inch long, they eat it. The women pulling the net are as innocent of clothing as angels in Heaven, and as modest and moral as any of their sisters in the civilized world. They told me it is the men who will not allow them to use any clothes, except a small screen.

"The spirited Kavirondo belles draw water in baskets for drinking purposes from Victoria Nyanza. A week ago a crocodile at this very spot grabbed a boy of seventeen by the leg and bit it clean off; yet these plucky girls go into the water as carelessly as if nothing had happened. To reach an open place they must go about two hundred yards in the papyrus swamps, which make a kind of barrier between the open lake and the solid shore. The swamp harbours the dreadful crocodile, the huge hippopotami, the lurking hyena and even the lion.

"*Jan. 20th:* It is good sport to shoot hippopotami in the Victoria Nyanza, off a raft. It is not safe to shoot them from boats, for they can overturn a boat and throw the men in to the crocodiles.

"I fired twenty-eight high-powered soft-nosed bullets at such heads as popped out of the water for a second or two, wounding some, I think, but killing none. It was a bad job, and I was sorry for the waste of ammunition. Towards evening I got the raft again; but the herd seemed to bear none of the effects of my last shooting. Spotting the leader bull, which happened to put its head high out of the water, I took a steady aim right under the eye and fired, with a .405 Winchester, solid-nosed bullet. The animal turned over and for about ten minutes kept swimming in a circle, spilling blood and gradually weakening itself. The bullet penetrated the brain. To pierce the brain the bullet must enter under the eye or the ear.

"The bulky hippopotamus, with six bullets through its massive head, was dragged out of the Lake by one hundred and twenty men and women. All were like hyenas, eager to slash a big piece of meat from the carcass. The natives living close to the lake are very fond of hippopotamus' meat. The men only are allowed to eat it, yet the women will fight to secure a piece for their lords. A husband will sell one of his wives for a slice of it. This animal must have been about two tons in weight. In an hour there was nothing left. Like vultures they fought for it. I had great trouble with my porters to keep them from securing too much meat. I had my suspicions as to what they were to do with it all. They certainly could not eat it up. They wanted wives! The women dragged its head (as big as a Saratoga trunk) away out to the village. It is a big head, but the brain weighs only two pounds.

"The hippopotami always live near the papyrus swamps, where the cows bear calves, and guard them from the ferocious crocodiles until the baby hippopotamus gets strong enough to follow its mother into the water. The cow with its young upon its back is a ferocious animal, and looks out for crocodiles, and for men armed with spears; but the latter hardly ever dare to come near her on a raft or boat. She goes for them like a submarine, upsets the craft and bites the men in two with her pair of jaws. Crocodiles leave alone full grown hippopotami, but a young one is lost against the combined attacks of a crowd of these terrible reptiles.

"This is one of the shores of the immense Victoria Nyanza that has not as yet been depopulated by the deadly sleeping sickness, brought by the tsetse."

(Mr. Dutkewich went on from Kavirondo and photographed the Ripon Falls. Here he shot a huge crocodile, and fought a leopard hand to hand. The leopard mauled Dutkewich, but he first shot it and then put an end to its fierce attack by the stock of his rifle.)

CHAPTER XVIII

THE VICTORIA NYANZA

VICTORIA NYANZA, the largest fresh water lake in the world, with the exception of Lake Superior in our own country, is partly German and partly English. The boundary between the two governments runs across the lake at 1° south of the Equator. The whole extent of the Victoria Lake is from 3.5° South to 1.5° North. Nyanza means "water" or "lake" in the Bantu language.

The blue waters extend on all sides and only a few islands are in sight as we stand on the pier at Port Florence. The islands are of different types — some high and rocky, some bordered with papyrus swamps filled with strange birds and black hippopotami.

Here we are right over the Equator in Kavirondo Gulf, and yet the air is as cool as on Lake Superior in the summertime. The English Government has on the Lake eight steamers of from six hun-

A FIRST GLIMPSE OF VICTORIA NYANZA.

dred to one thousand tons burden. They are very comfortable, snug little craft, lighted by electricity, with a cuisine as fine as that on the vessels of our own Great Lakes. I crossed on the steamer "Clement Hill," named after Sir Clement Hill, one of the English statesmen of "Newest Africa."

At Port Florence our ship was loaded by natives with only breechcloths, which they wore out of respect to the prejudices of the passengers. The Uganda Railway brings one directly to the lake on a siding which comes down from the pretty station of Port Florence. The naked porters took our luggage on board. I remember the natives singing as they worked; and the play of every muscle on the black statues was to be seen.

We sailed in the late afternoon through Kavirondo Gulf which is about forty miles long and fourteen miles wide. Then we entered the lake proper. The way is girt about with volcanic hills, some of which kiss the sky, some are rounded and cone-shaped. Those toward the South are especially noticeable. Toward the North the country generally is lower and the hills are spotted with straw villages. There are a number of islands in the Gulf itself, which narrows at its entrance and also at its opposite end. Near the end of the Gulf there is a string of strange-shaped islands. We anchored at one of these islands over night, it being dangerous to travel on the waters of the lake except in daylight.

Victoria Nyanza is in the heart of East Central Africa. Along the Equator, it is at a distance of about seven hundred miles from the Indian Ocean. To the westward, that is, to the Atlantic Ocean, it is about twice that distance. The Nile starts towards the Mediterranean at the northern end of it. The great river of Egypt in all its windings is about four thousand miles long. It is over two thousand five hundred miles in a straight line southeast to the Cape of Good Hope, and just five hundred and eighty-four miles by the Uganda Railway to Mombasa — where nearly everyone enters East Central Africa. The headwaters of the Congo River are only a few hundred miles away; and less than two hundred miles from the southern shore one may reach Lake Tanganyika, from which Lake one might enter a tributary of the Congo and float to the Atlantic Ocean.

The Victoria Nyanza and Lake Superior are the two largest fresh-water lakes in the world. The great Lake of Africa has never been thoroughly surveyed but it is known to be over thirty thousand square miles in extent, and geographers are not as yet certain as to its exact area. Pick it up and put it over New England, and it would drown the States of Massachusetts, New Hampshire, Ver-

The Victoria Nyanza

mont, Rhode Island and Connecticut. Lake Victoria is more than half as large as all of our Great Lakes combined. It has three times the area of Lake Erie. It is about twice the size of Tanganyika, although it is only half as long. The shape of Victoria is almost quadrilateral. Tanganyika is a narrow trough between high hills. Nyassa is long and narrow and so are Lake Rudoph and Albert Nyanza in the North. Victoria Nyanza is more like our own Lake Superior than any of the great fresh-water Lakes. It is six times as high as Lake Superior above the level of the sea and more than seven times as high as Huron and Michigan. It is lifted nearly four thousand feet above the Indian Ocean.

It was three hundred years after the discovery of Superior before a steamboat was seen on its surface. Forty years after Speke discovered Victoria Nyanza steamboats and telegraphs were being used throughout the whole section. Many natives of this region will take their first ride in an electric car or a flying machine and do their first telephoning by wireless. Such are the advances between the opening up of America and that of Africa. The bottom of the Great Lake has not been thoroughly sounded, but there are several places which are known to be more than six hundred feet in depth. Victoria has a mighty volume of water and its surface rises forty or fifty inches during some years. The volume is so great that a dam might be placed at the source of the Nile, and by a proper system of damming, such as the English are doing at the Assouan Dam, the whole of the vast territory along the Nile from Jinja to Alexandria would be completely irrigated during the whole year.

It is estimated that one hundred and thirty-six billion tons of water annually fall into this great inland sea. It is said that if the whole of the River Nile ran back into Victoria Nyanza for a year it would not raise the level of the water more than one foot.

Until very recently this region has been the blackest of all Africa. Slavery was common everywhere, and cannibalism rife. No one knew there was a Lake here until 1858 when Speke discovered the southern shores. For two thousand years men had been searching for the headwaters of the Nile. Speke was sailing upon the Lake and saw signs of a current. He followed the current until he heard the thunder of falling waters. Sailing on at last he came to a green bank, where he landed — first of white men to behold the great, white, foaming wonder of the fountains of the Nile. He called it Ripon Falls. The whole civilized world was thrilled by Speke's discovery. Henry M. Stanley went

The Victoria Nyanza

around Victoria Nyanza in 1875. No man has as yet ever sailed directly across it from North to South. Contrary currents and dangerous reefs are feared. Some fascinating discoveries may still be made upon this equatorial Lake.

At the present time almost the only inhabitants are these queer tribes of African natives who in certain regions are still warring with one another. North of the Victoria Nyanza and of the Kavirondo are natives as different from the Kavirondo as an American is different from a Japanese. On the South are other tribes with strange customs and the whole Lake is surrounded by a dozen or more tribes, each differing from the others in appearance and in various grades of civilization.

No European boat had ever been upon these waters until Stanley came. The natives told him it was such a large Lake it would take several years to go around it. The native boats are very primitive — made of boards sewed together with the fibres of the raffia palm, they can be kept from sinking only by industrious baling. I saw many of them at Jinja and Entebbe and they are used more or less all around the shores. The average boat is about twenty-five feet long, three feet wide and two feet deep. It is made without nails or any iron whatever and seldom has sails. A storm will easily capsize one of these boats, and often the boatmen jump overboard and hold on to the rim of the boat to keep from sinking until the storm is past. Sometimes when a storm is approaching the boatmen fill the boat full of water and drift like corks upon the uplifted waves.

The Lady Alice was the name of Stanley's big rowboat. He started at Speke Gulf and by the aid of a sail finally skirted the entire shoreline.

One of the steamers on the Lake is the Sir William McKinnon. It was brought up in pieces before the Uganda Railway was finished, and put together at Port Florence. It is still in commission and used by the British officials as a sort of despatch boat. Two other steamers are the Sibyl and the Winnifred, each of about six hundred tons, and finally the Sir Clement Hill, which is eight hundred tons and which was launched last year. The Sibyl and the Winnifred are sister ships. They make regular trips around the Lake in connection with the Uganda Railway, the voyage from port to port taking about ten days.

The Sibyl is a screw steamer, has a life-boat on deck, and has about a dozen cabins and a dark little dining saloon in the rear. The cabins are lighted by electricity and in each is an electric fan. The top deck has a double awning of canvas, and at midday we were advised to keep on our hats, while sitting under it. The sun's rays are strong in this latitude and one must protect one's head, even while indoors. The sailors are half-naked savages, who get wages of about ten cents a day; while the steward and cooks are Hindoos who get a little more. The head steward on the Sir Clement Hill was a Goanese, that is half Portuguese and half Indian — the name being derived from the Portuguese colony in India called Goa. There are twenty thousand Goanese in East Africa.

It seems that Victoria Nyanza is destined to be as well known to the traveller as one of America's Great Lakes. The expense of going there at the present time is too high for the average globe-trotter; but the man who can pay the bills will live as comfortably on board one of the African steamers as he can at home. There are, of course, many insects, cockroaches, rats and the like. Some one said last summer: " I have never seen so many and such wild animals of the roach kind before." Then among bugs infernal there is the jigger. This usually tries for a home in one's feet, and lays its eggs beneath the toe-nails, after boring a hole for this purpose. This cachè must be cut out at once, or else the eggs will grow to worms and may cause the loss of the toe. The insect is supposed to originate from South America and it has already gone over half of Africa and is especially bad around Lake Victoria.

The mosquitoes did not trouble me at all while on the water, but the common house fly was a plague and a living wonder. He was as myriad as the thoughts of men, and as cheerful as Satan is where sin exists. The shores are infested with the tse-tse fly, the bites of which cause the sleeping sickness. But they live only in swamps and cannot exist in the light of the sun. On land there are plenty of mosquitoes of all kinds and also plenty of midges. A swarm of these latter rising from the water of a swamp looks like a waterspout. These winged waterspouts are formed of millions of midges, who rise into the air as soon as they are born. They sweep over the lake in great numbers, raining down upon the boats like so much black pepper. They have to be swept up with brooms and thrown overboard. They get into the cabins and cover the dining tables — even when the ports are covered with netting and every open space apparently closed. They are, however, harmless and do not live more than a day. I went to supper one evening and when I returned on deck and sat down in my chair, in the dark, I had a feeling that I was crushing newspapers — not at all; only a few midgets!

The accommodations on the boats are good and the Hindoos cook well our five meals a day. The cost of meals is one dollar and sixty-five cents a day. The water of the Lake is quite safe to drink.

Nearing the shores of Uganda, the scene becomes more like a civilized settlement than one in the heart of the black continent. The landscape resembles the shores of green England at Dover. Much of the land is cleared and there are clumps of dark green woods. In one place it looked as if the corn and wheat had just been harvested, but I later discovered that what looked like yellow stalks of corn or wheat were really mounds of yellow clay, — homes of the white ants.

CHAPTER XIX

THE UGANDA PROTECTORATE

BEFORE we land at Entebbe I will anticipate a portion of the journey and explain some points of interest about Uganda, England's new pet colony of Central Africa.

Sir Harry Johnston, who for years was Governor of Uganda, says that the territories which comprise this Protectorate contain, within an area of some one hundred and fifty thousand square miles, nearly all the wonders, most of the extremes, the most signal beauties, and some of the horrors of the Dark Continent. Portions of their surface are endowed with the healthiest climate to be found anywhere in tropical Africa, yet there are also some districts of extreme insalubrity. The country has been ruled more or less by the British government since the battle of Omdurman and the opening of the Upper Nile, 1897. At the present time it is practically British territory.

Uganda offers to the naturalist the most remarkable known forms among the African mammals, birds, fishes, butterflies, and earth worms, one of which latter is as large as a snake, and is coloured a brilliant verditer-blue. In this territory there are forests of unmatched tropical luxuriance. Probably in no part of Africa are there such vast woods of conifers. There are other districts hideously desert and void of any form of vegetation.

There is the largest area of marsh to be met with in any part of Africa, and two of the highest points on the whole of the continent, namely, the lofty snow-peaks of the Ruwenzori range, named by Abruzzi after the Queens of England and Italy. Here also the largest lake gives birth to the longest river of Africa, and Mount Elgon is the largest extinct volcano in the world. The Protectorate contains over a hundred square miles of perpetual snow and ice; it also possesses a few spots, in the valley of the Nile, where the average daily heat is higher than in any other part of Central Africa.

Within the limits of this Protectorate are to be found specimens of nearly all the most marked types of African man — Congo Pigmies, and the low ape-like types of the Elgon and Semliki forests; the handsome Bahima, who are negroids as much related to the ancient Egyptians as to the average negro; the gigantic Turkana; the wiry, stunted Andorobo; the Apollo-like Masai; the naked Nile tribes; and the scrupulously clothed Baganda.

These last are enthusiastic Christians, while other tribes of the Nile Province are fanatical Mohammedans. The Bahima are, or were, ardent believers in witchcraft; the Busoga polytheists are burdened with a multiplicity of minor deities; while the Masai and kindred races have practically no religion at all. Cannibalism lingers in the western corners of Uganda; while the natives of other parts are importing canned meats, and are printing in their own language summaries of their past history. This is the country of the okapi, the whale-headed stork, the chimpanzee, and the five-horned giraffe; the rhinoceri with the longest horns; and the elephants with the biggest tusks.

Whatever drawbacks may be found in the Uganda Protectorate from the white man's point of view, monotony or lack of interest is not among them.

The Elgon district is one of the loveliest in the wild heart of Africa. The country is extremely fertile, traversed by the only three rivers entering the northern half of Victoria Nyanza. There is not much forest, although certain forests that follow the western slope of the Nandi Plateau are among the densest and richest in the Protectorate. There is evidence to show that this whole region was once forest land, — deforested through the agency of

Photograph by Peter Dutkewich, copyright, 1909, by Underwood & Underwood, N. Y.

IN THE NANDI COUNTRY, NEAR MOUNT ELGON.

man, only a few clumps of trees being left standing on hill tops, in connection with spirit worship.

The whole of the land is most grateful to the eye, consisting of rolling downs covered with the greenest of grass, and made additionally beautiful by the blending of the green with fleecy white, shining mauve or pale pink when the grass is in flower.

The villages are aggregations of huts surrounded by an immense floral hedge, consisting of the beautiful pink Acanthus Arboreus, mingled with coral-red aloes.

The sleek, humped cattle, often gray or white in colour, the parti-coloured goats and the brown sheep, the numerous fowls of black, white, piebald and gamecock variety, diversify these charming agricultural landscapes.

Where the land is not in cultivation, in the Elgon country, the prairies are gorgeous with wild-flowers at almost all times of the year. The sunflowers cause some of the hillsides to blaze with yellow.

The great interest in the southern slopes of Elgon lies in the caves, first discovered by Joseph Thomson. These recesses, with ceilings nearly thirty feet high, are generally situated close to the base of the awful mountain cliffs. Similar caves exist on the northern slope of the mountains, at much the same level and also at the base of precipitous overhanging cliffs.

Thomson inclined to the belief that the caves were the work of a vanished race, in search of minerals or precious stones. The negroes of the Nandi stock now make use of the caves — blocking them up in some cases by houses very much like those of the cattle-keeping Masai.

The scenery on the western side of the mountain is grander and more beautiful in its detail than on any of the other sides. Tremendous buttresses and precipitous cliffs of gleaming granite, quartz or dark basalt extend from the great crater wall into the Bukedi plains.

The inhabitants of west Elgon are a wild-looking and savage race, among whom are some stunted individuals with the facial features of the Pigmies of the Congo Forest, whom they closely resemble.

The flora of Mount Elgon resembles the Alpine flora of Kilimanjaro and Ruwenzori. Snow falls on the highest points but does not remain long. The greatest altitude is the rim of the crater — about fourteen thousand two hundred feet.

Uganda contains within its borders the very arcana of geographical mystery, — those sources of the Nile and Mountains of the Moon of which Rameses questioned, and Herodotus and Edrisi treated, and a host of geographers and explorers made the life-dream of closet speculation, and travel-quest. Here Hamitic and Nilotic Ethiopians dwell, "together yet apart," and Norseman, Gaul, Iberian, German, Celt and Ishmaelite, Hindoo and Punjabi, pure of blood, or blended by many generations of marriage or concubinage, present an endless variety of types of physique, intelligence, civilization, barbarism, religion and idolatry.

Danger lurks in the treacherous shallows of many a lake and the eddies of every river; where the horrible kitinda, the man-eating crocodile, lies in sullen silence awaiting his prey; where swarm mosquitoes, those winged lances of the water tipped with death; where the thick-set sluggish puff-adder suns itself amid sand and broken rock, slow to retreat, quick to strike and fatal beyond remedy; where even more deadly cobras dart from their lurking-places to implant the tiny twin punctures, which no leech may heal, as if the love of destruction and death impelled the lithe, flexible creatures to their venomous attacks. More insidious, but no less dangerous, the tsetse fly lurks wherever grateful leafage overhangs moist or watered territory, and its bite, not so painful as that of many other insect pests, is followed by fever, rheumatic pangs, lassitude, meningitic spasms, coma and death. Much more annoying is the bite of the little mbwa midgets that hover and hum where the broken waters of Lake Victoria pour down into the fissure at the head of the Nile. So virulent is the poison injected by the mbwa, that within forty-eight hours it results in large and very painful swellings. To add to the traveller's discomfort the " rest-houses " and native buildings of Uganda are often infested by a tick, whose bite is followed by a violent and dangerous fever. I always made my camp at least two hundred yards from the rest-houses and the villages.

Ichthyol and vaseline intimately mixed and rubbed over all exposed skin surface seemed, in my own case, to discourage all insects from attempting to draw blood at my expense. The odour was not especially entrancing, but I was saved much suffering and danger, and, when I bathed, the mixture was easily removed, leaving the skin soft and free from sunburn. I had one narrow escape from a serpent which struck at me near the head of the Nile, but happily missed, and when it failed, glided swiftly into its hole in the rocks. It seemed to be a cobra, but may have been of a less dangerous species.

Birds and butterflies; great parrots, resplendent in scarlet over gray and white; white-crested, metallic-sheened hornbills; plantain-eating birds, in royal blue, and others in violet and crimson, with bright yellow beaks; plump, fluffy quails; gorgeous flamingoes; snowy uncouth pelicans; the solemn-looking whale-nosed stork; and a host of smaller, many-hued thrushes and woodpeckers, give life and beauty to the forest and the shore. Enormous moths and butterflies of the most exquisite colouring, with numberless smaller specimens, many lovely in hue and of great scarcity in modern collections, attract the naturalist, and afford the entomologist a splendid field of operations.

Uganda contains within her borders a great number of representative tribesmen. Ankole, on its southwestern boundary, is the home of the Bahima, a very peaceable people, not especially powerful, although their King, Kahaya, in 1904 measured six feet six and one-half inches in height, and weighed three hundred and one pounds. He was of the Muhima or dominant caste, which is taller than the Muiru or peasant class. Their women always go closely veiled, and even those who are Christianized keep up the custom. The bridegroom never sees the face of his intended until he has paid seven cows to her father, and takes his wife to her new home. They are a nation of herdsmen, and to the Muhima all food is prohibited except beef, veal, milk and its products. Even mutton, goat's flesh, sweet potatoes, beans, and most other vegetable food are tabooed. The dress of the men is not unlike the toga of antiquity.

The Banyoro (people of Unyoro) were in Stanley's time the warlike subjects of that Kabba Rega who was the Napoleon of his limited sphere and fell before the victorious arms of England in 1899. He was banished to the Seychelles, where one of his sons is being educated to better things than the father knew, while another rules Unyoro under British supervision. This people dress decently in bark, cloth or skin garments, and despise the naked Bari and other Nilotic savages. All children when growing are deprived of the six front teeth of the lower jaw, and even the King receives this tribal mutilation. I think the custom must have originated in the fear of lockjaw, blood-poisoning being frequent.

A Banyoro presents his prospective father-in-law with a cow, which, if accepted, is followed without any talk or explanation by the gift of four or five more, the selection of one of the girls and her departure for her new home. They are agriculturalists, make earthenware, baskets, canoes, iron knives, swords and spears, and dress skins and hides. They use the throwing and the stabbing spear and war club, and carry shields of wood and buffalo hide.

The people of Toro (Batoro) live east of the Ruwenzori range and south of Lake Albert Nyanza in a very fertile and healthy country, which is, however, of volcanic origin, and subject to earthquakes.

They are wiry, light-brown in colour and strongly attached to the new order of things. Their "King," Kasangama, has learned to speak English, owns a horse and a typewriter, and employs several Hindoo artisans to teach his people carpentry. In Toro marriage is very leisurely consummated, the usual term of engagement being two years after the suitor has paid the usual price (two cows) for the girl. During this time, the affianced pair are not allowed to meet at all, and if the man dies, his brother succeeds him, if eligible.

The ancient burial rites of the Toro kings called for the sending "alive into the pit" of his two youngest wives, and also two men. The grave was covered, housed and watched by men only.

The Banubuddu, on the northwestern coast of the Victoria Nyanza, have been largely absorbed by intermarriage with the Baganda. They were formerly agriculturalists, but were likewise keen, bold and successful hunters. With their long, Danish flintlock muskets, they wasted few shots at close range, and the reputation of a marksman, who had to shoot a second time, suffered even when hunting the elephant.

Mukasa, the great deity of the Ba-Sesse, or Sesse Islanders, only a few years ago dominated the navigation of the Victoria. Her fanatical followers on rafts and in canoes bearing blazing torches, and hideously howling, so frightened the sailors who mocked at her power, that in 1879, so a French record states, lake navigation was closed for three months, until King Mtesa sent one hundred slaves, one hundred women, one hundred cows and one hundred goats to her temple. Kitinda, the god of Damba Island, received none but human sacrifices, which, having been disabled, were left on the beach to be devoured by a huge crocodile.

The Bakoki, (people of Koki,) live southwest of the Kagera River. They are good marksmen, especially with the bow, with which the boys will rarely miss a mark the size of a plum at thirty to forty yards. They smelt iron, and make their own hoes, hatchets, spears, knives, and arrowheads.

Among the Bakoki the would-be bridegroom pays two cows to the father of the girl, and the happy parent then prepares a feast. The husband, with a few friends, all of whom must fast until the next day, brings home the bride who is also kept without food. The young couple are given a live goat, and a thousand cowries, which are taken to the husband's father-in-law. After this "pretty marriage" the bride sees no company for three months, except her husband's brothers and sisters, and these must always bring a present for the privilege. Theft is punished severely, sometimes with death; but to steal bananas for food is no crime.

Photograph by Peter Dutkewich, copyright, 1909, by Underwood & Underwood, N. Y

BUSOGA HUNTERS BELOW THE RIPON FALLS.

The Busoga, of Usoga on the right bank of the Nile at Ripon Falls, were always friendly to Europeans, and to-day it is the custom for the local chief to visit the traveller and bring him supplies of food.

The Ripon Falls lie between high hills, and, for thirty miles below them, rapids and rocks break the Nile into a treacherous, dangerous torrent. The river is infested with crocodiles, and, although hundreds have been shot by vengeful hunters, it is still extremely dangerous to be capsized in this part of the Nile.

A little village of fishermen's huts nestles just below the falls. The inhabitants living near the angry waters use the spear amid a tumult of cascade and spray, which makes it necessary to talk by signs and motions. The sleeping sickness, smallpox and other diseases have greatly desolated Usoga, and its population probably does not exceed ninety thousand people.

Family and social usages in Usoga are interesting and unique. As marriage is the foundation of even savage states, I always made inquiry into laws regarding it. In this primeval tribe the man goes to some dance, generally given in honour of a departed Busoga, and, having danced and feasted with his charmer, he elopes and brings his fair bride to his own house. This ends all ceremony, except that the brother of the bride visits them the next day, and is received by the brother or some other relative of the bridegroom, who makes him a present of a cow or whatever he can afford to give. This the girl's brother keeps until he gets married, and pays it over to the brother of some other girl.

Men already married carry away a second wife in the same way, and with like etiquette and payment, and sometimes a married woman is carried off, but this breach of custom is generally condoned as a "mistake," and atoned for by the payment of a cow.

The Bakongo people inhabit the slopes of Mount Ruwenzori, and are of fine physique, peaceable and industrious, coming into the Uganda provinces to find work. They file their front teeth to a point, work in iron, and dress very lightly, live on simple food, and buy their wives in much the same way as the Batoro. Their section is good hunting ground and the scenery is, of course, magnificent, although great clouds of mist sometimes veil the mountains for days.

The Baziba already mentioned, a strong, hardy race, industrious and good tempered, living in German East Africa, send thousands of young men to Entebbe and other parts of Uganda, seeking employment. Their splendid physique, intelligent faces and peculiar dress of long fibre fringes, make them marked characters in the rather cosmopolitan population of Uganda. They are probably the most moral people in the world. The birth of an illegitimate child seals the fate of both its parents, who are bound hand and foot and thrown into Lake Victoria, or buried alive in a quagmire. If the man is unknown, his paramour is put to death.

The Basukuma, of Usukuma, at the south end of Lake Nyanza, also come into British territory for work and to trade. They are said to number five hundred thousand. They are almost purely pastoral, and suffer much from an insufficient rainfall, both in loss of crops and cattle. The prospective bridegroom in this tribe must first give the girl's father a beautifully woven bead belt, which is really for the girl to wear, and then the dowry is fixed by her father and brothers. The first instalment of sixty sheep is paid and the man becomes the servant of the girl's father for two years in further payment. He builds a hut and his wife lives with him, after he has paid a sheep to the oldest woman in the village for good fortune to his house; another to the oldest man "because of his gray hairs;" a third to the principal bridesmaid, who arranges the bridal chamber, and a fourth to the bride's eldest sister.

The Manyuema or Manyema, who occupy the eastern part of the Congo Free State, are largely found among the Uganda provinces. They scar the face in patches, but apply a dark pigment which lessens the effect of the scar. The native dress for both sexes is the viramba, a belt of long grass tassels reaching from the waist to the knee, but they are very apt to copy the Swahili women in dress and ornament.

They are a race of cannibals, who, on the death of a relative, summon their blood kin from the next village by the beating of a drum. Four men come over with a bier on which the body is carried away to be roasted and eaten by affectionate relatives. Sometimes, but rarely, the remains are stewed instead of being roasted. Of course all enemies slain in battle are eaten, as Stanley and others found when white men first forced a way through their country.

The Lendu have a few villages in Uganda territory, and many of them may be seen at times about Entebbe; indeed, the Entebbe police and soldiers are largely composed of members of this tribe. In the country villages, the Lendu girls wear a belt of heavy fringe reaching about half way to the knees. A loose cloth after marriage is often used in which a baby may be carried. The husband often wears only a single goatskin, but clothing and ornaments are being rapidly introduced.

Karamojo, north of Mount Elgon, is not as yet officially administered, and really is but little

The Uganda Protectorate 313

known. The people are a tall, finely formed race much resembling the Masai, and like them rely on the spear and shield. The region abounds in large game. It is one of the few places where the elephant hunter may be quite certain of finding his noble quarry. The men are a race of fearless hunters, and it is said that one of them has a record of five lions and sixty elephants, killed with the spear alone and unaided.

The men wear spiral necklets, armlets and bracelets, and the women earrings, but no garments whatever.

The Acholi, Bari and Latuka in the Nile provinces are naked Nilotic negroes, living largely on porridge made of millet or sorghum seed, and the game and fish captured. All have suffered much in the past from the raids of slave traders and the Mahdist wars, but they are now gradually acquiring some ideas of decent garb and modern civilization. In another generation they will become at least a semi-civilized people.

I visited Bukedi late in the year 1908 in the company of Archdeacon Buckley of Jinja. He knows the country and the people better than any other white man living.

Bukedi and Lobor probably constitute at the present time the wildest and least known parts of the Uganda Protectorate. Bukedi is south of

Lobor, is thickly populated, and consists mainly of vast plains of rich grass and huge swamps bordering the rivers or choking up the lakes that serve as reservoirs and backwaters for the Victoria Nile. Bukedi is a Uganda word meaning "The Land of Naked People," and it has been found convenient to apply it to this district, inhabited by the Lango and Miro tribes, who differ little in appearance and scarcely at all in language from the Acholi of the Upper Nile. Bukedi is now under the administration of a Uganda chief and has been thoroughly subdued in connection with the rout and dispersal, by Major Delme Radcliffe, of the last remnants of the Sudanese mutineers, who took refuge here in 1897.

Kasunguru, the chief, received us. He is a very clever politician. Buckley, who is an Irishman, has made so deep an impression on the ruler of Bukedi that the latter had his wife arrayed in a green silk dress, greener than the greenest green of the dear old Emerald Isle. When I told Kasunguru that England was on one side of the Atlantic and America on the opposite side, he asked incredulously: "Where, then, is Ireland?"

We travelled southward, and everywhere the kindly missionary was received with heartiest good will by the primitive inhabitants. Food and drink were always placed before us wherever we stopped,

GOVERNOR BELL OF UGANDA AND TROPHIES OF THE CHASE.

The Uganda Protectorate 315

and the Bukedi towns turned out to honour the simple, devout priest who seemed to them to be a friendly visitant from some supernal realm.

A remarkable description of the life and conditions in the Eastern Province of Uganda was presented a few months ago in a report issued by the British Colonial Office at London. It was written by Sir H. Hesketh Bell, Governor of Uganda, whose literary ability is well known among English authors.

Describing Bukedi, he said that the country is densely populated by primitive and war-like tribes, who possess no political organization, and who for the most part are absolutely naked and unashamed.

The district was a revelation to him.

I quote from his report:

" Though I had heard already of the enormous density of the population, and of the remarkable pitch to which they had carried their cultivation of the land, my trip filled me with amazement.

" We travelled for four days through enchanting scenery, and traversed a country the like of which is, probably, not to be seen in any other part of Africa. The great green mass of Mount Elgon, fourteen thousand feet high, towers up into the clouds, and its mighty buttresses stretch far out into the surrounding plain. Between these spurs lie broad and gently sloping valleys, each with its swiftly-flowing stream of limpid water.

" But instead of the tangled luxuriance of wild tropical vegetation, which would usually characterize such a scene in mid-Africa, the eye was equally charmed by the sight of almost unparalleled cultivation. Dotted all about, in wondrous profusion, are the neat dome-shaped huts of the Bagishu, looking like immense hives, each one flanked by one or two smaller huts serving as granaries. So clearly and neatly marked are the boundaries of all the plots that the countryside reminded me of the vineyards of Switzerland or of Southern France, and the whole scene gave me an impression of calm security and peace.

" In this dense crowd of over four hundred thousand negroes, living in an area about the size of Yorkshire, there is barely a trace of organization of any kind. It is every man for himself, and in most cases, every man's hand against his neighbour.

" Not only do they eschew clothing of any sort, but they are addicted to cannibalism of a particularly revolting kind. They do not hunt and kill people for the sake of their flesh, but they consider that burial is a wanton waste of food. . . .

" The northern people take amusing precautions with regard to bachelors. All the lads and unmarried young men are made to sleep in small specially constructed huts raised high up on posts. The doors of these huts are so small that the occupants have to wriggle in on their bellies. Access is only gained by a ladder which is carefully removed as soon as the young men have been safely disposed of for the night.

"I was told that among some of the tribes, fine ashes are strewn under these human pigeon-cotes so that tell-tale footprints would indicate any attempt at a nocturnal excursion.

"The people are polygamous, and each man secures as many wives as he can purchase or capture."

In the south of Bukedi are those extraordinary marsh-lakes, Kwania, Kamoda, and Kioga. Lake Kioga receives the Victorian Nile after its descent down the rapids which follow the Ripon Falls. The current of the Nile forms a discernible channel up the western part of this winding lake, though the water is often blocked with sudd. There is a good deal of clear water in the south and central parts of the lake, but the banks are almost unapproachable, through the growth of papyrus and reed jungles.

Between Bukedi and Mount Elgon, the land, although occasionally swampy, has excellent soil; and a good proportion of it has been put under cultivation by the tall, naked tribe of the Elgumi.

In this country there are many ant-hills and it

CHAPTER XX

ENTEBBE THE ENGLISH CAPITAL

ENTEBBE is the English administrative capital of Uganda. The mud hotel we occupied was called the Equatorial, and if we straddled a certain line in it we would bestride the equator. But the town is four thousand feet above the sea and the cool breezes from Victoria lake make the place as delightful as Massachusetts in June. In the garden are oranges and lemons, great beds of feathery papyrus are waving to and fro, and palms can be seen everywhere. This is on the edge of Victoria Nyanza, and right in the heart of the continent.

In the native houses you must take care lest the lizards and scorpions fall on you from the thatched roofs. You must also tie your shoes tight, lest the jiggers get hold of you. You can see a black stripe moving down the path; it is an army of warrior-ants who will attack you if you get near and whose bites feel like red-hot pincers. Their heads will tear off before you can pull them from the aching flesh.

ENTEBBE.

Entebbe the English Capital

Though the lake was discovered about sixty years ago, much of the surrounding territory remains as yet undiscovered.

The equator goes right through the lake and about sixty miles south the German territory begins. This part of Africa belongs to Great Britain, and from here to the Mediterranean, including Uganda, the Sudan and Egypt, the whole country is under British control. Every foot on each side of the Nile is English from Victoria Nyanza at Ripon Falls four thousand miles to the Mediterranean. The country contains some of the richest lands upon earth. Egypt has never been so rich as since Britain took possession. The Sudan has vast territories equally fertile and Uganda at the Nile's source is in some respects the richest of all.

The English officials say that Uganda is the cream of the African continent. I believe they are right. In no other part can so many valuable crops be grown. In some places the natives grow grain with almost no cultivation, and in others coffee grows wild. There are tropical fruits everywhere. There are great possibilities in cotton, and wonderful prospects in stock-raising, which promise to make Uganda an important meat market.

This is a land of vast forests as well as of rich plains covered with grass. It is a land of rubber, and has immense resources in fibres for the making of paper, rope and cloth. A million or more of the natives use bark blankets as dresses, and there is a raffia fibre which shipped to England brings one hundred and fifty dollars a ton. The country can produce as good hemp as can be found in the Philippines, and china grass and sisal thrive as well.

The Protectorate is wealthy in minerals. Hematite ore is almost everywhere, copper has been found in the central part, and gold is said to have been discovered in some places. There are extensive deposits of white china clay of considerable value in some localities, and the natives themselves make pottery from it.

Uganda lies on the roof of Africa. At the lake's borders it is as high as the tops of the Alleghenies; and Mount Elgon rises one hundred feet higher than the top of Pike's Peak. To the east are Kilimanjaro and Kenia and to the west are the highlands of the Ruwenzori, which rival those of Kilimanjaro itself.

The kingdom is almost surrounded by water. On the south is Victoria, on the west Albert Edward and Albert Nyanza, joined by the Semliki, and further down is the Nile. On the east is Lake Rudolph, and throughout the whole country are beautiful little lakes, ponds, rivers and creeks.

The general nature of the country is rolling. Hills, hollows, swamps and undulating plains.

Entebbe the English Capital 323

The hills are covered with grass. The swamps are spotted with woods and the papyrus is always to be seen — the material of which the Egyptians made their paper.

As to size, it is larger than New England plus New York, Pennsylvania, New Jersey, Delaware, Maryland and Virginia. There are between four and five millions of inhabitants and considerably over three hundred thousand are said to be Christians. Such are the semi-civilized Baganda.

Five provinces comprise this territory — the kingdom of Uganda, the central province to the east, the western province between it and the lakes Albert Edward and Albert and the Rudolph and Nile provinces at the north.

The central province directly north of Victoria Nyanza is fertile in the extreme. It borders on the Kavirondo country and many of its people go naked. It is densely populated and the people raise cattle, sheep and goats. These also do much farming. A characteristic feature of the province is Mount Elgon, ranking as one of the highest peaks of the continent. It is an enormous volcano whose slopes are covered with forests and on whose tops are frequent snowstorms, — although almost on the equator. Among the curious features of the mountain are its caves, which have been inhabited by the cave-men for ages — as homes, and as stables for cattle, sheep and goats. The cattle caves are never cleaned — they swarm with fleas and the stench is intolerable.

The native chiefs are now cutting roads through this province; so that travelling is made comparatively easy.

Uganda province is traversed by roads made long ago by the natives and a bicycle can go over much of it. Many of the British officials own wheels and also the richest of the natives are now using them.

The poorest part of the Protectorate is to the north. Not far from Rudolph the country fades out into a desert, and the Nile province is somewhat like the Sudan. As to the Western province, it is high and healthy. It is broken table-land, about a mile above the sea, and contains high mountains. The country is well-watered and much of it is covered with a tropical forest, filled with monkeys and swarming with beautiful birds. The people as a rule are well-developed negroes devoted to stockraising. The horns of the cattle are so large they seem to be leading the beasts. Here also we saw the Pigmies, just like those Stanley describes in the Congo forests.

These western natives are not so advanced as those of Uganda proper. Many go about naked, and others have only aprons of cloth bark tied about their waists. The natives of this northern part ornament their bodies with scars — sometimes cutting their stomachs and breasts in a manner to resemble Persian shawls. Many of them file their teeth and they are generally rather low in African civilization.

Uganda has more than half as many people as there are in the Philippines; and some have been noted for ages for their warlike character. The English government keeps order with a few score of officials and about twenty-five hundred soldiers. The soldiers are almost all native blacks and most of them recruited from the country itself. There are a few East Indian Sikhs, but the army is mainly made up of the King's African Rifles, commanded by British generals, colonels and captains. This force consists of fifteen hundred blacks and in addition about one thousand native constabulary — a small army to control four millions of people. Nevertheless the country is kept in perfect quiet and there are law courts in all provinces. There is also a supreme court to which appeals may be made. The people pay their hut taxes. In some provinces there are schools, and they are altogether far better off than they have ever been before.

Entebbe contains the greater part of the white population, which consists of just four hundred souls, including eighty-three women. The men are principally British officials, — well educated young fellows, fond of sport and devoted to tennis and golf, which they play daily. The women are their wives and daughters — fine-looking English girls. They dress as well as they do at home and their clothing would not be found out of place anywhere.

Their houses are of sun-dried brick, roofed with galvanized iron. Few houses have more than one story, but they have large rooms and large verandahs. Many are surrounded by gardens filled with all sorts of tropical trees and plants. The houses are built far apart along one of the wide, red-dirt roads of Uganda. Some of the roads are lined with flowering trees, the most common being the cape lily, which bears a mass of blue flowers. Indeed there are so many flowers and plants that one seems to be going through a botanical garden as one walks along the streets.

The business part of the capital is given up to the East Indians. There are half a dozen stores, roofed with galvanized iron. Many of the merchants come from India; and the money is the Indian rupee, about thirty-three cents. The brown-skinned merchants wear little yellow skull caps, calico pantaloons and long coats, buttoned high to the neck. They have yellow-brown faces, dark eyes and black curly hair.

THE RESIDENCE OF GOVERNOR BELL.

Entebbe the English Capital

The government buildings are scattered over the hills. They are usually roofed with galvanized iron; but they have brick walls and wide porches. There are no native huts in the town proper and as a rule very few buildings thatched with straw. The police barracks form the one exception. These lie on the western edge of Entebbe and consist of rude Nuba houses, with cone-shaped roofs.

The hotel at Entebbe is about the only one in this part of Central Africa. In other places one has to have one's own tents or stop at the official house. It is made of mud and grass with walls twelve feet high — the roof beginning about a yard above them, leaving a space of about a yard for air. The main building of the hotel, about fifty feet square, contains a dining room, parlour and billiard room, with kitchens off at the side. The bedrooms are bungalow-like sheds made of mud and thatched with straw. They are at some distance from the hotel itself and run around the walls of the compound. The bedrooms are floored with mud, and each has a rush mat, made from papyrus reeds from the lake, running across it.

The beds themselves are a rude framework of wood to which are woven strips of antelope skins. On these, rush matting is laid and then a thin mattress of Uganda cotton. Every bed has its mosquito netting. This region is very malarious and so no one would think of sleeping here without such protection.

The hotel food is fairly good for Central Africa, although it would be poor anywhere else. The chief trouble is the cooking, which is universally bad. The fare is quite varied; for instance, at the last dinner, we had a soup, fish, fried brains, beef, potatoes and green peas. Our dessert was a slice of paw-paw, a delicious melon-like fruit, and the dinner ended with coffee. The hotel rate is three dollars and fifty cents a day, including room and board.

The British govern as far as possible through the native chiefs — each petty locality having its own methods of government — and the machinery is adapted to these systems. In Uganda proper the work is done through a native council and the little king or officers appointed to represent him. The council consists of twenty chiefs, each with his own district and court, and these counties are subdivided until there is a chief to perhaps each village of any size.

The chiefs receive money from the British government and in return they collect the taxes and turn them into the treasury. The taxes are assessed so much to each hut, — usually about a dollar a year. This seems low, but when it is considered that it takes a month of good hard work to make a dollar in Uganda it is rather high, after all.

The Baganda chiefs are very intelligent, and many of them can read, having learned in the mission schools. One has written a book and some are writing out the court proceedings on the typewriter — the Roman characters having been adapted to the needs of the language.

The scene at Entebbe in the brief twilight of the Equator is one of great serenity and beauty. I walked up past the English Governor's house and looked across the blue winsome waters of the Great Lake. From afar came the solemn sound of the Ngoma or drum, and the soft music of the Uganda harp. Hills shone resplendent in the distance; the lights of home began to twinkle in the Government house close by. Footpaths were seen through green fields; the hum of insects and the song of birds were heard in the luxurious hedgerows. In the gentle landscapes of Central Africa I could never see any of the horror or the mystery of which I had read in books. And I cannot but believe that advancing science will conquer easily the worst plagues of the country and make it the happy home of rejoicing millions.

CHAPTER XXI

KAMPALA THE HISTORIC CAPITAL

MADE the journey from Entebbe to Kampala, twenty-five miles, in a motor car. The car came out on the very ship that brought me from England to Zanzibar, and a young English engineer named Stanford, who was also on the vessel, was managing the car between the two Uganda capitals. For Kampala is the ancient capital of Uganda, and the English government, with its customary diplomacy, has established the European administration at Entebbe in order not to offend the native monarch or his court.

My companion at this stage of the journey was Professor Palazzo of the University of Rome. He was travelling among the tribes, studying their manners, laws, history and customs. We were carried across a splendid road on a fine English car, and as the professor and I were the only passengers, we were able to stop the car from time to time and make little excursions into the native villages. We passed through some lovely rolling country, and the remnants of an ancient forest.

The air was soft and gentle, like that of Connecticut in the early summer, and the scene was so home-like that I never dreamed I could be twelve thousand miles from Boston. The bark-clad women were working in the fields, and some of their number were engaged in road building. The men of Central Africa, thus far, have not learned the nobility of manual toil; but it is the persistent effort of the missionaries and the Government to teach the tribes that the men should work as well as the women.

When we were half way on our journey, I saw a group of women working on the road near a huge ant-hill. When I stopped the motor car and endeavoured to make a photograph they all ran away shrieking into the bushes. One of them in her dismay left a little child, and I noticed that there was a sore on the child's hand. Picking it up I rubbed the wound with ichthyol and vaseline. When the women saw that we were perfectly friendly they came out from their hiding places and stood around us looking on curiously whilst I bandaged the child's hand. Presently one of the women went back into the jungle but returned with another child, which also had some form of skin disease on its arm. In a few minutes the road was covered with natives, both men and women, bringing the sick and afflicted to be cured. When I had exhausted all the stock of medicine I had ready, I found that there were still many people desirous of being helped by the salve.

After this little episode the professor and myself were invited to make all the photographs we desired; and I quote the incident to show how easy it is to manage the natives of Central Africa, if one will only use a certain amount of diplomacy and kindness.

We arrived at Kampala, which is a city set on seven hills. We were kindly received by an Italian merchant, Mr. Parenti, a native of Milan, who is there representing a great New York firm, and is engaged in buying and exporting hides. In fact, it may interest Americans to know that our country buys eighty-five per cent. of the hides of Uganda, nearly a hundred per cent. of the first class ivory of Africa, and a large per cent. of the diamonds. Some wit has said that so important are the United States to Central Africa that when there were bank panics in this country the price of wives in far Uganda went down from ten dollars to three dollars a head.

Of the seven hills of Kampala there are four that stand out distinctly in my memory. The first is Namirembe Hill, where the Church of England

Kampala the Historic Capital 333

Missionary Society have built their famous cathedral, capable of containing five thousand worshippers. There is a splendid hospital in this mission managed by the two brothers, Doctors Cook. I visited the mission and had a delightful interview with one of the doctors. He informed me that his brother and he looked after no less than fifty thousand patients a year. They make a charge for each visit of three cowrie shells, which is about one-fifth of a cent. This charge is made to prevent the people applying who are not sick.

The work of the Church of England Mission was the direct result of a letter from Stanley in 1875, when the great explorer was being entertained at the court of the famous King of Uganda, Mtsesa. As a result of the work of the English missionaries since 1877, there are now one hundred and fifty thousand Christians in Uganda. There are fifty thousand native teachers; and the entire school system of a country of five million inhabitants, where three hundred thousand of them can read and write, is conducted by the missionaries of the Protestant and Catholic churches.

The second of the famous hills of Kampala is Nysambia, where is located the Mill Hill Mission of the Catholic Church. I visited the Mill Hill Mission, and was very courteously received by Bishop Hanlon and the fathers of the mission. In fact the welcome everywhere in Africa was warm and sincere. Most of the priests are Dutchmen and Frieslanders. They are doing a mighty work in the country between Kampala and the Rift Valley. The good Bishop informed me that there were eighty-six thousand Catholic Christians in his diocese, and the work goes on apace. The missionaries of both Catholic and Protestant churches are working in harmony and doing a noble service for humanity in Equatorial Africa. There are probably no less than five hundred thousand native Christians in Central Africa to-day.

The missionaries are teaching the dark-skinned natives the Brotherhood of Man and the Fatherhood of God. But they are no longer teaching these untutored minds that they are equal socially and politically to the Caucasians. They are quietly and determinedly putting the question of political equality in abeyance, and seeking by the kindly sunshine of Christian morals and precepts to advance the backward moral springtime of their less fortunate brother Africans.

At the Nysambia mission, there is labouring to-day a noble American woman, Mother Paul, who has a very efficient school of four hundred native girls. The girls are learning reading, writing, sewing, household duties and the finer sanctities of womanhood. There are several English sisters as-

CATHOLIC SCHOOL OF THE MILL HILL MISSION.

FATHER PRENTISS AT THE ALGERIAN MISSION.

sociated with Mother Paul in the high work of the redemption of the women of Uganda. In all my trip through Africa I saw nothing more touching, beautiful and bordering on the sublime than the heroic efforts of these White Nuns of the Nysambia mission.

The third historic hill of Kampala is Ngambya and here the French Algerian Fathers have a beautiful mission overlooking the Uganda country that rolls away towards the Congo in waves of voluptuous green. The Algerian Fathers work from Kampala to the borders of the Congo Free State. They told me they had about fifty thousand native Christians in their various missions. They are building schools for native preachers and sending out rivers of gladness into cruel heathen wastes. I lingered long about the missionary establishments of Kampala, because they typify to me the best that has been done in Darkest Africa.

The missionary converts are sometimes criticized by the merchants as being lazy and intractable. Of course a change from rudest barbarism to ripest civilization must confuse many of the moral concepts; but the really fine examples of converted pagans stay at the missions, while the lazy and unpromising ones, although they know English, are often useless to the pioneers. The worst ones of all are those who work for the merchants.

The Mohammedans have been fanatical and profoundly in earnest in Africa. Their polygamous customs and their sensuous heaven appeal strongly to the primitive races. In fact, there are well-informed men who say that the Mohammedan religion must finally conquer Africa, and that Christianity is making hardly any headway compared to the oceanic length and breadth of the wave of Islam teaching. I think there is reason in this statement and that at the present time the Mohammedan religion suits the African better than the Christian. I saw in the Mohammedan missions much to admire; but I am convinced that the finer, clearer and superior tenets of the Christian faith will in the end make a complete conquest of the country.

The fourth of Kampala's hills is called Mengo. This is the home of the young King and some of his leading councillors. A few days after I arrived in Kampala, and while I was at the mission on Nysambia Hill, a Uganda boy handed me the following letter:

"KAMPALA, UGANDA, August 20, 1908.

"DEAR MR. MACQUEEN: The King of Uganda will receive us at 3.30 this afternoon. If you will return here at once we can go together to the Palace.

"LUIGI PALAZZO,
"Professor of Meteorology, University of Rome."

Kampala the Historic Capital

Accordingly I took a 'rickshaw and proceeded at once with the Professor to visit the young King, Dauda Chwa, or David I. The ride up to Mengo Hill is a very impressive one. The whole town is buried under the leaves of innumerable plantations which give food and shelter to the people. When our 'rickshaws reached the hill-top, we stopped, and passed through a pavilion, beautifully constructed of stout elephant grass, like thin polished canes, woven together with curious art. Crossing a court, and attended by native soldiers, we entered a second pavilion where we met the young king. Dauda Chwa, the Kabaka, or King, of Uganda, is a graceful, distinguished looking lad, twelve years old. He was simply dressed in a flowing black robe with a little white gold-rimmed hat. Beside him were his English teacher, Professor Sturrock, and Sir Apolo Kagwar, Prime Minister, a powerful, determined-looking man, who wore a crimson, gold-laced robe on which shone many decorations. The little Kabaka sat in his Chair of State and talked to us in English. He was greatly interested in America, and in the coming visit of ex-President Roosevelt. He showed me a map of Uganda he had himself drawn; and upon it he had marked the places where the best elephants could be shot. He seemed a little shy at first, but this shyness gradually wore off. He had a plaintive, sweet voice, and usually expressed his interest or admiration by saying in a boyish treble — "Oh, yes!"

The Kabaka gave us a reception in his own house. It is a comfortable building, quite small and modest, but nicely furnished and adorned with pictures, among which I noticed portraits of Queen Victoria and King Edward. The boy-king of Uganda can write very well in English. He rides a good pony and will no doubt become a refined, well-educated, and accomplished ruler. He is already a member of the Christian Church. He was a bright and pleasing figure to find in the centre of Africa, amid so much squalor and violence; like a little root of roses growing undefiled amid the wreckage of a battle field.

It is only yesterday that the grandfather of this boy, Dauda Chwa, the great Mtsesa, was marking his reign with savage massacres. King Mtsesa, descended from many war-like and cruel ancestors, ruled absolutely over the lives and properties of his subjects. The Baganda are the Japanese of Africa and, before Cameron or Stanley made them known to the world, they far excelled the surrounding tribes in cleanliness, neatness and decency, in sanitary living and comfortable dwellings. Nevertheless the people were in the bond of a most galling tyranny.

King Mtsesa, when the white men saw him first,

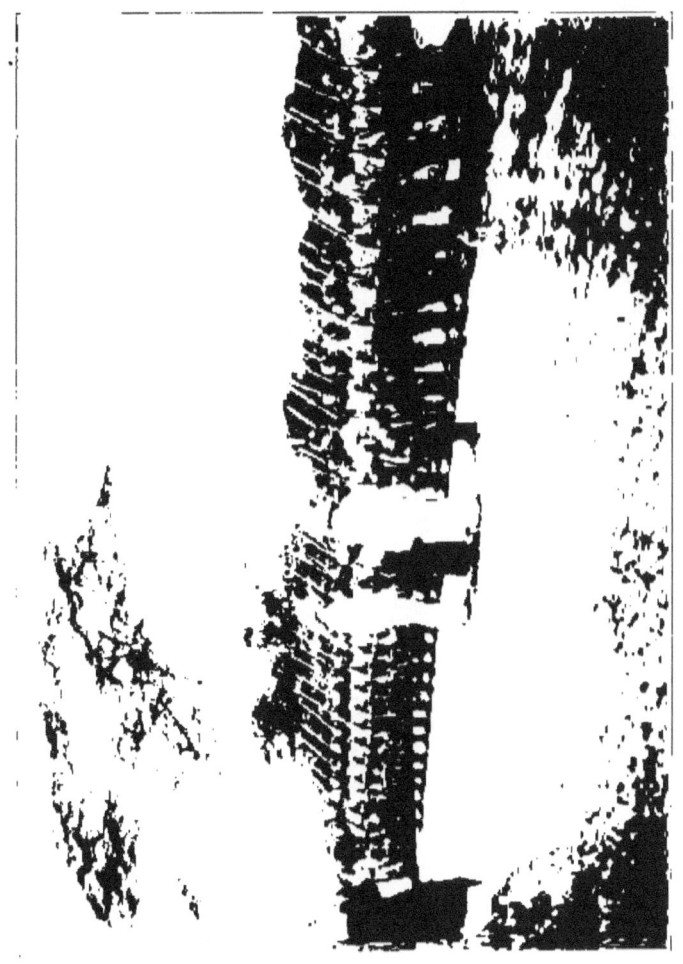

DAUDA CHWA, KING OF UGANDA, REVIEWING HIS TROOPS.

Kampala the Historic Capital 339

had conquered nearly every tribe on the West Coast of Victoria Nyanza. He had a method of advancing his empire very much resembling that of Ancient Rome. The conquered tribes were amalgamated with the ruling race. Each chief came to the king's court, and gave to the king one of his daughters to wife. All the children of the daughters of the chiefs were brought up at the court.

When a king died, and the time came to appoint his successor, all the children but two were ruthlessly put to death. The reason for preserving two alive was that one might be retained for the throne in case the successful candidate died.

The executions which attended the first audiences given the white men by Mtsesa; the massacre of thousands of men and women to appease his " ancestral spirits " or allay his fears of too powerful subordinates; and the murder of men and women for petty offences, blackened the memory of a ruler who did much for his people.

King Mtsesa welcomed to his dominions all men who came to tell him of a purer faith and better things for himself and his people. He also set aside the burial rites of his kingly ancestors. Until his own burial, every dead king of Uganda had been swathed in bark cloth by his successor and borne by the Court Executioner and the Keeper of the Tombs of the Kings to Emerara in the Country of

Busiro, where thirty-seven such tombs are still preserved.

The under jaw was removed and the mutilated body placed on a wooden bier or bedstead in a conical structure whose thatched roof reached to the ground. Its door once closed was never again opened.

Then the Court Executioner seized the King's Chief Cook and the Chief Herdsman, with three women of corresponding rank, and, slaying them, left the bodies before the royal tomb to be consumed by vultures. The King's jaw, cleansed and ornamented with cowrie shells, was placed in one of several new huts within an enclosure near the tomb, and the chief who built them became the life guardian of this relic of the dead ruler. Another chief and the King's wives were set to keep watch over the tomb, living in a hut nearby until all died.

Mtsesa, in defiance of all the traditions of his race and line, ordered all the remains and jawbones of his dead ancestors to be collected and buried, and directed that he himself should be decently interred in a simple grave with a few of his best spears planted about it in the form of a palisade, over which his wives should keep guard during the rest of their lives. His body was not to be mutilated, nor was anyone to be slaughtered as formerly.

A large structure built over his grave forms the

Kampala the Historic Capital

tomb of Mtsesa, the floor of which is carpeted with fine grass, laid down evenly blade by blade. Visitors are frequently admitted, and Mtsesa's wives carefully replace every blade displaced by their feet. The shrines of his ancestors, some of which are centuries old, however, ancient and dilapidated, are still watched over by devoted attendants.

These remains of a barbaric past contrast with brighter conditions existing in Uganda to-day, for, when Mwanga succeeded to the throne, he brought with him many of the superstitions and vices of his father. These, with the religious dissensions arising from the fanaticism of the Mohammedans, gave rise to civil wars and revolutions. As a result, the wars, in which Mwanga was by turns victorious and defeated, continued until the British Government took charge of the country and banished Mwanga to the Seychelles Islands, where, surrounded by his family, he lived until his decease in 1903. Dauda Chwa, Mwanga's son, was made King under a regency.

I have already spoken of the twenty-five mile road which reaches from Entebbe to Kampala, the native capital of Uganda. This, in itself, is a fine example of perfect road-making, but another road from Kampala to Lake Albert Nyanza is a magnificent sample of what has been achieved by the government and people of Uganda. A 'rickshaw or automobile may traverse the whole distance, two hundred miles, with much more ease than on the same length of road in any rural district of the United States. This has made possible the easy transportation of commodities between the different tribes composing the people of the Protectorate.

The natives of Uganda, in co-operation with the Imperial Government, have established a confederation of the Nile, Rudolph, Western and Central, Uganda and Kisumu provinces.

The territory is also divided into twenty counties, each presided over by a county chief, and is ruled by the Kabaka as we have seen. The second brother of the present King was not sacrificed. The English Government would not tolerate such cruelty. Moreover the Baganda themselves are ashamed of the barbarism of the past. This boy is about the same age as Dauda Chwa and lives on terms of intimacy and friendship with him. The King is under the guardianship of three regents. His income is four thousand dollars a year; and when of age (at eighteen years), he will have a salary of seven thousand five hundred dollars. The Lukiko, or native Parliament, consists of three regents drawing two thousand dollars each annually; twenty County Chiefs, paid a thousand dollars each annually; sixty Notables, three from each county, selected by the King, subject to the veto of

Kampala the Historic Capital

the Imperial Government; and six Persons of Importance, also selected by the King, subject to veto. The King's successor in case of death is to be chosen, by vote of the Parliament, from among the heads of the royal family, with the consent of the Imperial Government.

The Kabaka of Uganda is called "His Highness," and entitled to a salute of only nine guns, in strong contrast to the state and honour of Mtsesa, whose every act of importance was heralded by great military display, an extravagant burning of gunpowder, and very often by the sacrifice of many human lives. Polygamy has been largely done away with, and the practical selling of women as wives, almost universal amongst the tribes of Uganda, has been modified by an act of the Parliament to payment to the father, where the parties are willing to contract, of thirteen shillings and four pence sterling or about three dollars and thirty-seven cents. This amount may be slightly exceeded by a chief or person of consequence. As a result, the choice of the parties, and especially of the women, is consulted largely nowadays, whereas formerly it was simply a matter of bargain and sale, to which the women were supposed to submit without question.

Professor Palazzo and I made many journeys from Kampala into the interior of Uganda. We visited Mtsesa's tomb and the missions as well as the Royal Palace. The Professor, a very learned and erudite man, was of the opinion that this remarkable nation had many traits of the ancient Egyptians. I noticed features among them that strongly recalled the old sculptured faces I had seen at Cairo in the museum. It is impossible for me to believe that a nation great enough to build the Pyramids would live five thousand years beside the Nile and never find its source. I think therefore that the Baganda are a race of lost Egyptians who have mingled with Bantu tribes and in the course of many generations have become assimilated to the negroid race.

CHAPTER XXII

THE DEVELOPMENT OF UGANDA

WHEN the people of Uganda and of the Sesse Islands first came in contact with the white race they were undoubtedly the most advanced of all the tribes of Africa. Nevertheless, in their country were to be found some of the most cruel and detestable customs that have cursed humanity in its ascent from beasthood.

For example: When Christianity first spread among the people of the Sesse Islands nothing was so strongly resented by them as the burial of the dead. The British Government found it necessary to keep armed guards over newly made graves for six or eight days after the burial. In 1899, a French priest labouring alone among the Basesse died suddenly; and an associate was sent to bury him. He was told by the natives that the priest was already buried, but they refused to point out the place of sepulture, which remains unknown to this day. It is supposed, in plain words, that the missionary was eaten by the natives.

While I was on the shores of Victoria Nyanza last year, I knew of several people who died. But I could not find, after the most careful search, where their remains had been buried. There is no doubt but that even at this day a cult of man-eaters exists all through Central Africa, and, though they do not put to death their fellow men to feast upon them, they assuredly eat the bodies of the dead. I found traces of this decadent cannibalism from Zanzibar to the Nile.

British authority and the modern laws of Uganda, together with the obloquy and detestation now encountered by the supposed members of this horrible cult, have restricted its operations to out-of-the-way villages and the small islets of this beautiful archipelago.

The islanders raise crops of bananas, beans, potatoes, wild coffee, maize and tobacco, and many fowls. There are no carnivorous pests, and the hippopotamus and crocodile are the only dangerous beasts. The Basesse go decently dressed, even the women wearing ample robes of bark cloth, which, however, generally leave the bust and shoulders uncovered.

The scenery among the Sesse Islands is remarkably beautiful when viewed from the steamer's deck and, when seen from an eminence like Mount Bagola, presents a vista of blue water, reflecting

The Development of Uganda 347

bold headlands, shaded creeks and lagoons and wooded islets, stretching away in almost limitless variety to the horizon and gradually softened and attenuated by the glories of dawn, the splendours of the setting sun or the soft haze which, even in the hottest tropical day, gives a magical charm to distant scenery.

The people of Uganda as a rule seem to live very happily. They are always laughing and smiling, and the men and women go about hand in hand. They have good homes; they live in villages where every hut has its garden, growing bananas, sweet potatoes, and other vegetables.

The houses are of different sizes. Those of the chiefs are quite large and are elaborately made. Those of the ordinary people are made of reeds with thatched roofs, the latter being upheld by poles. Even the poorest house has two apartments, one at the front and the other at the rear. The rear apartment has bunks around the wall upon which the people sleep.

Such huts have but little furniture: two or three stools, a half dozen earthenware pots, and some wicker or grass basins constitute a complete outfit.

As to food, the chief staple is the banana. There are many varieties of these in Uganda, and they are more important to that country than wheat and corn are to ours. The banana, which serves as the chief food, is much longer than any that come into our markets. It is a sort of plantain. It is sometimes made into Pembe, a delicious cider. It is eaten green, the fruit being first peeled and then cooked with a little water in an earthenware pot. After it steams some time the flesh softens and soon becomes a solid mass of mush. When done it is taken off the fire and turned out upon some fresh banana leaves. These serve as a tablecloth.

The family now gathers around and gets ready for the meal. Each first washes his hands and gives them a shake to get off the superfluous water. The father then takes a knife and divides the pile of banana pulp into as many divisions as there are members at the board. In the meantime a bowl of soup or fish gravy has been placed inside the ring. This is used in common.

In the fields grow Indian corn, peas, beans and sweet potatoes. Chickens, sheep and goats are raised. The people do not seem fond of eggs, and the women are not allowed to eat them after they are married. They are not permitted to eat chicken or mutton, such viands being reserved for the men of the family. They may, however, eat beef or veal. The eating of chickens is supposed to render the women barren. The Baganda, however, are beginning to laugh at such superstition and everybody will soon be eating chickens.

The Development of Uganda 349

The Baganda also have fish from Lake Victoria and from their numerous streams. They eat locusts, and are especially fond of white ants. The ants are caught by smoking their hills about nightfall and trapping them as they come out. They are eaten both raw and cooked.

Now in Uganda the farmers are growing sugar cane. They are growing tomatoes and a green vegetable much like spinach. I saw little fields of tobacco here and there. The soil is as red as that of Cuba, and the plants grow without much cultivation. The tobacco is used for smoking, and is consumed by both men and women. They gather coffee from the wild trees and chew the pulp, but so far have not learned to use it as a drink.

Since the British have taken possession of Uganda they have introduced many kinds of foods which are becoming popular, and they are gradually creating a market for the white man's goods. Some of the natives are using tea, and jams and biscuits are gradually coming into demand. This is, of course, among the wealthier people, and especially among the chiefs, who buy these things to serve at their teas or dinner parties.

Another article which is becoming common is the umbrella. Both women and men use it, and I often saw a crowd of a dozen or more of well-to-do natives going along with umbrellas in their hands.

All through the heart of Africa the people want to wear the white man's clothes and to eat his food.

Within the past few years the missionaries have taught many of the Baganda to write and a demand for writing paper has been created. The people want cotton goods, and they especially like our American sheeting.

Little stores are now springing up in the more highly populated centres, and there are a score of such establishments between Entebbe and Kampala.

Indeed, the British are making a new nation of the Baganda. Only a few years ago the whole nation was warring with its neighbours and enslaving the weaker tribes. Mtsesa had a large army and his predecessors had many wars. Justice was then practically unknown and human life was of no account. The people had no incentive to work. They lived upon the bananas which they grew in their gardens; they made their clothes from the bark of the fig tree and their houses came from the cane of the swamps.

To some extent such conditions still prevail, but the people each year want bigger houses and better homes. They are beginning to use kerosene, and the huts of the chiefs are lighted by lamps. Some even have little patches of carpet, and a few are beginning to use modern furniture. Shoes and

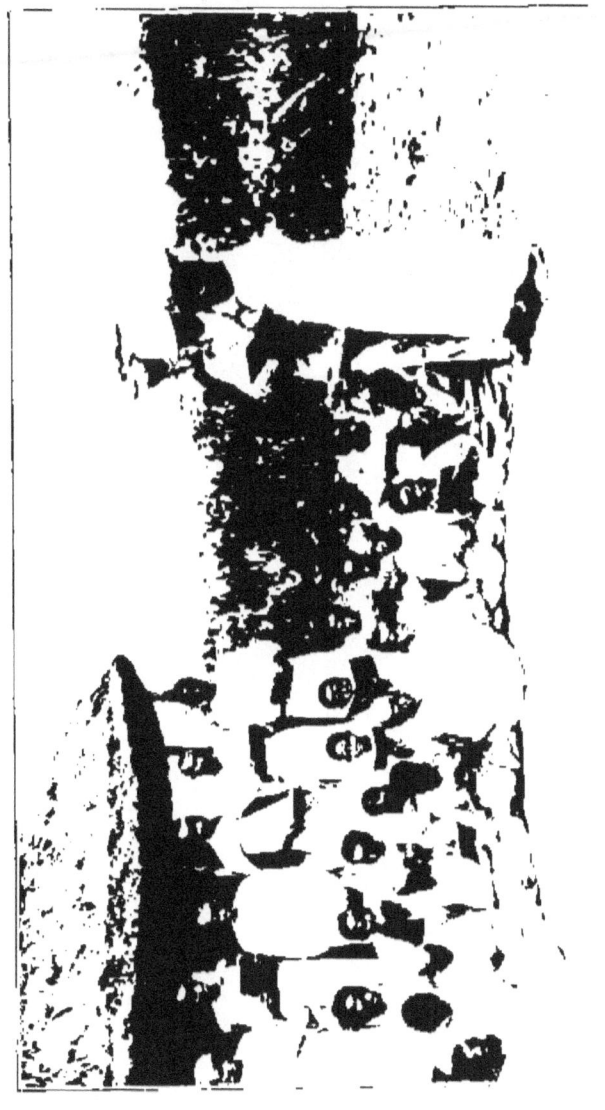

stockings are beginning to be worn, and the desire for all foreign things is becoming an incentive to work. So far the advance has been slow and the low wages, amounting to only four or five cents a day, are not particularly favourable. As time goes on this condition will change, and in a generation more there will be a fine, self-supporting semi-civilized nation at the head of the Nile.

It has been the Government's policy to grant but few concessions for the exploitation of Uganda. The lands are held by the natives and also by the British Government. Some of the chiefs own large tracts. The native Prime Minister, for example, has about a hundred square miles of land. He owns a thousand head of cattle, and his income is over five thousand dollars a year. Other chiefs have smaller tracts, and the King himself has a considerable property.

All forests over two miles square are supposed to belong to the British Crown. The timber is especially valuable, and the rubber possibilities are untold.

At present the British authorities are planting rubber trees along the principal roads. There are such all the way from Kampala to Entebbe. The trees are carefully set out and are guarded by fences of wicker work or cane. Those who labour on the roads cultivate these trees and they are now growing luxuriantly. They will probably yield a considerable revenue to the government within a very few years.

The Baganda are called the " prudes " of Africa. Their bark clothing is made in great sheets the size of a bed quilt, and it is wrapped about the body, extending in the case of the men from the neck to the feet, and in the case of the women from the arm-pits to the ankles.

The Baganda men are seen dressed in cotton. The bark cloth does not resist the rain so well as cotton. The men come more in contact with Europeans and hence adopt civilized clothing quicker than their wives.

The women do not seem to regard the exposure of their persons above the waist as indecent, although they are usually clad from armpits to ankles. I am told that many of them take off their clothes when dining inside the house, in order to keep from soiling them.

It was quite naive, the manner in which the Uganda girls wore their terra cotta sheets. The bark cloth was wrapped tightly about their bodies, leaving their plump arms and shoulders bare. It was often tied in at the waist with a bark cloth sash and gathered up at the front so that a great fold hung over and fell half way down to the knees. It gave forth a swishy rustle as the women moved, and they seem to delight in this noise as our girls delight in the swish of their silk petticoats.

The tree from which bark cloth is made is a species of the fig-tree. The bark is cut in such a way that it comes off in sheets. If it is properly stripped from the tree another coat will grow.

The bark comes off in strips from six to ten feet long and as wide as the circumference of the tree. These strips are soaked for a time in water, until they become damp and soft. They are then spread out on skin mats and hammered with mallets. This makes them thinner and broader.

The finished cloth is composed of many fibres which cross each other like the woof and warp of a web; and when it is dried it seems like a sheet of real woven fibre. It can then be sewn together into blankets and used as clothing.

Since the country has been opened to Europeans many of the richer natives have begun to wear cotton, and, interesting to note, they prefer American goods to any other. These goods have long gone by the name of "Americani." Both men and women wear long gowns like the Arab burnouses, so that any large crowd forms a mixture of whites and tans. The whites are the American cottons and the tans are the bark cloths.

As I went about in the towns and villages I noticed that the people are well-made. They are shorter than the average Caucasian, the men being not more than five feet four or five inches tall, and the women still less. Every one holds his head up and throws back his shoulders. This may come from the hilly nature of the country and from the fact that the people do much walking up and down hill. The younger women have beautiful necks and arms. Many of them are like ebony statues, and almost every girl has a form that would be coveted by their white sisters across the sea.

The land already begins to hum with industry. On the road to Jinja I passed hundreds of men and women carrying loads. The men went along on the trot with firewood, bunches of bananas, and bales of hides balanced on cushions of leaves upon their heads. Women carried gourds of water upon their crowns, so carefully poised that the water did not spill, although the gourds were untouched by their hands. Now and then we passed a girl going along the road with a glass bottle balanced in the same way.

All the highways of the country are kept by the natives, under the direction of their chiefs. Back of the chiefs are the British officials, who work through them. Every person in the country, male and female, is subject to one month's work during the year, as a road tax. Each chief is responsible for the roads of his territory, and he calls upon

The Development of Uganda 355

every householder for the requisite amount of labour.

The householder, as a rule, sees that the most of the work is done by the women. Everywhere there were girls down on their knees pulling out weeds, or bending over and smoothing the roadbed with short-handled hoes. In a few places men were at work, but, as a rule, the hard labour was done by bare-shouldered and bare-footed females clad in bark.

Uganda has some of the best cotton soil in the world, and it is as big as Alabama, Louisiana, Mississippi, South Carolina and Georgia combined. Several years ago the British began to experiment with cotton and there are now thousands of little plantations all over Uganda — the seed having been distributed to the chiefs. I have walked through cotton fields where the plants were higher than my head.

The amount of seed first used was one thousand pounds and the product last year from this was two million pounds, and the output of the current year will be five million pounds of seed cotton.

This cotton movement is being engineered by the Uganda Company, Limited. It is an association of British capitalists and they have active, up-to-date men there in their employ. They are putting up a big ginning plant at Kampala with modern machinery. Twenty-four gins are already running, operated by steam engines, one of a hundred horsepower. Last year Uganda and Egypt sent into the markets of the world an amount of cotton equal to one per cent. of the entire output of the United States.

The cotton of Uganda is said to be equal to any upland cotton that we can produce. The company is installing hydraulic baling presses and other machinery. It has purchased a location at Ripon Falls at the head of Napoleon Gulf, where the Nile flows out of Lake Victoria. The falls will furnish a big electric power and it is the intention to build ginning mills and factories there which will be run by Nile power. The farmers are paid for cotton in the seed only two cents a pound. The pay is considered too small and a raise in the price will be necessary to make the people work.

The native farmers, of course, have no idea of intensive cultivation. All the cotton thus far grown has been from American seed, the wild cotton having too coarse a fibre. Egyptian cotton has been tried, but has not proved as suitable for the climate and soil as the American upland. The Government itself is aiding the movement by distributing seeds. It has also put up hand gins in different parts of the country and baling presses for public use.

There are fibres in Africa which may later be

A FOREST OF UGANDA.

The Development of Uganda 357

made into silk as fine as that of the silk-worm. An official at Kampala stated that he had seen these fibres growing wild and they reach a height of five or six feet. The bolls look like cotton but are far more soft, fleecy and glossy. This may produce a revolution in the trade of the world later on.

Regarding the forests — they are magnificent. As my boys pulled my 'rickshaw from Kampala to Jinja, I often saw mahogany trees a hundred and fifty feet high, and four and five feet in diameter. They are perfectly straight, running up to a great distance without a branch. We passed, on the way, a species of wood resembling teak, and a hard wood that almost resists the blows of an axe.

There are rubber vines and rubber trees; some of the latter were a hundred feet high and of large girth. Expert rubber gatherers have been brought from Ceylon to show the Baganda how to tap the trees properly. I passed a very fine rubber concession about sixteen miles from Ripon Falls. Uganda, like Congo, will soon supply the rubber tires for the motor-cars of the millionaires of America, and the nabobs of Europe.

Uganda, governed by England, has within herself the seeds of a great empire and increasing wealth; schools, churches, hospitals, courts, libraries, public gardens, rubber-trees, cottons, spices, fruits and valuable trees, — all this and more.

Here a handful of masterful Englishmen have taken up "the white man's burden" and borne it under stress unutterable — when mutiny and massacre threatened, surrounded by innumerable savages in the heart of a wild continent; when multitudes were dying around them of the terrible and incurable "sleeping sickness;" when the bubonic plague, brought by some sordid ignorant coolie out of the poisonous East, crept like a serpent into the heart of Africa, and began to reap where the smallpox and fever had gathered victims; and when drought and blight cut off the only sources of food supply, and men, women and children died by thousands before relief could come.

And those Englishmen, though stern and severe, when necessary, are just and law-abiding in their dealing with the helpless aborigines. No one may strike a native except he be punished by a verdict of a court, and this punishment must not be brutal or excessive. It is a joy to know such men — doughty fighters, hearty, genial hosts, mighty hunters before the Lord, who, for the honour of the English name and flag, and the desire of doing the work given them to do well and faithfully, bear exile in a savage land bravely and cheerily to the end.

Uganda herself has myriads of men, savage men, if you will, who in form and stature, if not in features, recall the sculptured manhood of Phidias and Praxiteles in the golden days of Grecian art. For here, sooner or later, drift representatives of every race, and every hybrid, that peoples Africa from the lower Congo to the Indian sea. From Congo, and from other colonies where white men sometimes take too many privileges with the Kiboko whip, the natives come to English territory, willing to do hard work, where no man uses them cruelly or dares to do them wrong.

One sees also chiefs, decorated for loyalty in rebellion and gallantry in action, draped in " Americani," with wives and children who no longer fear that the caprice of a despot will loose upon them the spears of his legions, or the greed of some rival court. They meet in council now to debate and legislate for the good of the common people, and, if the chief has some privileges above his poorer neighbour, it comes from the hand of the administration in a moderate salary or a permission to be a little more liberal in giving away his substance.

I heard much of the noble charities of last summer, when the bananas were blighted and the rice was blasted by the drought. The truth was not known in due season until hunger had so done its work that, first and last, four thousand men, women and children died of hunger or the weakness which no relief could repair. One learns with pride of how Catholic prelate and Protestant priest heroically fed the multitude with that temporal bread which alone could preserve the body alive to profit by the spiritual teachings of those Christian co-labourers.

When you see such an evolution in so short a space of time; of despotic caprice supplanted by just laws, and grovelling bestiality replaced by brotherly love, " it makes you think better of you and your race and the work that they have to do."

FAMINE SUFFERERS IN UGANDA, RELIEVED BY BISHOP HANLON AND ARCHDEACON BUCKLEY.

CHAPTER XXIII

SLEEPING SICKNESS IN UGANDA

MR. PARENTI very kindly procured for me a jinrickshaw and four stout Uganda boys, and I left my friend, Professor Palazzo, at Kampala, and proceeded by 'rickshaw to Jinja, at the fountains of the Nile. About twenty miles on the way lies the hospital of Kyetume, where I was told there were seven hundred patients suffering from sleeping sickness. I decided to stop over night at the hospital.

The boys went cheerily singing over the road. We ran into a terrific thunderstorm characteristic of Uganda; but before night we reached the hospital, where I was most hospitably received by Dr. Claude Marshall, who was then in charge.

Sleeping sickness came into Uganda about four years ago. It is caused by the bite of the tsetse fly, which was brought from the Congo by the caravans passing through with ivory to the coast. In four years two hundred and fifty thousand of the most promising natives of Africa have died from the terrible disease. No man who has had an attack of sleeping sickness has ever yet authentically recovered. The appearance of such a malady, in a colony governed by the most progressive white men of Europe, has spread a thrill of horror through civilization.

When the sun came out after the heavy rain and my bronze human steeds trotted into the gardens of the English Hospital, I was again impressed, as I had often been before, with the homelikeness of the surrounding country. It was an hour before dark and the birds were out among the tree-tops, singing as sweetly as they do in England or in Maine. The bird-notes seemed familiar and the scent of shrubs and flowers was delicious.

The young doctor, like most of England's picked men, was an absolute gentleman and a perfect sportsman. After he had regaled me with the best his table afforded, he brought out two guns, summoned a couple of gun-bearers, and we started for a tramp out in the bewildering woods. We came across many of the tracks of wild buffalo and saw the flash of glorious pinions among the leafy branches. The doctor brought down a few plantain-eaters and we ran across an antelope and bagged it for the pot. I never cared much for the hunt, because I do not want to be happy through the misery of some innocent thing.

This is not said in criticism of other men, who with kind, tender hearts are often fond of the excitement of the chase.

We returned in the lucent light that precedes the darkness on the Equator. The doctor had many interesting stories to tell me of hunting and colonizing in the heart of Africa. He invited me to remain a week at the hospital, which I was very willing to do because I wanted to study from the doctor's knowledge the ravages of sleeping sickness.

The hospital is laid out among beautiful gardens, on a hill overlooking a splendid agricultural section. Most of the patients are treated in a village which the English Government has established. Those who are not seriously ill are kept in the village until the disease has made considerable progress. After that they are brought into the general buildings of the hospital itself. The disease will kill a man in any space of time, running from two days to two years. No authentic cure of the disease has yet been found.

Great Britain is making gigantic efforts to thwart the power of this dreadful foe. Already she has under the care of skilled physicians no less than twenty thousand patients. The people living along the shores of Lake Victoria Nyanza have been removed back into the country several miles, and every possible attempt has been made to exterminate the tsetse fly. The most successful attempt yet made has been the planting of a certain shrub in the marshes where the fly lives. The shrub is certain death to the tsetse fly.

The area infected by the sleeping sickness thus far has been confined to the islands in the northwest of Lake Victoria Nyanza, and the shoreland from Entebbe to Jinja, a distance of about ninety miles. But the fear is that the disease will spread through all the provinces of the Upper Nile; and at the present rate of decrease in population it is estimated that in twenty-five years the entire population of Uganda will have disappeared. It might also spread to the Sudan, Rhodesia and Portuguese Africa and decimate half the continent.

The tsetse fly, whose scientific name is *glossina palpalis*, breeds in moist and swampy land. Scientists believe that it gets some of its virus from the body of the crocodile. Dr. Koch declares that it also feeds on the bodies of water fowl frequenting swamps. If it bites a person after it has imbibed this virus, or after it has bitten a human being infected with the sleeping sickness, that person is almost certain to develop the fatal malady.

On the island of Buvuma it was estimated four years ago that there were twenty thousand healthy people; to-day I am told there are less than twenty individuals. In the Sesse Islands of a population of thirty thousand four years ago, only twelve thousand remain to-day. These are examples of the devastation of this gruesome pest. Alongside of its blighting power, the wasting grasshopper and the eating caterpillar are as motes in a sunbeam. It cuts down human generations as the reaper mows the grain. In front of it are myriads of healthy, happy human beings; in its wake is a universal charnel house; and the griding of its terrible wings are as the beating pinions of death.

The British authorities have established six great hospitals or stations in Uganda for the treatment of sleeping sickness. They contain nearly twenty thousand patients and are located as follows: (1) Sesse Island; (2) Kyetume, near Kampala; (3) Busu in Usoga; (4) Bulumasi; (5) Island of Buvuma; (6) Entebbe. The treatment followed in these hospitals is an injection of atoxyl, composed of arsenic, anyline and carbolic acid, discovered by Dr. Koch, the famous German specialist on tuberculosis.

During 1908, in his official report to the Minister of the Interior with regard to the progress made by the German expedition sent to East Africa to investigate the sleeping sickness, Professor Koch announced that he had discovered a specific against sleeping sickness similar to that which the doctors already possess against malaria in quinine. The remedy, which is a preparation of arsenic, is called atoxyl, and destroys the trypanosomes, the germs of the disease.

Professor Koch's close inspection of the habits of the *glossina palpalis* insect, which British investigations had already proved to be a disseminator of the disease, led him to the conclusion that the sleeping sickness can be spread also by other insects, such as, for instance, the *glossina fusca*. The *glossina* lives principally on the banks of lakes, among stones, dried branches and plants; and feeds on the blood of the waterfowl and fish frequenting the surface of the water, and also on the blood of crocodiles. These latter animals, Professor Koch declares, are one of the chief reasons for the existence of the *glossina* in the Victoria Nyanza territory.

In order to study the *glossina* and the sleeping sickness together, Professor Koch availed himself of the offer of an empty mission-house placed at his disposal by the British authorities at Bengala, in the Sesse Islands, to the northwest of the Victoria Nyanza.

The professor came to the conclusion that the only remedy which would be efficacious would be one that destroyed the trypanosomes in the infected persons, as quinine annihilates malaria parasites. After various experiments Professor Koch decided to employ atoxyl injections of half a gramme in solution, which proved most efficacious and caused no harm. Six hours after the subcutaneous injections had been made the trypanosomes were unchanged, but eight hours after there was no sign of trypanosomes, while the general condition of the patient had improved. In three weeks patients who were seriously ill when the treatment began, and who, without atoxyl, would certainly have died, had improved to such an extent as to leave no doubt in the professor's mind of the efficacy of the remedy.

Unfortunately, a week after Dr. Koch's report appeared, Sir P. Monson wrote to the Times that it was optimistic, that a relapse invariably occurred, and that trypanosomes were found in the blood even after a year's alleged cure. He gave cases where monkeys who had been inoculated with the blood of patients who had undergone arsenic treatment soon weakened and died of sleeping sickness.

In August, 1907, Sir Hesketh Bell, the Governor of Uganda, put forward a scheme for the suppression of sleeping sickness and the Treasury authorized the expenditure of the funds required for this work. According to Sir Hesketh Bell's plan, the natives are to be removed from the fly-infested district on the shores of Lake Victoria to healthy locations inland. The sick are to be placed in segregation camps, where they will undergo the so-called atoxyl treatment. It is estimated that some twenty thousand people will have to be dealt with in this manner. It is further intended that all landing stages along the shore of the Victoria Nyanza shall be freed from the presence of the tsetse fly by means of a complete clearance of all vegetation. Fords, ferries, and waterholes will be similarly dealt with, and it is hoped that, by constant and consistent efforts in this direction, sleeping sickness will gradually be stamped out in Uganda. It is a matter for satisfaction that the chiefs fully appreciate the steps that are being taken, and are working loyally with the Government in helping to stamp out what has already proved such a terrible scourge in Uganda.

Replying to a question in the House of Commons in September, of the same year, Mr. W. Churchill said that he was unable to state the weekly number of deaths resulting from sleeping sickness in Uganda. The question of the measures to be taken to prevent the spread of sleeping sickness was not in his opinion one for the English Government alone, but for all the Governments in whose African possessions the disease unfortunately had appeared, and the only prospect of dealing with it effectively seemed to be by international co-operation. The International Conference which met in London in June, 1907, had taken some steps in this direction, and when it should meet again Mr.

Churchill hoped that it would be possible to arrive at a definite agreement on the whole question of the investigation and control of the disease.

It should, however, be added that the problem of controlling an epidemic of this kind affecting vast areas in the heart of Africa is one which presents enormous difficulties, and that, while every exertion will be made, too much must not be expected even from international co-operation.

The work that I saw interested me very much. Twice a day the doctor went through the hospital, treating the patients, cheering and encouraging the downhearted, ordering food and medicine for the weak. Attended by an interpreter, he asked the various symptoms and explained to me, as we went along, the course and ravages of the disease. It was a sight not wanting in quiet heroism, this young English aristocrat, from Pall Mall, away from his real environment and amid the inconveniences and annoyances of Equatorial Africa, doing his duty by the Empire in that quiet, assured way which makes the Englishman the greatest governor of colonies the world has known.

The hospital itself consists of a series of buildings in the native daub and wattle style, common to Uganda, with palm thatched roofs and overhanging eaves. Down the centre of each building there is a wide aisle, and on either side of it are rows of beds, of native manufacture, whereon the patients lie, covered with a blanket. Fires are kindled at intervals down this aisle, and most of the patients are not too sick to do their own cooking. Some of the victims are young men and women who have strength to go about, and these live in the village in clean sanitary huts, of the ordinary Uganda type. The course of the disease runs anywhere from two days to two years. I have seen patients brought in one night and buried the next day. On the other hand, the doctor showed me men who had had the disease for nearly two years and who were still able to keep on their feet.

Dr. Marshall also told me that his chief, Capt. Grey, R. A. M. C., had divided the patients into four classes, according to the extent of the ravages of the disease. Class A are patients who do not know that anything is the matter with them, but have enlarged glands on the neck. Class B, typical gland enlargement of the neck and the man is not so strong as he used to be. He has body itch and general debility. Cannot walk as far as formerly. If you look at his tongue it is tremulous. Class C, the glands are large, the patient has body itch all over, cannot walk at all, tongue tremulous and the man sleeps a great deal. Class D is a case where a man has all the foregoing symptoms emphasized and in addition has meningitis. It is from the latter affection that sleeping comes, and this case is always hopeless. Many cases have no sleeping symptoms apparent. At this stage some of them go mad.

I visited the madhouse and found about twenty patients in it. Some òf them had to be tied, but few of them were violent. To most of them, the terrible happiness of insanity had come. There is also a deathhouse, where they keep the sick who are in the last stages of the malady.

Let me quote from my notebook:

"The doctor goes his rounds along with an interpreter. Here are some questions and answers at random:

Q. "What is the matter with this man?" Ans. "He has a pain in his head."

Q. "What is the matter with this boy?" Ans. "He has pain in his stomach."

Q. "What is the matter with this woman?" Ans. "She has pain like rheumatism in her shoulders and chest."

Q. "What is the matter with this old man?" Ans. "He has fever, chills and rheumatic pains." So the exciting drama goes, seven hundred people condemned to death, yet nearly all of them are quite cheerful. They do not seem to believe that they are going to die, yet the doctor says to me, "Not one of these people will ever leave this place alive. All are condemned to death absolutely within two years."

It seemed to me the jolliest deathhouse that I had ever seen. The boys were playing a kind of football; the women were sitting in the court, chatting and gossiping, as if disease and death were the farthest from their minds. The red clouds of evening arched low on the horizon and amid bird songs and the chirruping insects the tropic night came down. The country was as sweet as Maine or Massachusetts in the springtime, yet here were all the terrors of wasting madness and annihilating death.

Next morning, a chief who had walked two hundred miles came to the hospital. His name was this — Mbugakutwala — and he came from Lake Kioga. He was a man evidently young, yet disease, which turns the sweet-eyed girl into a spectre, had touched him with its thumb. He showed his tongue to the doctor. It was tremulous — symptom of the sleeping sickness. The doctor took some blood from the swelled glands of the neck. He put it under the microscope, looked for a few minutes in the field of vision, turned and offered me the instrument. I looked intently through the microscope; confused images were there, like volcanoes in the moon seen through a telescope. At last, I could discern a living thing, darting about in one of the

TAKING BLOOD FROM THE NECK OF A SUSPECTED MAN.

DR. MARSHALL INJECTING ATOXYL.

white globules. It was the germ of the sleeping sickness; and the man in the prime of life, a human being like myself, loving the sun-light as dearly as any alive, was condemned to the dark house and the narrow grave.

CHAPTER XXIV

AT THE FOUNTAINS OF THE NILE

MY Baganda boys started bright and early one morning from the Kyetume Hospital for a trip of sixty-five miles with me to Jinja, at the Fountains of the Nile. It was not without a thrill of enthusiasm that I started on this little journey towards the source of that historic and alluring river which has touched the imagination of many men — from Herodotus to Chinese Gordon.

I took four Baganda boys along with me — two to pull and two to push the little Pullman car. The road lay through the forest lands, papyrus swamps and green meadows of Uganda. The boys kept singing the entire day. They seemed to have only one song of about two thousand verses. Later I heard some of the verses translated and I give a few lines

"White man is the iron; Baganda is the wood.
What is the use of iron without wood?
What is the use of an axe without a haft?
White man pays rupees; Baganda brings him to his home."

At the Fountains of the Nile

Often we stopped at the Rest Houses and I was delighted at the soft tones of the language as I heard the people chaffering with my boys. My bronzed Baganda steeds were high mettled young fellows, and many a fight they had along the highway. They would rush through a village shouting and singing; some little urchin would come out and poke fun at them, and then I would hear a good slap, as one of my boys would strike the cheeky offender on the face with his open hand.

There were native shops beside the road at which my boys bought *pembe*, a delicious banana wine. I bought them about two gallons of this *pembe* in the heat of the day. We rested from twelve until two. We drank up all the *pembe* and the boys after that seemed to have more spirit than any native Africans I have ever seen. Thenceforth their love and loyalty towards me was unbounded. When we stopped at a village I could hear the boys telling the natives what a splendid Msungu (white man) their master was. One sentence I was able to translate. It began with the words " Bwana Mzuri kidogo " or " Our good master is a small man." I cannot remember the native words for the rest of the sentence; but the purport of it was that though this white master was small of stature he had a great heart and wonderful intellect; he gave them banana wine and ant pie and plenty of time to rest when the sun was hot. Any man who contradicted them or doubted their word they served with thwacks upon his back or resounding slaps upon his face.

The boys made forty miles the first day, and we camped for the night beside a delicious stream in a cool grove. I had a light tent for myself, while the Baganda found shelter in a neighbouring village. Though I was entirely alone and in a district infested with buffaloes, leopards, lions and other dangerous neighbours, yet I fell soundly asleep shortly after dark and did not wake till dawn. I kept no fire. This shows how we become accustomed to the strangest and most dangerous environment. When first I started on my journey, only the strongest body-guard, with lighted fires around me at night, could make me able to sleep with a sense of security, and here finally I went to sleep with no protection and no camp fire, with wild beasts possibly only a stone's throw distant, as nonchalantly as though I were in the finest hotel in Paris.

I could not find my Baganda boys until late the next afternoon. We had to make twenty-five miles to reach the home of Archdeacon Buckley at Jinja. I had been commended to the Archdeacon both by the missionaries and business men of Kampala and by the young doctor at Kyetume. The doctor had said to me, "If that Archdeacon Buckley does not quit Africa soon, I will be a Christian myself."

At the Fountains of the Nile

So I set off for the house of Buckley, the Irish missionary. The people knew where he lived; my Baganda boys had heard his name, for they constantly inquired, as we went from village to village about "Bwana Inglesa Backley" — "the English Master Buckley."

At sunset we came to the shores of Napoleon Gulf. As I looked out on the blue water, I heard like the "roar of a rain fed ford" the roar of the Ripon Falls, where the great lake of Africa is hurled into the Nile. It was a delightful moment for me to realize as I did that soon I would look upon the most fascinating and interesting river-source in the world.

But the night was falling and darkness was only half an hour away. We must cross the Gulf, which is nearly half a mile wide at the point where I stood, or else spend the night in a mosquito-haunted swamp and among the tse-tse flies.

I saw a ferryman approaching from the Usoga side. We called upon him and he drew his long boat up on the sand. It was one of those leaky and dangerous craft, made of boards, that I have already described. My Baganda lifted the jinrickshaw and tried to put it in the boat. Then the Busoga ferryman ordered them to put it out. This they refused to do, telling him what a good man I was and how big, though I looked small, and how much *pembe* they had drunk at my expense along the road. The more the Baganda talked of my good qualities the more enraged they became at the Busoga ferryman; and turning to me exclaiming, " The Busoga are Shensi dogs," they lifted the man bodily and flung him into the lake which at this place was full of crocodiles. I rushed down to the water and ordered the Baganda boys to pull the dripping and chastised man out from his perilous position. This they did, and the Busoga man made no further objections to carrying my 'rickshaw in his rickety boat.

The Baganda rowed the boat themselves; two of their number being detailed to bail out the water. It was all we could do to keep the flimsy craft afloat and, looking over the edge of the boat, I noticed the sleepy, cynical, devilish eyes of leering crocodiles in the waters close by. We reached the Jinja side of the gulf just as the last ray of light was fading from the landscape. We still had two miles to go before we could reach the home of the friendly missionary. A new argument started between my men and the Busoga ferryman. The latter wanted fifteen cowrie shells extra for carrying the 'rickshaw. The Baganda explained to him that the 'rickshaw was part of their master and that he must be content with one fare for both the carriage and the man. Fifteen cowrie shells is

At the Fountains of the Nile 379

equal to one cent in American money, so I could not let the argument go on all night, and therefore I paid the man his importunate demand.

We were now in the Province of Usoga. It was very dark and, as the Baganda despise the Busoga, the boys would not ask anybody the way to the missionary's home. Accordingly, they took about two hours to go the two miles and felt their way along the hedges, with which they were apparently familiar. At last the lights of the mission gleamed in front and at about half-past eight we reached the house of Archdeacon Buckley.

I alighted, knocked at the door and was met by the missionary himself. Buckley is a short, stout, round-faced, genial Irishman, with an accent as rich as old Port wine. I pulled out a handful of letters to tell him who I was and what I was doing, but he waved the letters aside, saying in his kind Irish way, "I do not want to know who you are, you are a white man and a gentleman and are welcome to anything I can give you in the house." I was made very comfortable by the good priest and slept very soundly until the morning. Just as I was awaking I heard the bird-songs clear and sweet in the plantation; then, above their chanting murmurs, a loud roar like that of artillery or like great waves breaking on the ocean's shore. It was the Ripon Falls.

Greatly refreshed by the slumber of the night, I

breakfasted in the mission. The Archdeacon himself accompanied me through the village of Jinja, across the waving fields of corn and grass, through shrubs all bent and chewed by the hippopotami; then out on the ridge in full view of the great white wonder — the foam and cataracts of Ripon Falls.

Never shall I forget the glories of that summer morning, at the headwaters of the Nile. Away below us for miles and miles glimmered the rapids of the Victorian Nile under a sky of limpid blue. The green banks on either side were drowned in freshets of verdure. The woods were full of strange bright birds. There were also the cormorant, the hawk, and that queer comedy of nature's work, — the whale-headed stork.

Looking down from our high platform above the river we saw the beginning of the rapids and heard the roaring thunder from the Fountains of the Nile. In the middle distance there were little islands in the channel and the current poured over in three separate rivers, reminding me of Niagara, where the waters are parted by Goat Island; and in the background rose swelling ranges of hills that faded in purple distance away back into the very heart of Africa.

As at our American falls, the current is comparatively quiet above, but when it leaves these islands it drops down in a boiling, bubbling, seething mass,

Photograph by Peter Dutkewich, copyright, 1909, by Underwood & Underwood, N. Y.

THE RIPON FALLS.

At the Fountains of the Nile

The spray rises high into the air and falls back like rain on this tropical forest. It goes up in a mist and the dazzling sun of the equator paints rainbows in it. We watched the glory of the angry waters and tried to estimate their power and limit.

Thus at last I looked upon the Fountains of the Nile, discovered in the pagan centuries by the Pahars of the Pharaohs. So for millennia had they gushed under the Mountains of the Moon. My mind drifted down the river of Lotus dreams, and was lost in a mirage among the meadows of asphodel that wind through the Milky Way of the old alchemists.

In that mirage I saw the Akkads conquer and crush; then raise a stately and luxuriant civilization. Thence came the palaces and temples, the pyramids and obelisks. The great God Ammon-Ra was mistily dim, Osiris and Horus ruled over a race of beaten slaves. Isis never lifted her veil until with her black breasts she suckled the infant Christ. Then, following the mirage of my thought, I saw, upon the background of the younger centuries, the prophet-son of Pharaoh's daughter, grandiose and austere; the homesick Hebrew; and that dainty princess of Utopia, the Queen of Sheba.

Then the conquering Alexander and the world-defying Romans. There rose from the mist of Egypt's waters the flawless Grecian features and the burning wonderful eyes, hued like a Cyprian violet, of her who ruined Antony, seduced Cæsar and gave the empire of the world to Octavius — the great Queen Cleopatra. Called a wanton, squandering the wealth of Egypt in chariots and perfumes; her fair face was the sweetest of all that ever blossomed on this historic river. In her met all the sweetness that has been given woman for her glory and all the genius that man has wrested from the sky. Yet, fearing nothing and making mock of righteousness, she took empire for her place of play; staked kingdoms where the pawns were men; and "poisoned the wholesome breath of life with the doom of her desire." Grand as the storm, lovely as the lightning, cruel as the plague; and yet with the tender heart of a child. That vision filled the picture I was watching for two thousand years.

Cleopatra was a flash of lightning that served to intensify the gloom of two millennia. Then out of the dust of war and fear, and the gleam of Moslem spears, flashed the artillery of Napoleon; and when that had cleared away, I saw brilliant rule of England.

For this is the River of the Future as of the Past. Where Cleopatra's useless barge floated on the languid waters yesterday, to-morrow the Anglo-Saxon's ships will float an argosy of gold and make the wide land smile.

At the Fountains of the Nile

There are many fish in the lake, and they often swim down the falls. You can see them jump high out of the current, turning somersaults, as it were, as they go over the rocks.

Where the Nile flows over the falls the channel is only about twelve hundred feet wide, and the rocky foundation is such the lake can be easily dammed. The stream is deep and narrow, and it passes on over a series of cataracts which continue almost forty miles. During this distance it is so swift that boats cannot live on it. These waters of Victoria Nyanza rush onward with a terrible force, and this continues until within about thirty miles of Lake Chioga. Here the land is almost level and the lake is shallow and quiet. It has swamps filled with crocodiles and hippopotami, and the Nile flows peacefully through. It then goes onward traversing the Protectorate, taking two other great jumps on its way to Albert Nyanza. The first of these is at the Karuma Falls, and the other at Murchison Falls, which is about two hundred miles north of Jinja.

This description gives an idea of the electrical possibilities of the Nile away up at its source. The British are surveying it and are estimating its value in the industrial development of the country. An English syndicate has a concession for the little island just below the falls, and it expects to invest a half million dollars in establishing a cotton factory there. There are big lumbermen, who are exploiting the forests on both sides of the Nile, who want power; and I am told that other parties are after concessions.

The government is opposed to leasing power stations at the falls proper, as it may be necessary to build a dam here to regulate the outflow of the Nile. They do not object, however, to works bordering the rapids below the falls, and a series of power stations might be made thirty or forty miles long which could do all the manufacturing for this part of Africa.

Indeed the electrical possibilities of the Nile in connection with Uganda are enormous, and the manufacturing possibilities are equally great. The country has plenty of iron ore, and the British officials say that it can raise as good cotton as that grown in our Southern States. They predict that there will eventually be cotton plantations all the way from Lake Victoria to Lake Albert, two hundred miles, with ginning plants and cotton mills at Murchison Falls and along the Upper Nile.

The whole of Lake Victoria is tributary to this region, and the vast population which surrounds it could be supplied with cotton woven at these factories.

At present one of the great troubles in getting

At the Fountains of the Nile

the natives to raise cotton is that of transportation. It is now carried into Kampala on the heads of porters and the long march eats up the profits.

By establishing ginning plants along the Nile much of the cotton will go to them in boats, and more will be carried across country on the excellent roads which the British are inducing the natives to build. There are already hundreds of miles of road in Uganda which could be used by an automobile, and one can travel thousands of miles on a bicycle.

One of the interesting problems of this part of the world is as to whether the Nile can be regulated at Lake Victoria. The Assouan dam has added millions to the wealth of Egypt. Some of the best of the world's civil engineers look upon Lake Victoria as the great future reservoir of the river Nile. Sir William Garstin, the chief engineer of the Egyptian public works, says that a regulator could be put in at Ripon Falls and the water let out through sluices into the Nile. That river is the only outlet for Lake Victoria, and a slight dam at its source would produce enough water to irrigate a large part of the Sudan and to add millions of acres to Egypt.

As it is now the lake is estimated to have one hundred and thirty-eight billion tons of new water every year. The most of this is lost by evaporation and only eighteen billion tons go into the Nile. The present yearly discharge of the Nile at Alexandria is less than fifty billion tons, so that Lake Victoria could double its discharge and not feel it.

There are, however, many engineering problems connected with such regulation, and there are also political ones. The damming of the lake, for instance, might cause it to flood the shores of German East Africa, and for this reason the German government would be likely to object.

All along this part of the Nile are dense forests. The trees come right up to the river. Some of them are about one hundred and fifty feet high, rising forty or fifty feet without a branch. There is a great deal of mahogany and other hardwoods, and lumber mills will probably be established along the Nile to supply the demands of British East Africa, Uganda and the other countries about the lake as they develop. Some of the timber is so valuable that it could be sawed up and shipped across the lake to Port Florence and thence over the Uganda railroad to Mombasa, to be carried by steamship to Europe and South Africa.

A big rubber syndicate has a concession of one hundred and fifty square miles of forests in this region. It has been laying out its estate and is endeavouring to establish good labour conditions.

After a delightful visit to the Archdeacon and a

journey into Bukedi, of which I have spoken in an earlier chapter, I turned my face once more towards the coast. I had to leave my comrade in Africa because I had to meet engagements in America. But I left Africa with a feeling of great regret. My boy, Osmanie, had been with me on Safari for fifteen hundred miles. Salim, Mahomet and the other boys I left with Mr. Dutkewich. But Osmanie refused to leave me.

When I returned to Nairobi I procured the poor fellow a place with a Scotchman there. When a little later I came back from a short journey to Juja Farm and Fort Hall, Osmanie was looking for me at the hotel. He had become a great dude and was wearing, in noble style, the cast off clothing I had given him on our various safaris. From a beautiful, naked, untutored savage, Osmanie in six months, had become a degenerate swell; an affair of white waistcoats, knee breeches, and patent leather shoes.

So far had Osmanie carried his foppishness that when he returned to the Masai village of his birth he would not speak to the boys and girls with whom he had grown up. Accordingly, they had him arrested, and sent back to the police at Nairobi in order to ascertain if he had come honestly by so much elaborate clothing. Our meeting at the hôtel was quite heartfelt. Osmanie was accompanied by a tall, Irish dragoon, and he carried a paper containing an account of his foppishness and his suspicious irregularity in garments. I put the honest fellow at his ease with the British authorities at Nairobi and he came into my room and besought me very earnestly to take him back into my employ.

I told him I was going to England and he said, "Well, let me go to England, too." Then I explained that I was going, still further, to America, and he, simple soul, all unaware of our immigration laws, said that that was better still. "Amerika Mzuri sana bwana" — "America is still better, Master," but I had to refuse his urgent offer.

I left Nairobi for the last time with the utmost regret. The place is full of fine, generous, open-hearted pioneers. There were Vice-Governor Jackson, Mr. McMillan, Mr. Heatley, Harry Edgell, Lord Delamere, Mr. Currie, the manager of the Uganda Railroad, and a dozen others that I was beginning to know and to feel a hearty friendship for. There was the beautiful wide rolling equatorial plain, that I had come to love; its freshness, its freedom, its newness, its appeal to the homesickness of a wanderer like myself.

Of all the countries I have visited, no one has made such an appeal to me as Central Africa.

Of course the camera cannot do justice to such panoramas. In pictures the vast expanses look flat and common, monotonous to the eye and melancholy to the soul. Equatorial Africa is a botanical and zoological garden, where nature's central laboratory is working day and night through seasons that know no decadence of winter. The common flat photograph poorly pictures the fairyland of glades and vistas, that might conceal the cities of a busy population.

I make no doubt that this Central Africa, so wild and dark through all the past millenniums of man's life, will in the near future be the site of one of the most eager and commanding civilizations on the globe. With the ripening of progress and culture on the Equator much of the sweetest charm of wildest Africa will pass, but it will be the happy home of rejoicing millions of free men, white and black. It is a thesaurus of rich minerals; it is a garden of superb fecundity; it is a fairyland for the lotus eater; it is a mart for the merchant. But, for the man who hates the dust of cities and the mad clash and recoil of selfish and contending interests, Africa is a haven of rest.

Oh, land of Africa, how I have loved thy sunny days and starry nights; thy great free, untrammelled wilderness; thy glories of eternal ice and perpetual summers; thy simple people of the unspoiled lives. Thy memories crowd upon me in the busiest hours like echoes of an unforgotten song. Even thy savage monsters that tear each other in their slime have a fierce gladness as from the uprushing life of the old primordial earth. Thy glorious forests are as islands of enchanted rest, and thy hot fevers are but nature's nepenthe to the worn out hunter. Thy lure and fascination will never leave me, until my feet at last, worn out with many travels, have sought and found the poppied path to sleep.

THE END.

Bibliography

ALEXANDER, B. — From the Niger to the Nile. 2 v. 1907.
ANDERSSON, C. J. — Lake Ngami.
BAKER, S. W. — Albert Nyanza. 1864.
BAKER, S. W. — Ismailia: a narration of the expedition to Central Africa for the suppression of the slave-trade.
BALDWIN, W. C. — African hunting. 1863.
BENTLEY, W. H. — Pioneering on the Congo. 2 v. 1900.
BETTANY, G. T. — Dark peoples of the land of sunshine. 1890.
BRODE, H. — Tippoo Tib: the story of his career in Central Africa. 1907.
BROWN, R. — The Story of Africa and its explorers. 2 v. 1892-3.
BRYCE, J. — Impressions of South Africa. 1897.
BURROWS, G. — Land of the pigmies. 1898.
BURTON, R. F. — First footsteps in East Africa. 2 v. 1894.
CAMERON, V. L. — Across Africa. 1877.
CASATI, G. — Ten years in Equatoria and the return with Emin Pasha. 2 v. 1891.
CHURCHILL, R. S. — Men, mines and animals in South Africa. 1892.
CHURCHILL, W. S. — My African journey.
COLVILLE, Z. — Round the black man's garden. 1893.
CONGO, THE: a report of the Commission of Enquiry appointed by the Congo Free State Government. 1906.
DAVIS, R. H. — Congo and the coasts of Africa. 1907.
DENHAM, D. and others. — Travels in Africa. 1822, 1823, 1824.
DRUMMOND, H. — Tropical Africa. 1889.

Bibliography

REID, T. W. — Land of the Bey. 1882.
SANDERSON, E. — Africa in the nineteenth century. 1898.
SCHILLINGS, C. G. — Flashlights in the jungle. 1905.
SCHNITZER, G., ED. — Emin Pasha, his life and work. 1898.
SCHWEINFURTH, G., ED. — Emin Pasha in Central Africa. 1889.
SCHWEINFURTH, G. — Heart of Africa. 2 v.
SELOUS, F. C. — African nature notes. 1908.
SELOUS, F. C. — Travel and adventure in South East Africa. 1892.
SKINNER, T. — Adventures during a journey to India by way of Egypt. 1837.
SOUTHWORTH, A. S. — 4000 miles of African travel. 1875.
SPEKE, J. H. — Journal of discovery of source of the Nile. 1864.
STANLEY, H. M. — The Congo and the founding of its free state.
STANLEY, H. M. — In darkest Africa. 1890.
STANLEY, H. M. — Through the Dark Continent. 1878
STARR, F. — Truth about the Congo. 1907.
STEVENS, T. — Scouting for Stanley in eastern Africa. 1889.
THOMSON, J. — Through Masai Land. 1885.
VANDELEUR, S. — Campaigning on the Upper Nile and Niger. 1898.
VINCENT, F. — Actual Africa. 1895.
WACK, H. W. — Story of the Congo Free State. 1905.
WARD, H. — My life with Stanley's rear guard.
WHITE, A. S. — Development of Africa. 1890.
WILLOUGHBY, J. C. — East Africa and its big game. 1889.
WISSMANN, H. VON. — My second journey through Equatorial Africa from the Congo to the Zambesi in the years 1886-7. 1891.

Index

Aberdare Mts., 11
Abruzzi, Duke of, 299
Abyssinia, 24, 27, 29, 109
Acacia, 11, 164
Adder, Gaboon, 129
Africa, vi, vii, 1, 2, 3, 4, 5, 11, 12, 13, 15, 17, 20, 21, 22, 23, 38, 55, 61, 73, 94, 97, 98, 99, 100, 103, 114, 115, 116, 118, 124, 125, 144, 145, 146, 149, 152, 154, 156, 168, 170, 177, 183, 187
Ahlbory, Dr., 194, 206, 209, 212
Aigrets, 124
Albert Edward Nyanza, 6, 49, 156
Albert Nyanza, 3, 6, 8, 128, 137, 156, 188, 291
Alexandria, viii, 19, 73, 292, 386
Algeria, vii, 22, 30
Algerian Fathers of Nairobi, 248
Ali bin Hamoud, 70, 72
Amenti, 18
American Fibre Company, 159
American goods in Africa, 251, 353
American machinery in Africa, 251
Angola, 27
Ankole and its People, 305
Ants, 129
Antelopes, 4, 106, 123, 124, 127, 129, 136, 139, 164
Arabs, 5, 6, 42, 43, 50, 61, 63, 64, 67, 70, 71, 72, 73, 78, 79, 80, 87, 91, 92, 97, 107, 166, 177, 179
Arabia, 64
Assegais, 25
Asses, Wild, 128
Assouan Dam, 99, 385
Athi Plains, 101, 124, 235
Athi River, 108

Baboons, 173, 174, 175, 272, 273
Bagamoyo, 7
Baganda, 156, 329, 338, 344, 349, 350, 352, 374, 376-379
Bagishu, 316
Bagola Mt., 346
Bahima, 300
Bahr-el-Gazal, vii, 8, 188
Bailey, Councillor, 123, 244
Baker's Roan Antelope, 138
Bakoki, 308
Bakongo, 310
Balthazar, Father, 185, 217
Bambarras, 21, 30, 43
Bantus, 5, 6, 256, 344
Banubuddu, 307
Banyoro, 306-307
"Bao" game, 181
Bark Cloth in Uganda, 352, 353
Basesse, 307, 345
Bast, Herr, 134, 186
Bata, 220
Baziba, 148, 149, 310
Bell, Sir H. H., 315, 367
Bellefonds, Linant, 48
Bello, Sultan, 33

Index

Berbera, 5, 56
Beza, Rabbi Ben, 24
Big Game, 121-138
Binns, Rev. Dr., 97
Birds, 305
Boats, 15
Boers, 28, 57, 99, 110, 123, 272
Bondou, 30
British East Africa, 3, 108, 121, 123, 127, 158, 222
British Government in Uganda, 328, 346, 349, 350, 351, 357, 358, 359, 363
Broken Hill, viii, 99
Bububu, 65, 69, 74
Buckley, Archdeacon, 128, 313, 376, 377, 379
Buffaloes, 4, 122, 125, 128, 197, 222-227
Bukedi, 127, 137, 313-317
Bukoba, 96, 128, 150
Bumbireh Island, 48-49
Burra, 159, 162, 164, 221
Busoga, 300, 309, 378, 379
Buvuma, 47, 49, 153, 364

Cairo, vii, viii, 24, 30, 56, 88, 99
Camels, 15, 74, 122, 184
Cane, Diego, 23-24
Cannibalism, 51, 300, 345, 346
Cape Bojador, 23
Cape of Good Hope, 23, 24, 80, 90
Caravans, 21
Carre, Bro., 185
Cattle, 4, 12
Caves of Elgon, 301, 324
Central Africa, v, vi, 2, 3, 14, 17, 21, 31, 40, 58, 79, 147, 154, 290, 329-331, 346, 380-388
Chaga (see Wachaga)
Chandler's Reed-buck, 110, 121, 129, 136
Cheetahs, 124
Chimpanzees, 4, 128, 300
Church of England Missionary Society, 75, 97, 128, 333
Churchill, Hon. W., 368, 369

Classes of Patients in Sleeping Sickness, 370
"Clement Hill," Steamer, 289
Cloves, 62, 69, 78, 94
Cobra, 129, 303
Coffee, 95, 193, 246
Colobus Monkey, 122, 123, 128, 168, 177, 178
Colytam, Vizier, 26
Congo, 1, 3, 5, 19, 23, 35, 39, 42, 46, 52, 53, 54, 55, 66, 94, 152, 169, 290
Copra, 62, 69, 74, 78, 94
Coptic, 17
Cranes, White, 139
Crocodiles, 4, 13, 124, 233, 303
Cook, Rev. Dr., 333
Cotton, 95, 246, 355-356
Coudenhove, Count, 168, 171, 173-175, 178, 219
Covilham, Da, 24-25
Currie, Mr., Manager Uganda R. R., 388
Customs, 324-325
Cyrene, 19

Danda Chwa, 337, 338, 342, 343
Dar-es-Salaam, 7, 69, 77, 188
Delamere, Lord, 123, 129, 244, 245, 388
Development of Uganda, 345-360
"Dhows," 68, 97
Diaz, Bartholomew, 24
Donkeys, 4, 122, 132, 159, 166
Donyo Egare, 10
Drummond, Henry, vii, 227
Dutkewich, Mr. Peter, v, vi, 157, 158, 160, 172, 195, 196, 199, 205, 206, 207, 208, 210, 211, 215, 217, 261, 287, 387
Duyker antelope, 138

Eagles, 110
East Africa, v, 6, 58, 66, 67, 69, 78, 85, 89, 92, 95, 103, 107, 108, 112, 116, 123, 134, 136, 145, 154, 187
East African Coast, 5, 18, 54, 88

Index

East African Mammals, 124-125
East African Protectorate, 3, 6, 92, 100, 112, 123, 235
East Central Africa, 48, 139
East Indians, 237, 238, 325-326
Edgehill (or Edgell), Harry, 119, 221, 243, 244, 388
Edrisi, 20
Education in East Africa, 113
Egypt, 1, 3, 14, 15, 17, 29, 56, 57, 99, 321, 385
Eland, 222-227
Eldama Ravine, 110, 126, 127
Elephants, 4, 110, 122, 123, 124, 127, 128, 136, 169, 170, 172, 195
Elgon, Mt., 4, 8, 127, 137, 299, 300, 302
Elliott, Sir Charles, 132
Elmenteita, Lake, 119
Elmina, 23
El Moran, 267, 269
Emin Pasha, 12, 100, 255
Entebbe, 6, 111, 128, 137, 188, 293, 320-329
Equatorial Africa, 12, 243, 321, 334, 369, 389
Europeans in Uganda, 326, 327, 328, 353

Family Life in Uganda, 348
Farm-lands of East Africa, 109
Fascination of Africa, 389-390
Fassman, Rev. Dr., 191, 212-213
Ferig Pasha, 56
Fezzan, 21, 30, 31, 32, 34
Fishermen, 16
Fleischer, 123
Flora, 16, 103-105, 301, 302, 320
Fola Rapids, 8
Fort Hall, 112
Fort Ternan, 108, 111, 120
Foulahs, 21
Frere, Sir Bartle, 97

Galleys, 15
Gama, Paulo da, 25
Gama, Vasco da, 25, 26, 27, 81, 85, 87, 90, 92

Game in East Africa, 106-109, 121
Garstin, Sir William, 385
Gazelles, 123
German East Africa, 3, 7, 93, 109, 121, 122, 148, 150, 155, 158, 168, 188, 191-193, 223, 321; Government, 190; Railroads, 188
"Ghary-boys," 83, 85
Gilsanez, 23
Giraffes, 4, 28, 101, 108, 124, 127, 128, 129, 138, 164, 232
Glossina Fusca, 366
Glossina, Palpalis, 364, 366
Gnu, 121, 122
Goanese, 63, 84, 106, 108, 131, 295
Goats, 4, 12, 194
Gold, 21, 45
Gondar, 29
Gondokoro, 99
Gordon, Charles George, 55, 56
Gorillas, 4
Grant Gazelle, 107, 121
Gregory, Professor, vii, 105, 125
Grey, Dr., 370
Guaso Nyiro Country, 263, 266, 268
Guinea fowl, 122, 137, 159

Hamitic, 17
Hanlon, Bishop, 128, 333
Hannington, Bishop, 84
Hartebeest, 107, 127, 136, 164, 232
Hausa, 5
Health of whites, 261
Heatley, 126, 388
Henry of Portugal, Prince, 22-23
Herodotus, 17
Hinde, Capt., 146
Hindlip, Lord, 247
Hindu, 113, 130, 170, 238, 239, 243, 248, 296, 303
Hippopotami, 4, 7, 13, 122, 123, 124, 128, 138, 139, 233, 254, 285, 286, 287, 288
Horneman, Conrad, 30

Horses, 4, 5, 15, 21
Houses in Uganda, 347
Hunters, Native, 313
Hurlburt, Rev. Mr., 109
Hyde-Baker, 169-172, 218-219
Hyenas, 4, 122, 129, 160, 164, 166, 168
Hyrax, 197

Ibn Batuta, 20, 21
Imitation of Animals, 227-233
Indian Ocean, 4, 86, 88, 93, 100, 186
Insect Pests, 320
Ituri Forest, 169
Ivory, 21, 67, 68, 94, 171
Izchia, 21

Jackal, 121, 123, 129, 183
Jackson, Gov., 114, 388
Jaluo, 154
Jinja, 111, 127, 292, 293, 313, 374
Jinrickshaw in Uganda, 361
Jipe, Lake, 122, 176
Johnston, Sir Harry, vii, 168, 215, 216, 298
Journalism in Nairobi, 249, 250
Juba River, 6, 92
Juja Farm, 241

Kabaka, 47
Kaffirs, 25
Kagera River, 148
Kagwar, Sir Appollo, 337
Kahaya, King, 305
Kampala, 6, 330-345
Kapiti Plains, 108
Karagwe, 7
Karamojo, 312
Kasangama, King, 307
Kasunguru, Chief, 313
Katakiro, 47
Kavirondo, 12, 93, 100, 111, 112, 149, 157, 254, 257-260, 276-287; Doctors, 283; Husbands, 282; King, 278; Maidens, 281; Marriage, 258; War-dance, 278; Warriors, 280; Women, 277

Kavirondo Gulf, 289
Kedong River, 118
Kenia Falls, 274
Kenia Mt., vi, 1, 4, 8, 10, 11, 55, 112, 116, 126, 146, 147, 234, 236, 263-275
Khartum, 8, 14, 56, 57, 99
Khedive, 55
Khem, 15
Kibo, 8, 9, 10, 183, 186, 193, 201, 204, 207
Kibwezi, 107
Kijabe, 109, 118
Kikuyu, 6, 101, 109, 111, 118, 154, 157, 236
Kilifi, 89
Kilima, 185, 186, 199, 217
Kilimanjaro, vi, viii, 3, 4, 7, 8, 9, 55, 93, 95, 106, 112, 121, 122, 137, 158, 168, 174, 177, 178, 183, 184, 186, 187, 189, 194-216, 235, 273
Kilwa, 89
Kimawenzi, 8, 9, 11, 17, 201, 204
Kinancop, Mount, 270, 271
King's Rifles, Uganda, 255, 325
Kioga, Lake, 317
Kirunga, 4
Kisumu, 111, 120, 255
Kites, 110
Kiu, 106, 108
Klein, Max, 123
Kob, 138
Koerfer, Herr, 159, 162, 163
Kongoni, 122, 136
Kudu, 110, 127, 196
Kwazi eagle, 8
Kivu, Lake, 4, 188
Koch, Dr., 364, 365, 366, 367
Kungungu, 220, 221
Kyetume Hospital, 361

Labour in Nairobi, 247
"Lady Alice, The," 47, 50, 53, 294
Lamu Archipelago, 70, 89
Lango Tribe, 314
Lendu, 312

Index

Leo Africanus, 21
Leopards, 4, 107, 122, 124, 128, 129, 160, 163, 166, 168, 175, 195, 196
Limoru, 117-118
Lions, 4, 101, 102, 121, 124, 128-133, 138, 160, 168, 172, 177, 182, 250
Livingstone, Dr. David, 29, 38, 39, 40, 42, 43, 44, 45, 50, 58, 59, 73, 75, 83, 97
Londiani, 110, 127
London, Thos., 96
Longanot, Mount, 118
Lukiko, The, 342
Lumi River, 164, 166, 167, 168, 176

Machakos Road, 108, 114
Mackenzie, Bishop, 40-41
Madagascar, 60, 66, 115
Madeira, 23
Magassa, 47
Mahogany, 357
Mail Systems in Central Africa, 187-188
Makelingu, 96
Malindi, 89, 90
Mandara, 215
Manyuema, 311-312
Marangu, 158, 185
Marriage in Africa, 180, 305, 306, 308-312
Marshall, Dr. Claude, 361, 370
Martini, lion killer, 166, 172, 173, 175, 182
Marabous, 110, 124
Marangu, 123, 218
Masai, 3, 6, 8, 10, 54, 101, 111, 139, 140, 141, 142, 143, 144, 145, 147, 148, 153, 156, 162, 167, 177, 189, 190, 236, 243, 264, 267, 269
Mau, 108, 109, 119, 153
Mauck, 211
Mbale, 127
Mbiri River, 112
Mbugakutwala, 372

Mbwa fly, 303
McMillan, W. N., 114, 126, 241, 242, 243, 244, 388
Melikanoi, 167, 177
Melindi, 27
Mengo, 6, 336
Meroë, 17
Meru, Mt., 11, 122, 188, 189, 197, 200, 213
" Meseeka," 73
Meyer, Hans, 206, 215
Mimosa, 11, 159
Minerals, 321
Mir Ali Bey, 91
Miro Tribe, 314
Missionaries, 334, 335, 360
Mweru, Lake, 2
Moffatt, Robert, 39
Mohammedan, 65, 85, 137, 179, 336
Molo, 110
Mombasa, 7, 20, 26, 27, 64, 69, 73, 77, 79-98, 100, 101, 106, 120, 134, 147, 170, 188, 192
Mombo, 7, 187
Monchardi, Mr., 123, 184, 218
Monkeys, 4, 175
Monomapata, 27
Monson, Sir P., 367
Moschi, 95, 121, 123, 134, 169, 170, 183-193
Motor-cars in Uganda, 300
Mozambique, 20, 24, 26, 27, 28, 60, 90
Mpalas, 164
Mtate, 159, 221
Mtesa, King, 47, 48, 308, 333, 338-341, 344, 350
Muazi Moji Road, 76
Mukasa, 307
Mumias, 127
Muscat, 64, 78
Mwanga, 84, 341
Mwanza, 12, 128
Myita, 90

Nairobi, vii, 94, 107, 108, 111, 112, 113, 114, 116, 117, 123,

126, 127, 134, 205, 234-253, 388; Climate, 248
Naivasha, Lake and Country, 109, 118, 126, 139, 140, 271
Nakuru, Lake, vii, 110, 119, 133
Namirembe Mission, 332
Nandi, 6, 101, 120, 153, 236, 300
Napoleon Gulf, 7
Natal, 25, 45, 46
Nellat, 127
New, Rev. Chas., 215
Ngambya, 335
"Ngoma" dance, 94
Niger, 21, 30, 36, 37
Nile, v, viii, 1, 3, 7, 8, 14, 17, 19, 22, 29, 42, 44, 47, 48, 56, 73, 94, 99, 100, 111, 127, 148, 169, 290, 292, 321, 374-390; Sources of, 292
Nilotic tribes, 313
Njiri Plain, 9
Njoro, 109
Northern Africa, 19, 20
Nyassa, Lake, 3, 40, 41, 291
Nysambia Mission, 333, 334

O'Hara, Mr. and Mrs., 129
Okapi, 128, 138, 169, 300
Ol Kononis, 190
Omdurman, 57, 157, 298
Oryx, 110, 127, 196
Osmanie, 217, 219, 220, 387-388
Ostriches, 4, 108, 109, 122, 124, 129, 164, 183

Paa, 121, 136, 164
Pahars, 15, 18
Palla antelope, 138
Palazzo, Prof., 256, 330, 336, 343, 361
Panthers, 4
Papyanos, Mr., 170
Papyrus, 13
Parenti, Mr., of Milan, 332, 361
Park, Dr. Mungo, 30, 31, 35
Parri Forest, 173
Parri Mts., 122, 164, 168, 173, 205

Parrots, 318
Parsees, 63
Partridges, 122, 137, 159, 162
Patterson, Mr., of Marangu, 184, 218
Paul, Mother, 334, 335
Pease, Sir Alfred, 114
Pemba, 7, 69, 70, 92
Pembe wine, 347, 375
Peters, Dr. Carl, 168
Pharaohs, 15, 18
Piava, Da, 24
Pig, Wild, 123, 196
Pigeons, 122, 137, 159
Plantain-eaters, 137, 318
Polo, Marco, 90
Polygamy in Uganda, 343
Port Florence, 96, 100, 101, 111, 120, 254-262, 288, 386
Porto Santo, 23
Portuguese, 22, 23, 24, 26, 29, 34, 41, 80, 84, 91, 92, 94, 133
Prester John, 23
Ptolemy, 19, 89
Puff-adder, 229, 303
Python, 129

Quails, 276

Rabai Hills, 81
Railroading in East Africa, 252-253
Rebman, Dr., 17, 214
Red Sea, 2, 18, 20, 24
Rhinoceri, 4, 101, 108, 122, 123, 127, 128, 164, 165, 240-241
Riches of Africa, 321
Rift Valley, 3, 4, 109, 118, 140
Ripon Falls, 7, 99, 127, 292, 309, 377, 380, 385
Roads in Uganda, 341, 342
Rodentis Macqueeniensis, 213
Roosevelt, Ex-President, 101, 107, 109, 112, 114, 115, 126, 132, 242, 337
Rovuma River, 7
Rubber, 94, 95, 193, 218, 357
Rudolph, Lake, 2, 3, 291, 334

Index

Ruvana River, 12
Ruwenzori, 3, 4, 93, 299, 310

Sadler, Gov. Sir James K., 114, 123, 244-245
Safari outfitters, 240
Sahara, 3, 4, 5, 30, 31
Said Khaled, 72
Salisbury Bridge, 103
Sandig, 30
Sataspes, 18
Segou, 30
Semitic, 17
Semliki, 3
Senegal, 30, 36-37
Seringeti Plain, 158, 164, 168
Sesse Islands, 345, 346, 364, 366
Seyidie, 107
"Shambas," 69
Sharp, 15
Slave Trade, 16, 21, 38, 41, 67-68, 313
Sheep, 4, 12, 109
Shimba (see lion)
Shirati, 96
Shirwa, Lake, 40
Silva, Da, 133
Simba, 107, 130, 131
Sleeping Sickness, 361-373; Hospitals for, 365, 371; Treatment for, 365, 367
Snowstorms in Africa, 324
Sobat, 8
Sofala, 24, 27
Somaliland, vii, 112
Somalis, 63, 94, 95, 169, 236, 243
Speke, 12, 17, 41, 59, 291, 292
Speke's Tragelap, 137
Spirillum fever, 170
Stanley, 18, 43, 44, 47-54, 59, 75, 83, 100, 255, 292, 293, 333
Stanley Falls, 52
Steamship facilities in Central Africa, 111
Steinbuck, 138
Stork, Whale-headed, 300
Sturrock, Prof., 337
Sucota Game Reserve, 126

Sudan, 5, 56, 66, 122, 155
Sudanese, 169, 314
Sulima, Sultan, 187, 194, 215
Supper-time in the Jungle, 268
Swahili, 5, 62, 63, 65, 73, 75, 81, 94, 101, 106, 136, 137, 155, 164, 179

Taborah, 188
Taita, 159
Tanga, 7, 77, 119, 187
Tanganyika, Lake, viii, 2, 3, 7, 41, 42, 44, 50, 96, 148, 152, 188, 191, 192, 290, 291
Tangier, 20, 21
Taru desert, 121, 164
Taveta, 122, 148, 168, 169-182
Tetal, 127
Thika Falls, 274
Thika River, 275
Thompson Gazelle, 107, 121, 136
Thomson, Mr. Joseph, 168, 215, 216, 302
Tigre, 29
Timbuctoo, 21, 23, 30, 36
Tobacco, 246, 264
Toro, 3
Tripoli, vii, 30, 31, 32, 34
Tsavo, 101, 102, 106, 107, 166, 167
Tsetse fly, 4, 113, 166, 303, 361, 364-368
Tunisia, vii, 22
Types of Natives, 299, 302, 303, 305

Uasi Ngishu, 110, 127
Uganda, 6, 12, 47, 49, 71, 84, 92, 95, 100, 111, 112, 115, 121, 122, 127, 128, 137, 148, 149, 154, 297-325, 345-360; Future Prospects, 319; Government, 328; Hotels, 327-328
Uganda Railway, vi, 73, 80, 95, 99-120, 121, 139, 192, 261, 289, 388
Ugaya, 12
Ujiji, 7, 42, 43, 46, 50, 188, 192

Ukerewe Island, 128
Umba River, 6, 7, 92
Umbrella, Use of, 349
Unyamwezi, 3
Usavara, 47-48
Usoga, 111, 127, 318
Usukuma, 192
Usumbara, 93
Uzukuma, 12

Victoria Falls, 45, 46
Victoria Nyanza, vi, vii, 2, 4, 6-8, 12, 13, 41, 47, 54, 73, 93, 95, 96, 99, 100, 107, 111, 128, 139, 148, 149, 158, 188, 191, 192, 254, 276, 287-297, 364, 368; Area, 290; Discovery of, 292; Insect pests, 296; Steamers on lake, 288-289, 294, 320; Trade, 255; Water capacity, 292
Victorian Nile, 380
Voi, 95, 106, 121, 129, 158, 159, 170, 184
Von der Decken, Baron, 215
Vultures, 110

Wachaga, 9, 175, 186, 190, 191, 193, 194, 196, 199, 200
Wakahe, 190
Wakamba, 107, 111, 156, 237
Wakavirondo (*see* Kavirondo)
Wakwafi, 167, 168

Wambuka, 190
Wambulu, 190
Wameru, 190
Warumbu, 190
Warusha, 189
Waparri, 173
Wart-hog, 121
Wataita, 159, 162
Wataturu, 190
Wataveta, The, 166, 173, 176-182; Dance, 178
Water-buck, 267, 284
Wayanika, 96, 107, 156
White Fathers of Algeria, 84
White Nile, 19
Wildebeest, 107
Wolfe, Herr, 186, 209, 211
Wolves, 124
Wright, Rev. G. W., 85

Zambesi, 1, 20, 28, 39, 40, 41, 45, 46, 99, 118
Zanzibar, vi, 7, 20, 21, 41, 42, 43, 44, 59-78, 89, 92, 96
Zaire River (*see* Congo)
Zareba, 159, 166, 176
Zebra, 4, 106, 107, 109, 119, 121, 123, 124, 128, 129, 136, 138, 139, 164, 222-227, 232
Zebroid, 119
Zimbas, 91
Zenecke, Commissioner, 186
Zulu, 155

www.ingramcontent.com/pod-product-compliance
Lightning Source LLC
Chambersburg PA
CBHW031247230426
43670CB00005B/74